be returned on or before
amped below.

27

MAN AND HIS ENVIRONMENT
VOLUME I

MAN AND HIS ENVIRONMENT

VOLUME I

Proceedings of the First Banff Conference on
Pollution. Sponsored jointly by The University of
Calgary and the Engineering Institute of Canada
Held in Banff, Canada, May 16 and 17, 1968

Edited by M. A. Ward.

PERGAMON PRESS
Oxford   New York
Toronto   Sydney   Braunschweig

PERGAMON PRESS LTD.,
Headington Hill Hall, Oxford

PERGAMON PRESS INC.,
Maxwell House, Fairview Park, Elmsford, New York 10523

PERGAMON OF CANADA LTD.
207 Queen's Quay West, Toronto 1

PERGAMON PRESS (AUST.) PTY. LTD.,
19a Boundary Street, Rushcutters Bay, N.S.W. 2011, Australia

VIEWEG & SOHN GMBH,
Burgplatz 1, Braunschweig

Copyright © 1970 Pergamon Press Inc.

First edition 1970

Library of Congress Catalog Card No. 70–113396

Printed in Great Britain by A. Wheaton & Co., Exeter

08 015763 7

CONTENTS

CONTENTS

PREFACE

THE First Banff Conference on Pollution was held May 16 and 17, 1968, at the Banff School of Fine Arts, Banff, Alberta. The Steering Committee was composed of Chairman H. W. Klassen, H. W. Klassen and Associates Ltd., Calgary; Secretary D. G. Colley, The University of Calgary; K. Aziz, The University of Calgary; R. F. Comstock, Stanley Associates Engineering Ltd., Calgary; G. A. Engbloom, Calgary Power Ltd.; J. H. Hole, Lockerbie and Hole Western Ltd., Calgary; M. F. Mohtadi, The University of Calgary; H. R. Skinner, Reid, Crowther and Partners, Calgary; W. A. Smith, T. Lamb and McManus Ltd., Calgary; and the editor. The four conference sessions were covered by members of the Steering Committee.

The purpose of the conference was to bring together all parties who have an interest in pollution but at different levels; the politicians, the planners, the industrialists, the engineering profession, the biologists and the medical profession. It was hoped that the interchange of ideas between the various groups would lead to a clearer understanding of the whole problem by all and thus assist in its solution, in any given circumstances.

Seventeen invited papers were presented which covered a wide range of topics dealing with air and water pollution. Two keynote papers were presented to give some thematic order to the Proceedings in the water and air pollution sessions by Dr. E. F. Gloyna, University of Texas, and Dr. A. T. Rossano, University of Washington, respectively. Each of these review papers introduced a session where a number of research and practical papers were presented and discussed.

There were approximately 150 registrants for the conference. Although the majority of participants came from the prairie provinces, British Columbia and the northern states, the conference had attendees from many points of North America.

The complete program follows:

Thursday, May 16, 1968

<table>
<tr><td></td><td align="center">*Session 1: General*</td></tr>
<tr><td>9.00 a.m.</td><td>The Provincial Government's Role in Environmental Quality Maintenance
J. D. Ross,
Minister of Health, Province of Alberta</td></tr>
<tr><td>*Convenor:*
H. W. KLASSEN
Chairman:
R. A. RITTER
Dean of Engineering,
The University of Calgary</td><td>The Quality of Man's Environment
J. B. CRAGG,
Killam Memorial Professor, Head, Department of Biology and Director, Environmental Sciences Centre, Kananaskis,
The University of Calgary

Progress Toward Control of Air Pollution in the United States
D. J. BORCHERS,
Special Assistant to the Director of Air Pollution Control,
Department of Health, Education and Welfare,
White House, Washington, D.C.</td></tr>
</table>

12.00 noon	Discussion

Session 2: Water Pollution

1.30 p.m.

Liquid Waste in the Pulp and Paper Industry
D. R. STANLEY, President,
Stanley Associates Engineering Ltd., Edmonton

Convenor:
 M. F. MOHTADI
Chairman:
 J. B. CRAGG,
 Professor and Head,
 Department of Biology,
 The University of Calgary

Petrochemical Waste Disposal
E. E. KUPCHANKO,
Head Water Pollution Control Section,
Environmental Health Services Division,
Department of Public Health, Government of Alberta, Edmonton

Pollution from Municipal Sources
P. D. LAWSON,
Reid, Crowther and Partners Ltd., Calgary

K. J. BRISBIN,
Underwood and McLellan and Associates Ltd., Calgary

Unsolved Engineering Problems in Water Quality
(Keynote Address)
E. F. GLOYNA, Professor
Department of Environmental Health Engineering and Director,
Centre for Research in Water Resources,
University of Texas at Austin

4.00 p.m.

Panel Discussion

6.00 p.m.

Conference Dinner
Guest Speaker:
 G. W. GOVIER, Chairman,
 Oil and Gas Conservation Board of Alberta, Calgary

Friday, May 17, 1968

Session 3: Air Pollution and Urban Waste

8.30 a.m.

Fundamental Concepts of Atmospheric Pollution
(Keynote Address)
A. T. ROSSANO, Professor,
Department of Civil Engineering, Air Resource Program,
University of Washington

Convenor:
 K. AZIZ
Chairman:
 H. L. HOGGE, Director,
 Division of Environmental
 Health Services,
 Government of Alberta,
 Edmonton

Meteorology and Air Pollution
R. E. MUNN, Supervisor,
Micrometeorological Research Unit,
Meteorological Service of Canada, Toronto

Ventilation and Mixing in Alberta Cities
K. D. HAGE, Professor,
Department of Geography, University of Alberta

R. W. LONGLEY, Professor,
Department of Geography, University of Alberta

Wind-Tunnel Modelling of Stack Gas Discharge
G. R. LORD, Professor and Head,
Department of Mechanical Engineering, University of Toronto

H. J. Leutheusser, Associate Professor,
Department of Mechanical Engineering, University of Toronto

Numerical Simulation of Atmospheric
Pollution from Industrial Sources
D. G. Colley, Research Associate,
Department of Chemical Engineering, The University of Calgary

K. Aziz, Associate Professor,
Department of Chemical Engineering, The University of Calgary

11.30 a.m.   Panel Discussion

Session 4: Air Pollution and Urban Waste (continued)

1.30 p.m.   Air Pollution from Bivalent Sulfur Compounds in the Pulp Industry
F. E. Murray, Head,
Division of Applied Chemistry,
British Columbia Research Council, Vancouver

Convenor:
K. Aziz

Management Views on Pollution Control

Chairman:
P. J. Bouthillier, Professor,
Department of Civil Engineering,
University of Alberta

J. E. Baugh, Vice-President,
Canadian Fina Oil Ltd., Calgary

Effects of Air Pollution on Health
A. J. de Villiers, Consultant in Charge,
Biomedical Unit Occupational Health Division,
Department of National Health and Welfare, Ottawa

A Systems Engineering Approach to Urban Solid Waste Collection
and Disposal
J. W. MacLaren, President,
James F. MacLaren Ltd., Toronto

D. P. Sexsmith,
James F. MacLaren Ltd., Toronto

Pollution Control and Abatement within the Planning Process
W. T. Perks, Chief,
Long Range Planning, National Capital Commission, Ottawa

4.00 p.m.   Panel Discussion

5.00 p.m.   Adjournment

The quality of the papers presented at the conference and the lively discussion that ensued during the scheduled discussion periods and in informal meetings was most gratifying for those who were involved in the tedious, and generally overlooked, job of organizing the technical and social aspects of the conference program.

I am sure all who attended the conference will join me in expressing appreciation to Calgary Branch, Engineering Institute of Canada, and the Faculty of Engineering, The University of Calgary for their sponsorship. I would also like to thank K. Aziz and M. F. Mohtadi for acting as academic editors for the technical sessions. I owe much to Brian Langan, Research Associate in Civil Engineering at The University of Calgary, for his contribution of time and effort during the tedious process of editing the conference papers.

Finally, I express my thanks to the three girls in the editor's household for their forebearance during the preparation of the final manuscript of the Proceedings.

Department of Civil Engineering   M. A. Ward
The University of Calgary   Editor

FOREWORD

THE Banff Conference on Pollution reaffirmed the value of a multi-disciplined approach to a multi-faceted problem. A number of excellent technical papers covering the political, legal, medical and some general aspects of the overall problem of pollution were submitted by prominent and concerned men from throughout Canada and the United States. These proceedings document the formal program of the Conference but the exchange of ideas and the stimulating discussion will, hopefully, influence our attitude towards a major social problem.

To the Hon. J. D. Ross, Dr. J. B. Cragg and Mr. D. Borchers, the guest speakers, I offer the thanks of the Conference for their participation. Their broad and imaginative views added appreciably to the proceedings.

To keynote speakers Dr. A. T. Rossano of the University of Washington and Dr. E. F. Gloyna, University of Texas, I should like to express the gratitude of the University of Calgary and the Engineering Institute of Canada, for their astute appraisal of the technical papers and their leadership in the discussions which followed each session. The University of Calgary must be thanked for their enthusiastic support and the very generous contribution of time on the part of many individuals of the Engineering faculty. Without this support and the financial and organizational assistance rendered by the Calgary Branch of the Engineering Institute of Canada, the Conference would not have been possible.

More than anyone I am aware of the very special thanks due to Dr. M. A. Ward of The University of Calgary for his perseverance and skill in directing the proceedings to a worthwhile conclusion. To him I extend the thanks of the Steering Committee for the accomplishment of a difficult task.

H. W. Klassen and Associates   H. W. KLASSEN
Calgary, Alberta   Chairman
                                                              Steering Committee

GENERAL

THE PROVINCIAL GOVERNMENT'S ROLE
IN ENVIRONMENTAL QUALITY MAINTENANCE

J. D. ROSS, B.A., M.D., M.L.A. *Minister of Health, Alberta*

ABSTRACT

The "environment"—air, water, and soil, is essential to man's survival and also is important to the development of our society and the people of it. The urban and industrial areas of Alberta are centres of concentrated activities of man and thus are subject to concentrated pollution of the environment. The Provincial Government's role in controlling pollution and maintaining a useful and desirable quality of environment includes overall planning, assessment of current air and water quality, provision of adequate legislation, and where necessary, enforcement of the legislation. The environment affects all segments of our Province's society and thus there is real need for co-ordination and exchange of ideas. The "Alberta Advisory Committee on Pollution Control" was set up for this purpose in 1967 and will be a continuing Advisory Committee to the Government.

INTRODUCTION

Man's environment is the combination of those physical circumstances in which he lives, which are essential to his health, enjoyment of life and the opportunity to develop his individuality and purpose of life. The air, which he breathes some 25 times per minute, is essential for existence; freedom from toxic or noxious materials will help to avoid respiratory and other illness which would shorten his life; and freedom from offensive odors will allow him to enjoy the air, rather than create apprehension about polluted air. Water isn't required every few seconds to sustain life, but about two quarts are consumed every day of our life. Again, freedom from toxic materials is basically a must and the absence of materials offensive to taste and smell is pretty essential. The other basic requirement for life which can be endangered by pollution or adverse environmental quality, is food. Food-producing vegetation and livestock can be destroyed or damaged in quality by airborne and waterborne materials foreign to nature.

Basic maintenance of life is essential, but it is not the only purpose in life today, anymore than it has been in any of the past ages. Man is a reasonably intelligent being, and requires an environment which will allow him to maintain his self-respect, develop his individual personality, house his family and allow him to enjoy his life. Here the environment at his house, his town or city, and place of recreation, are all important to him.

Another aspect of the environment which we must consider is the possible effect on man's work, whether it be the farm, its crops and livestock, the warehouse, the manufacturing plant, or the "heavy" industry. In each case air and water are important to their operation to a greater or lesser degree, whether it be an adverse effect on the operation itself or the need to release or dispose of unwanted materials from the operation.

The other traditional fundamental needs of man are warmth and shelter. The heating of houses and other buildings in Alberta is not the serious environment problem that it has been in other places because of the availability of natural gas as a fuel, however, the products of combustion—carbon dioxide, nitrogen oxides and water vapor, are still released to the atmosphere.

It is apparent that the environment is important to people in all aspects of their life, and it is evident also that it is the actions of man that impairs or despoils the quality of it.

SOURCES OF POLLUTANTS

Our current problem areas are those where man's activities are greatest, i.e. the larger urban areas and the industrial areas. The urban areas are increasing in size rapidly, particularly Calgary and Edmonton which are the fastest growing cities in Canada. The industrial areas in and near these two cities are also growing quickly, and the increase in the gas processing, sulfur recovery, and chemical fertilizer plants in other parts of the Province has been equally rapid.

It is interesting to note the approximate amount of unwanted, discarded or lost materials in the larger urban areas. The solid refuse, i.e. household, business and commercial waste, is some five pounds per person per day and the amount is reported to be increasing at the rate of $1\frac{1}{2}\%$ per year. In a City such as Calgary, with a population of some 340,000 people, this would mean 1,700,000 pounds per day or 310,000 tons per year; in a sanitary landfill, packed to 800 pounds per cubic yard, and at a 10 foot depth, this would take up some 46 acres of land per year. The wastes flushed down the sewer have been estimated at up to $0 \cdot 5$ pounds per person per day, which would be 50,000 pounds per day for every 100,000 people in the city. Needless to say, 90% treatment would leave only 5000 pounds per day per 100,000 people to be released to the river. The amount of materials released to the air could not be measured as readily as they come from such a wide variety and large number of "sources" including home heating, apartment, office and store incinerators, automobiles, trucks and buses, manufacturing plants and the "heavy" industry. However, the amounts of air pollutants from the different types of sources have been measured and this, in turn, used as a basis for estimating the amounts in a city. This method was used in source surveys made by the Department of Health for the Calgary and Edmonton areas in 1964. The total amount of pollutants in Calgary at that time was some 382 tons or 764,000 pounds per day for a population of 304,000, and prorating this up to the 1967 population of 336,000 gives an amount of 422 tons or 844,000 pounds per day. This is about $2 \cdot 5$ pounds per person per day.

The amount of lost or waste materials at industries will vary with the type of the industry, the size and, of course, the number of them. The losses will occur in the refinement of products and the conversion from raw materials to the products. Both, but particularly the latter, are never 100% efficient and therefore pollutants are created. Some of our sulfur recovery plants produce 1500 tons per day of sulfur, thus if the efficiency is 90% there is a release of some 165 tons per day of sulfur, and if the efficiency is 95%, only 80 tons are lost per day.

CONTROL OF POLLUTION

The foregoing must lead us to the conclusion that we are going to have significant impairment of quality of the environment, commonly called "pollution", where we have concentrations of people or industries. The potential amount of the pollutants will be proportional to the number of people and if steps are not taken to control these pollutants the extent of the pollution will also be proportional to this density. Sooner or later control is going to have to be exercised or the effects of the pollution will be extremely serious. The amount of control required of similar premises in similar circumstances should, of course, be equal in order to be fair and the amount of control should be adequate to maintain a useful and reasonably enjoyable environment, but not excessive so that we have control for the sake of control. It should, however, be basically recognized that no one is entitled to operate in a manner which is detrimental to someone else.

The pollution or environment maintenance problem then would divide into certain fundamental manouvres as follows:

1. Assessment of the problem.
2. Invoke a certain degree of control as indicated.
3. Keep the problem under surveillance and assessment.
4. Invoke a higher degree of control when necessary to maintain a "useful" quality of the environment.

The participation of the various persons, corporations, or agencies will have to vary to provide an efficient and effective program under the different circumstances.

SOLID REFUSE DISPOSAL

Taking the solid refuse part first, it is a traditional and essential part of the urban municipalities' job to provide a collection service to the residential areas to keep the city in a clean and healthy condition. In commercial or industrial areas the municipality may provide the collection service, or it may be arranged by the individual premises by contract with a private firm. Either way, the operation is entirely within the municipality and there has been no need for outside control, and the cost is borne by the premises receiving the service. The disposal of the refuse may have serious effects on the environment and on other person's property, and the effects may well extend beyond the boundaries of the municipality itself. There is, therefore, a need for provincial or joint development of the ground rules for control of the disposal process. In Alberta, a joint urban-rural-provincial committee was formed in June 1967 to assess this problem and to develop the ground rules required for disposal without pollution of the environment or infringing on the rights and privileges of individuals.

WATER POLLUTION CONTROL

The control program for the water segment of the environment is not nearly so much a matter of importance to the municipal or industrial group releasing the pollutant as it is for the person, municipality or industry downstream. The municipality must provide a system of sewers to collect the waste waters, or water carried wastes, from the various homes, business, commercial and industrial premises in order to maintain healthy, orderly and pleasant conditions within the municipality itself. Similarly, the industry not served by the municipal sewers must have its own system to collect waste waters from various parts of the processing. In both areas the collected waste waters must be disposed of in some fashion and invariably the only practical means is to release them to the nearby river or other body of water. This may be quite satisfactory where the amount of pollutants is small and the body of water is large, in other words, the "solution to pollution is dilution". However, this is wishful thinking as far as Alberta is concerned because the annual flow in our rivers is relatively fixed and is not extremely large. Hydro and storage dams will give us larger flows during the winter, but this too is limited.

The control program must establish the degree of treatment or control of the released industrial and municipal waste waters so that the combined effect will not decrease the water quality in the receiving waters to the point where its usefulness is impaired. In Alberta the initial assessment of the quality of the water in the rivers and of the waste waters being released to them was started in 1950 by the Department of Health. The degree of waste water treatment required was assessed as being the minimum of effective primary treatment in the critical area. The need for additional treatment at Edmonton became evident in 1954, and at Calgary in 1966, in order to avoid serious adverse degradation of water quality. Industries have been requested, at the Provincial level, to provide a comparable degree of treatment in order to provide a suitable quality of waste waters.

In water pollution the determination of the need for waste water treatment has been made by the Province, as has the continuing assessment of water quality in the rivers and of the waste waters being released to them. The provision of the required treatment or control facilities and their operation is a responsibility of the municipality or industry.

AIR POLLUTION CONTROL

The air environment is not assessable to the same degree of precision as the land or water ones are. Lethbridge claims the greatest amount of clean fresh air in Canada because the wind never stops blowing and the average speed is greater than at any other meteorological station. (Some say they need all they can get.) The amount of dilution and the direction the pollutants travel is directly dependent on the speed and direction of the wind and the dispersion of them also varies with the temperature gradient of the atmosphere and the topography of the area. The effect of air pollution will also vary with the distance from the source and the presence of other sources. Needless to say, the winds are no respectors of municipal boundaries so that the control has to be on an "area" basis to be effective. The Regulations for the Control of Air Pollution in Alberta are Provincial, with the enforcement a joint City and Provincial program in City areas and basically a Provincial one in other areas.

Air quality monitoring facilities are provided by the Province and, with the exception of some of the more basic monitoring equipment, are operated by the Province. The data obtained is tabulated, summarized and evaluated using electronic data processing, and reports prepared. For the rural areas near industrial plants, two mobile air pollution laboratories are used to monitor air quality.

New "sources" of air pollutants are evaluated and approved at the Provincial level. Compliance with the conditions of approval are checked by making periodic stack sampling surveys by our staff and by requiring industry to assess their operation by use of plant records and also by making stack surveys themselves in the case of the larger industries. Industry reports are forwarded at monthly intervals to the Department.

ASSESSMENT OF METEOROLOGICAL FACTORS

The assessment of the pertinent meteorological parameters in the larger urban centres of Calgary and Edmonton is currently the subject of a research study sponsored by the Province. In Edmonton, temperature measurements are made on the CN Tower building at the top (370 foot level), at the middle (186 feet) and at the base (49 feet) and wind speed and direction equipment will be installed at the top. In Calgary, a 300 foot meteorological tower was constructed this winter on a site provided by the City. Temperatures are recorded at the 300, 150 and 33 foot levels and wind speed and direction at the top and bottom levels. In addition, a portable kytoon is used for measuring temperature gradients at other locations; stationary recording thermometers and also portable temperature measuring equipment is used to assess the heat island effect. These various meteorological parameter measurements are compared to the level of the pollutant concentrations with the overall purpose being to increase the understanding of the air pollution picture. Hopefully, also, it will lead to the reliable prediction of the frequency of occurrence of the higher pollution levels.

COMPLAINT INVESTIGATIONS

Another area that the Province is required to involve itself in is that of "complaint" investigations, whether they originate from organizations, corporations or individual members of the public. Each complaint is evaluated, often in conjunction with local authorities, and if required, corrective measures are requested of the person or corporation causing the conditions complained of. Should the problem not be resolved in this way, a formal Provincial Board of Health "Hearing" may be held and action taken before the courts of law to have the operation restrained until the correction is provided.

SUMMARY

In summary, the Alberta provincial functions in pollution control or environment quality maintenance are—overall planning, assessment of current air and water quality, special research studies, the provision of adequate legislation to clearly outline the "ground rules" and provision of an adequate program of enforcement of compliance with the ground rules. The cost of providing and operating the required pollution control equipment is that of the municipality or industry releasing the water or airborne pollutants. The effectiveness of any program, however, depends on the degree of co-operation of all agencies concerned—provincial, municipal and industrial. This past year we have formed an Alberta Advisory Committee on Pollution Control to assist us in developing and maintaining an efficient and appropriate program. This Committee has some 84 members who represent government, municipalities, industries, professional associations, and the public, and also is broken down into twelve Subcommittees, each having a specific area or subject of interest. The Committee will meet at least once a year and the Subcommittees one or two additional times. We are confident that this group will be very effective and ensure that the programs are efficient and appropriate.

THE QUALITY OF MAN'S ENVIRONMENT

J. B. CRAGG *University of Calgary*

ABSTRACT

Stress is laid on the need for biologists and engineers to understand each other's approaches to environmental problems. The biologist sees the following major threats to biological systems: alterations in the carbon dioxide and oxygen concentrations in the atmosphere; the effects of toxic chemicals such as herbicides, pesticides and radioactive wastes; many management practices, e.g. damming of rivers, clear felling of trees and other techniques for altering habitats. For every year of this century at least one bird or mammal species has become extinct. Species are unique creations of evolutionary processes and should be preserved both for scientific and aesthetic reasons. The study of natural systems is necessary, not only for an understanding of man's environment, but for the maintenance of its quality.

INTRODUCTION

There is much in common in the way in which biologists and engineers approach their respective studies. Years ago, when I taught comparative anatomy, I used engineering examples to make sense of animal structures which had evolved over many millenia. I would point out to students how the strands of spongy tissue in bone were correlated with the areas of principal stress; how the hollow cylindrical shaft of one of our long bones had its ends splayed out where it articulated with other bones, thus following sound engineering principles; how the vertebral column and the fore and hind limbs attached to it, demonstrated some of the principles of bridge construction.

Now, as an ecologist, I am once again concerned with the role of the engineer. The ecologist's function is to study the interrelationships between organisms and their environment. Many branches of engineering today are concerned with modifying the natural environment or attempting to correct the many errors which have resulted from man's failure to follow ecological principles in manipulating the environment. It is becoming increasingly evident that the principle environmental systems, air, soil and water, are not limitless, that in some parts of the world they are already severely if not irreversibly damaged by pollutants and other destructive agents. It is important, therefore, that biologists and engineers should come to understand each other's approach to environmental problems.

THE ECOSYSTEM CONCEPT

Perhaps, at the outset, I should make it clear that an ecologist is not just a person who collects and names organisms for the sake of filling museum cases. I have no wish to underestimate the importance of collecting and naming. A sound taxonomy is necessary in every science whether we are dealing with the identification of metals in chemistry, or the separation of closely related species in aspen woodlands.

9

Many ecologists today are concerned with the dynamics of whole living systems, we call them ecosystems. An ecosystem is a combination of plants, animals, their remains, and the total environment with which they are associated. The study of an ecosystem is fundamentally similar to the study of an engineering system and the outlook of the systems' analyst is common to both. Here at Banff we are situated in what is predominantly the coniferous forest ecosystem. It is possible to break the system down into a number of components: input of materials, their processing and utilization; output, made up of crop and dead material. The latter, through the activity of many thousands of decomposer organisms, is broken down to release locked-up chemicals which are put back into circulation.

One of the things which concerns ecologists today is the fact that important operations in some ecosystems are being altered by man's activities, and the possibility cannot be ruled out that there may be some disastrous consequences. We talk about the twin threats of the population explosion and the technological revolution. I want to examine some aspects of the latter, as they relate to the major theme of this conference.

Environmental pollution has been defined as ". . . the unfavourable alteration of our surroundings, wholly or largely as a by-product of man's actions . . ." [1]. Its effects are many, and I want to start by taking a global view of one aspect in which the role of the green plant, whether it is a huge tree or a microscopic alga, is of supreme importance.

CARBON DIOXIDE FROM FOSSIL FUELS

In the forest ecosystem which surrounds us, as in all ecosystems, light energy falls on the green vegetation and it is utilized to transform chemicals from the soil and carbon dioxide from the atmosphere into plant tissue. During this photosynthetic phase, oxygen is released into the atmosphere. There is a sensitive balance between the production of oxygen during photosynthesis and the utilization of oxygen by animals and plants in their respiratory phases. The carbon atoms, which are the essential constituents of living matter, come from the carbon dioxide in the plant's environment. In the case of terrestrial plants it is the $0 \cdot 03 \%$ carbon dioxide in the atmosphere which provides the necessary carbon molecules.

The carbon cycle has three major phases; first, carbon locked up as carbonates in rocks. The main bulk of the Rockies constitutes such a reserve, and the carbonates of these mountains are exposed to all the forces of weathering. The second phase is in solution, particularly in the sea and this in turn is in equilibrium, or should be in a state of equilibrium, with the third phase which is the carbon dioxide in the atmosphere.

Fossil fuels are now being burned at increasing rates and as Revelle *et al.* [1] states, "Within a few short centuries, we are returning to the air a significant part of the carbon that was slowly extracted by plants and buried in the sediments during half a billion years". The oceans of the world are not capable of adsorbing the present output. Something like half of the carbon dioxide which is produced by the burning of fossil fuels remains in the atmosphere. It is estimated that the atmospheric CO_2 will, by the year 2000, be increased by approximately 25% [1].

What are the long-term effects of this intervention by man? Carbon dioxide adsorbs longwave radiation, thus one possible effect of an increase of the carbon dioxide content of the atmosphere will be a reduction in the amount of heat lost to the outer atmosphere. Thus, we can expect the earth's average temperature to rise and this could bring in its train a raising of sea levels throughout the world, the obliteration of major ports and, at the same time, many parts of the earth's surface would be turned to desert. These are not the forecasts of science fiction writers, but possibilities which actually confront mankind and which require greater study.

Perhaps some figures may drive this home. Cole [2] points out that a Boeing 707 burns about one ton of fuel every ten minutes, producing over two tons of carbon dioxide. With increasing numbers of aircraft, the carbon dioxide trails, particularly over major cities, are mounting up. At the same time the vegetation cover of the surface of the earth is gradually being reduced by the expansion of cities and the constructions which go with them. As Cole states, we do not know at what point the homeostatic mechanisms which buffer the effects of man's activities, will cease to operate and so bring about a serious decline in the availability of oxygen.

EFFECTS OF POLLUTANTS ON ORGANISMS

As a biologist, I am particularly concerned with the effects of environmental pollution on animal and plant life. There is ample evidence to show that a wide range of pollutants from solid industrial wastes to a variety of toxic chemicals, which now include such things as herbicides, pesticides and radioactive wastes, kill many plants and animals. The techniques for rendering many of these materials harmless are known and the cures are largely dependent on economics and the stringency of the antipollution laws.

There are, however, many ways of polluting the total environment for which we have not yet got the necessary answers. The insidious effects of persistent insecticides is a case in point. Tarzwell [3] has summarized the situation as far as aquatic organisms are concerned. Measured in terms of recorded kills of fish, pesticides originating from agricultural and forest lands which have been treated with them, account for more kills than any single one of those other notorious agents of pollution, refinery, paper mill or plating wastes.

From the wildlife point of view some of the pesticides, of which DDT is the best known, are now distributed on a worldwide basis and occur far from the centres where they were originally used. DDT residues, for example, have been found in fishes from Alaskan rivers, from oceanic feeding birds, and even from penguins collected on the Antarctic Continent. The long-term effects of these materials cannot be forecast. They represent the results of blindly treating one part of an ecosystem without regard for the other parts of that system. In fact, in many cases the efficacy of a treatment for a particular purpose has been challenged. As Tarzwell [3] states, some two million acres of forest in Montana were sprayed to control spruce budworm. The measures were unsuccessful over large areas but made heavy inroads on the fish and on the invertebrates on which the fish feed. In one stream the number of aquatic organisms was reduced by over 80%.

Of special significance is the way in which pesticides can be concentrated with each successive step in a foodchain. Thus, Hunt and Bischoff [4] showed at Clear Lake, California, that the amount of pesticide residues rises as you pass from the microscopic plankton which is the basic food material, through plankton-feeding fish to the main predators, which are other fish and birds. In many parts of the world the large predaceous birds, which are among our most striking examples of wildlife have been reduced in numbers, in some cases to the point of extinction, as an indirect result of the load of persistent insecticides carried in the bodies of their prey.

The use of a toxic chemical has led to an increase in some pests rather than a reduction. Thus, attempts to control *Sminthurus viridis*, a major economic pest of Lucerne in Australia

[5] resulted in increased damage by the pest because its predators were more sensitive to the insecticide than the pest itself. In other cases, predators are being destroyed largely because of the way in which pesticides are concentrated with each step in the food chain.

INTERFERENCE WITH NATURAL SYSTEMS

So much of man's influence on the total environment derives from the fact that he operates as though he were not an integral part of the system and as though he regarded himself as immune from the results of his actions. As a biologist, I feel it necessary to point out how all of us are a part of the environment in which we live.

The vast assembly of plant and animal forms which occur on the earth today have been moulded and selected for the conditions in which they live.

We carry in our bodies the results of millions of years of evolution. Our sense organs, our biochemical machinery for processing and utilizing the materials of the environment, are the products of modifications and evolutionary experiments made over many generations.

But evolution has not been confined to the individual organisms. The way organisms interact, compete and live together, have also been subjected to those same forces of selection. In the Arizona desert you have communities of plants and animals highly adapted for desert conditions. Here in the Canadian Rockies you have organisms attuned to efficient living in what, to us, is a rigorous mountain environment. These communities are adapted to make the best use of their living conditions.

Man has felled trees to extend his prairie, he has dammed rivers and interfered with huge drainage systems, he has poured millions of tons of wastes into the seas of the world. All these acts are, at the ecosystem level, the equivalent of interfering in a crude, fumbling way with the biochemical processes of our own bodies. We are, in interfering with the environment, interfering with the outcome of countless evolutionary experiments.

Scarred mountain slopes from which the protective vegetation has been removed; wide flood plains as the aftermath of forest destruction—these are the obvious reminders of the destructiveness of man's actions. The effects of introductions such as the rabbit into Australia and the starling in North America are other examples of what happens when man interferes with the subtle interrelationships which exist in balanced ecosystems.

For every year of this century at least one bird or mammal species has been rendered extinct. I am Vice-Chairman of the Commission on Ecology of the International Union for the Conservation of Nature. One of the functions of that body is to collect information on threatened species and habitats. Over two hundred species of mammals and over three hundred species of birds are on our danger lists. The optimists among us hope that by adequate measures we shall be able to save some of these threatened species. There are, however, pessimists among us who feel that the lists will grow as more and more inroads are made into natural systems.

It is easy to be complacent about these happenings; to say that these things occurred in the past and, with modern knowledge, mistakes of this kind will not be repeated. I am not prepared to accept this argument.

THE NEED TO STUDY LIVING SYSTEMS

As Barry Commoner [6] has pointed out, the greatest single cause of environmental contamination of this planet today is radioactivity from test explosions of nuclear weapons. Commenting on the results of nuclear tests over the period 1948 to 1962, Commoner states that one constituent of fallout, strontium 90, increased the radioactivity of the environment by an amount equivalent to about one thousand million grams of radium. Our prewar knowledge of radioactivity was based on a world supply of a few grams.

Commoner draws a parallel between radioactive fallout and the contamination of the environment with a variety of toxic chemicals, particularly the synthetic pesticides. Modern physics produced the know-how of nuclear explosions; modern chemistry the extensive range of toxic chemicals. Both types of knowledge were exploited to the full because of mankind's demand for the products, bombs on the one hand and pest control on the other. Both types of knowledge were exploited before their biological effects could be worked out. Thus, living systems throughout the world, and man is dependent on those systems and is part of them, are faced with new threats.

To meet these and similar hazards there must be a considerable expansion of knowledge on how living systems operate. In biology, as in chemistry and physics, there has been a knowledge explosion but it has been centered on molecular biology to the extent that the letters DNA and RNA are almost as familiar as the names of household detergents. I have no wish to belittle the great achievements of molecular biology and their very great importance to our proper understanding of living processes, but fashions in science have got to be watched. René Dubos [7] of the Rockefeller Institute, in his volume of the Yale Silliman Memorial lectures called "Man Adapting", makes the following statement: "Any activity, however trivial, that deals with sub-microscopic particles or sub-cellular chemical phenomena is labelled 'fundamental' whereas efforts to formulate, investigate or teach the phenomena of life as experienced by whole organisms is considered scientifically unsophisticated."

If man fails to deal with the problems of environmental pollution then his chances of utilizing the advances in other areas of knowledge may be doomed to failure. There is a long record of civilizations which have become extinct and some of those extinctions, as in the case of Babylon and Greece, can be related to the destruction of local environments. Today the world is one and, with pollutants ranging from the Antarctic to the Arctic, the whole of mankind is exposed to their effect.

Natural systems attain their greatest degree of stability when there is a considerable level of biological diversity within them. On the whole, the effect of a pollutant is to reduce that diversity and produce a simpler system in terms of species content. That is why I see a basic similarity between the effects of rabbits on the landscape in Australia or New Zealand and the effect of a pollutant in air, water or soil. Both types of interference produce a reduction in variety and with it the distinct possibility that the system will cease to operate in a normal manner.

I realize that it is one thing to talk in the broad terms which I have been using, another to deal with problems of immediate and local concern. I am, no doubt, equivalent to the academic scientist who knows a great deal about the chemical makeup of a virus but is unable to help the doctor who has to deal with a virus-stricken patient. I do not deny that there is need for expansion in research at the technical level, of controlling particular pollutants, but there is at least an equal need for an expansion of research on the environment as a whole.

For practical purposes, problems of pollution are most readily dealt with by allocating them to one of the major divisions, air, soil, or water. From the long-term point of view, the links between these systems must be accepted otherwise treatments can become mechanisms whereby the pollution problem is pushed along the line, either to be forgotten, or to become another person's or another generation's problem. In this regard marine pollution deserves much greater attention than it now receives. Mankind takes a much too optimistic view of the capacity of the sea to cope with the by-products of man's technological activities. The recent misadventures of wrecked oil tankers have, I hope, given us some warning of what might happen.

It is the microscopical life of the oceans which is mainly responsible for the oxygen-carbon dioxide balance of the atmosphere. The seas, particularly those of the continental shelf regions, maintain an abundance of wildlife. Unpolluted estuarine areas probably have the highest organic production of all types of ecosystems yet, in many parts of the world, they are being polluted and turned into wastelands.

According to Hubbert [8] the U.S.A., with 6% of the world's population, consumes 30% of the world's total production of minerals. Many of the major pollution problems arise from the utilization of those mineral resources. As industrialization grows in the developing countries an even greater use of mineral products will take place and coastal pollution on the North American scale will become of world concern. Yet we are woefully ignorant of the effects of many effluents on marine life.

WHY PRESERVE WILDLIFE?

Some may ask, why preserve wildlife if much of what it does can be replaced by man-made systems? In brief, there are two reasons. I have not talked about aesthetic values because aesthetic and health values are the motivating forces in many operations concerned with pollution control. My first reason for conserving wildlife is in part aesthetic, part scientific. Organisms are unique creations of evolutionary processes. They are as much deserving of preservation as many artifacts which man preserves—old manor houses, paintings and other works of art. When a species becomes extinct, something unique has been destroyed. My second reason is that we know so little about the workings of these natural assemblages of organisms. Their study is not only of academic value. Organic communities represent the outcome of millions of years of evolution. By studying the flow of energy through such systems and the utilization of chemicals by them, we have much to learn about organic production and this should prove of use to us both in relation to food production and in the proper use of landscape. In fact, this is one of the major themes of the International Biological Programme which passed from the feasibility to the operational stage in July last year.

CONCLUSION

Twelve years ago a symposium was held in Princeton which led to a monumental source book called *Man's Role in Changing the Face of the Earth* [9]. At that meeting conservationists, biologists, geographers, town planners, engineers, economists, challenged each other. Dr. Kenneth Boulding, Professor of Economics in the University of Michigan, composed two poems—I shall only read a few lines which highlight the main argument of my paper.

A Conservationist's Lament started with the verse:

> The world is finite, resources are scarce
> Things are bad and will be worse
> Coal is burned and gas exploded,
> Forests cut and soils eroded.

and ended with the moral:

> The evolutionary plan,
> Went astray by evolving man.

The other poem was called *The Technologist's Reply*. It started:

> Man's potential is quite terrific
> You can't go back to the Neolithic.

It also ended with a moral:

> Man's a nuisance. Man's a crackpot,
> But only man can hit the jackpot.

There is a danger in the modern world of seeing things as juxtapositions. It comes to us in the form of modern art, in the opposites of teenage culture and the parent generation and in the two cultures of C. P. Snow. The lines which I have just quoted throw up another basic juxtaposition: "omnipotent man" versus his alienated defensive self acting as though separated from the evolutionary process.

In my opinion, we are in need of a new way of looking at things. There is no need to return to the Stone Age but, on the other hand, there is no need to allow man to stagger from one crisis to another. The picture I have drawn of man changing the form and content of environments is a real one. All I ask is that, in changing the environment, we do it as part of the natural process, not as some interloper playing at God.

Let us admit our ignorance of the natural scene. Let us accept the challenge of understanding the processes of nature. When the historians of the future look back on this age, how will they see us? As the generation before another Dark Ages or as the New Renaissance; when synthesis and the ability to harmonize provided us with new ways of living as part of the total environment. We have to work out a fresh approach to environmental problems of which pollution is only one aspect, but nevertheless an important one. In developing this new science, biologists and engineers have much to learn from each other. I am optimistic enough to believe we can fashion an environmental science which will pay due respect to the many living systems which have a place in the economy of this planet.

REFERENCES

1. REVELLE, R. (Chairman) Section on atmospheric carbon dioxide in *Restoring the Quality of our Environment*. (President's Advisory Committee) White House, (1965) pp. 317.
2. COLE, LAMONT, C., Can the world be saved? *N.Y. Times Magazine*, 31 March 1968, p. 34 et seq.
3. TARZWELL, C. M., The toxicity of synthetic pesticides to aquatic organisms and suggestions for meeting the problem in *Ecology and the Industrial Society*, Editors: G. T. Goodman, R. W. Edwards, J. M. Lambert, Blackwell, Oxford, 1965.
4. HUNT, E. G. and BISCHOFF, A. I., Inimical effects on wildlife of periodic DDD applications to Clear Lake. *Calif. Fish Game*, **46**, 1960, pp. 91–106.
5. WALLACE, M. M. H., Insecticides for the control of the lucerne flea, *Sminthurus viridis* (L.) and the red-legged earth mite, *Halotydeus destructor* (Tuck.) and their effects on population numbers. *Aust. J. Agric. Res.* **10**, 1959, pp. 160–170.
6. COMMONER, B., Conservation of the water resource: the responsibility of the scientist. *J. Water Pollution Control Fed.* Jan. 1965, pp. 60–70.
7. DUBOS, RENÉ, *Man Adapting*. Yale University Press, New Haven, 1965.
8. HUBBERT, M. K., *Energy Resources*. Committee on Natural Resources; Nat. Acad. Sci. Washington, D.C. 1962, p. 141.
9. THOMAS, W. L. (Ed.), *Man's Role in Changing the Face of the Earth*. Univ. Chicago, Chicago, 1956.

DISCUSSION

H. S. Hicklin (*University of Alberta*):

1. Your paper discussed the question of oxygen depletion in the atmosphere. Would you enlarge upon any calculations or observations you may have made concerning the ability of the photosynthesis process to return oxygen to the atmosphere at a rate comparable to that at which it is being used in the many combustion and chemical processes, in irreverseable chemical production and by living organisms?

2. From your paper it would appear that education in environmental conservation is urgently needed. I do certainly concur and to my mind this could be consecutively carried out at three levels, in each case, geared to the ability and interest of the age group.

(a) Grade 6; young children do influence their parents' thinking.
(b) Grade 12; older children, both urban and rural would benefit if their attitudes would bear on the problems of conservation.
(c) University level; in a number of disciplines, students are soon in a position to influence industry and their communities on the use of chemicals and the problems of waste disposal.

Would you please explain what is already being done in this regard and if you believe a program could and should be established for the 1968–9 school year encompassing the critical areas of immediate concern?

Author's Reply

1. *Oxygen depletion in the atmosphere.* There is no readily available information on this matter. The oxygen of the atmosphere is of biological origin and one can say that organic matter on the earth and free oxygen in the atmosphere are the two results of the photosynthetic process. Thus, if the total amount of organic matter is reduced, then the amount of oxygen in the atmosphere will be reduced to a corresponding extent. At the present time we have no adequate assessments of the organic matter component of the Earth system. It is our hope that the International Biological Programme, which is paying considerable attention to problems of organic matter production, will be able to provide the basic information on which calculations can be made. Certainly there is no direct evidence to suggest that the oxygen content of the atmosphere has been changed in the course of the last hundred years or so, whereas the carbon dioxide content has been markedly altered.

2. *Education in environmental conservation.* I agree with the comments on the need for education in environmental conservation. The difficulties which are felt at the present time are twofold. First, the absence of a solid body of teachers who are sufficiently aware of the scientific and social problems associated with conservation. There are bits and pieces of information available, but before much progress can be made in the educational field, special courses will have to be developed to give teachers the right attitude to the total environment, following which a solid basis for courses can be arranged. The new syllabuses which have been produced for school biology courses in Britain and U.S.A. go a long way towards providing the basic scientific information on which courses on conservation could be based. It is, however, important to realize that such courses should have a solid, scientific and social basis and should present an intellectual challenge both to the teacher and to the student. It would be too much to expect such courses to be introduced within a year or two,

but various experiments are being tried, certainly in schools in Britain, and as a result of such experiments coupled with sound common sense, instruction by way of television and radio, I think much will be accomplished. The very important area of pollution is already receiving attention both at the federal and provincial level as a result of the *National Conference on Pollution and our Environment* held in Montreal in 1966 [1].

REFERENCE

1. "National Conference on Pollution and our Environment", Canadian Council of Resource Ministers, Montreal, October 1966, (in three volumes), Queen's Printer, Ottawa, 1967.

PROGRESS TOWARD CONTROL OF AIR POLLUTION IN THE UNITED STATES

D. J. BORCHERS *Department of Health, Education, and Welfare, Washington, D.C.*

ABSTRACT

This paper outlines the provisions of the Air Quality Act of 1967 under which the United States is undertaking its most comprehensive effort to bring the Nation's growing air pollution problems under control. The Act's new concept in air pollution control is described which places the primary responsibility on the States and their subdivisions for developing and implementing regional control programs, while giving the Federal Government standby authority to take action where the States fail to act, or fail to take adequate action. The international aspects of the United States' clean air program is also covered.

I am very pleased to participate in this Banff Conference on air pollution, and to outline the efforts that are being made in the United States to deal with the relentless growth of this problem. It is timely, I think, that we look at where the United States stands with regard to air pollution, because the recent passage of the Air Quality Act of 1967 provides new challenges and new opportunities to come to grips with a threat to civilization the true dimensions of which both Canadians and Americans are just beginning to understand.

At the beginning of this century, when we closed the old frontiers in the United States and set forth on our great technological adventures, not even the most imaginative of science fiction writers could have conceived of how profoundly we were to change our society. In our singleminded devotion to achieving the benefits of science and technology, we plunged ahead with the abundant materials at hand, without a very precise notion of where we were going, and without serious attention to the possible adverse side effects of our new activities on our environment.

Belatedly, we begin to understand how dependent we are on our natural resources and particularly on our fundamental resources of air, water and land. We had to convert many of our beautiful rivers and lakes into practically open sewers before we concluded that we must control the pollution of our water resources, and we had to experience the tragedy of Donora and the anguish of Los Angeles before we began to realize that the seemingly infinite ocean of air that surrounds this planet has decidedly finite capacities for diluting and dispersing the wastes thrown up from civilization.

I think we can all agree that no industrial society can afford to make the same mistakes with regard to the air that have typically been made in the past with regard to other precious natural resources. The price of such negligence would be higher than any of us would be willing to pay and in a currency far more precious than dollars. We cannot set air aside in national parks, we cannot replenish the air as we replenish soil and trees, and we cannot purify the air, as we do water, before we use it. We must breathe the air as it comes to us—too often laden with pollutants which reflect the persistence of an attitude now tragically out of date.

Today, more and more Americans are becoming aware of this harsh reality of modern life. I believe it is being borne home to all of us more convincingly day by day that man cannot adapt, without basic biological and physical changes, to an environment which is far different from and, in many respects, more hostile than that which existed during most of the long period in which human evolution has taken place.

Today, the United States pays billions of dollars each year for the dubious privilege of living with—rather than controlling—air pollution. Air pollution soils, corrodes and damages a wide variety of structures in our cities and towns—from the guttering on a home to the suspension bridges that span our rivers. It threatens forests and farmlands as well. It constitutes a national health hazard of greater significance than many may appreciate. It contributes to the rising incidence of such important chronic respiratory diseases as lung cancer, bronchitis, and emphysema—the fastest growing cause of death in our Nation today.

We all know of course that the question of the *extent* of the effects of air pollution on human health has not escaped its share of controversy. But if there is any controversy concerning the fact that it is hazardous to breathe polluted air, I am not aware of it. The American Medical Society has stated that air pollution is a health hazard. So has the American Thoracic Society. We *know* that the death rate has increased markedly in acute air pollution episodes. We *know* that the transport of oxygen by blood is upset during periods of pollution, that pulmonary resistance and the work of breathing is increased, and that man's work performance is reduced. I do not believe I have to pursue the point any further. I think we can all agree that contamination of the air can cause and aggravate disease; that the total level of air pollution is increasing; and that we must do everything possible to remove the dangers from the air we breathe.

The first sure sign in the United States that the scientific community and the public were beginning to understand that the contemporary problem of air pollution is much more than a mere smoke nuisance or a mere inconvenience came into view with passage of the Clean Air Act in 1963. We have made progress under this legislation.

In 1963 expenditure for State and local air pollution control programs totalled $13 million. Last year they totalled $26 million. Prior to passage of the Clean Air Act, only 16 states had passed air pollution control legislation. Today, 46 of our 50 states have done so.

We have begun to control emissions from motor vehicles. Beginning last Fall when 1968 models were introduced, all new cars and light trucks sold in the United States were equipped to meet Federal exhaust emission standards. These standards will cover 1969 model vehicles as well. In January, we published proposed standards which would tighten and extend these controls beginning in the 1970 model year.

Under the Clean Air Act, we have also initiated several important interstate abatement actions in various parts of the country. These abatement actions have stimulated local and State control efforts and promise to help improve the quality of the air breathed by millions of people.

And under the Clean Air Act we have been able to add our efforts to that of Canada's in attempting to bring under control those international problems of air pollution which the two countries mutually share.

As you are all aware, the International Joint Commission has organized itself to deal with air pollution by creating two boards—the International St. Clair-Detroit Air Pollution Board, and the International Air Pollution Advisory Board. In December of last year the St. Clair-Detroit Board set forth the requirements of a study of international air pollution in that area. The study project, which will be carried on jointly by our National Center for Air Pollution Control and your Department of National Health and Welfare, is now fully staffed and proceeding on schedule. A technical report, on which abatement action can be based, is expected to be issued in the latter half of 1969.

The International Air Pollution Advisory Board has identified four other areas along the United States-Canadian border where air pollution may be international in scope. These are: St. Stephen, New Brunswick—Woodland, Maine; Niagra River area, Ontario—New York; Sault Ste. Marie, Ontario—Michigan; and International Falls, Minnesota—Ontario.

While our accomplishments under the Clean Air Act have been heartening, they have fallen far short of the need. Since 1963, the trends of urban, industrial, and technological growth, which are the hallmark of our era, have continued to rise. We continue to generate more electric power, to drive more automobiles, and to produce more products, and we promise to do more of the same in the decades ahead. Unless air pollution control efforts are greatly improved, a problem which is now serious in many places and critical in some, promises to become critical in many and tragic in some.

It was in recognition of these unpleasant but undeniable facts of modern American life that the Congress passed and the President signed the Air Quality Act last November.

The Air Quality Act for the first time gives the Nation the opportunity to control air pollution on the basis of scientific knowledge, and at the same time provides a means by which this knowledge can be translated into effective social and political action.

This Act should do away with most of the excuses for inaction we have all heard in the past. We now have written into law a comprehensive plan for the control of air pollution which will enable all levels of government, as well as the private sector, to discharge their respective responsibilities for controlling pollution, on a regional basis, in a logical and orderly way.

I would like to review just how we intend to accomplish air pollution control under the Air Quality Act of 1967.

First, the Department of Health, Education, and Welfare is given the responsibility of defining the broad *atmospheric areas* of the Nation. This step was essentially accomplished on January 16 when we marked out eight atmospheric areas covering the 48 contiguous States. Areas covering Alaska and Hawaii will be defined later. Each of the atmospheric areas represents a segment of the country in which climate, meteorology, and topography— all of which influence the capacity of air to dilute and disperse pollution—are generally homogeneous.

Second, the Act requires the Department to designate *specific air quality control regions*. These regions will be designated on the basis of factors which suggest that a group of communities should be treated as a unit for the purpose of setting and implementing *air quality standards*. Factors to be considered in making these determinations include meteorological, topographical, social, and political considerations, and the nature and location of air pollution sources. We are moving rapidly ahead on this work, and we hope to designate several of the more important control regions by the end of this fiscal year.

At the same time, the Department is required to develop and publish *air quality criteria* for a pollutant or group of pollutants, together with information on available control techniques applicable to the various sources of that pollutant or group of pollutants.

Air quality criteria represent the latest scientific evidence of the effects of air pollution on human health and property. The criteria describe the predictable effects of exposures to various concentrations of a pollutant for various lengths of time. As such they provide a

21

scientific basis for establishing what standards of air quality we must, as a minimum, achieve. They are, then, the scientific cornerstone upon which we will build our control efforts under the Air Quality Act.

I must say at this point that I cannot agree with those who declare that we do not yet know enough to publish criteria. It is true that we have not been able to define precisely the mechanism through which air pollution contributes to disease, and it is true that we have not been able to quantify precisely the contribution of air pollution to the incidence of disease. We may wait many years before our research efforts yield this kind of information.

But it is also true that there is abundant epidemiological, clinical, and laboratory evidence that air pollution *is* connected with the onset and worsening of disease.

A year ago, in testimony before the Senate Subcommittee on Air and Water Pollution, Surgeon General Stewart said, and I quote: "It would be foolish to say that we do not need more research on the health effects of air pollution. Of course, we do. It is rarely possible for us, at our present stage of scientific sophistication, to point to an individual case and say with certainty, "This man died because of air pollution," or "This man is unable to work because of air pollution".

". . . We are dealing with an extraordinarily complex set of phenomena when we seek the causes of the chronic illnesses which are our dominant health problem today. The old, familiar relationship of one-cause, one-disease—the formula upon which our success stories in communicable disease control and eradication have been built—no longer suffices. . . . air pollution is clearly and unquestionably a factor in the development of not one, but many, diseases affecting literally millions of our people. We have evidence of many kinds, from many sources, pointing inexorably in that direction. To ignore such evidence until the last 't' is crossed and the last 'i' is dotted would be dangerous folly."

The United States Congress does not intend that we wait until the last "t" is crossed and the last "i" is dotted. In the Air Quality Act the Congress directs the Secretary of Health, Education, and Welfare to publish criteria for those pollutants he believes harmful to health and welfare *as soon as practicable* and based on the *latest scientific knowledge*. Under the Act, air quality criteria must be published *before* the States can begin to carry out their responsibilities for controlling pollution in the regions designated by the Secretary.

The National Center for Air Pollution Control is pushing ahead with the task of developing criteria as rapidly as we can. As required by the Air Quality Act, we have established a National Advisory Committee on Criteria, with a membership broadly representative of industry, the universities, and all levels of government, and we expect to issue criteria for two major classes of pollution—the sulfur oxides and the particulates—early this summer.

Returning to the provisions of the Air Quality Act, as soon as a criterion and the related information on control techniques is published, the Act begins to have a direct effect on those States responsible for the air quality control regions that have been designated.

The Act sets up a timetable which States must follow in developing air quality standards and implementation plans for the designated regions. When air quality criteria and data on control technology are made available for a pollutant or class of pollutants, the States will have 90 days to submit a letter indicating that they intend to set standards, 180 days in which to set the standards, and a further 180 days to develop plans for implementing them. If the Secretary of Health, Education, and Welfare finds that the air quality standards and plans for their implementation are consistent with criteria and related control technology information, then those standards and plans will take effect. If a State fails to establish standards, or if the Secretary finds that the standards are not consistent with the criteria, he can initiate action to ensure that appropriate standards are set. States may request a public hearing on any standards developed by the Secretary; in such cases the hearing Board's decision will be binding. States will be expected to assume the primary responsibility for application of the air quality standards. If a State's efforts prove inadequate, the Secretary is empowered to initiate abatement action.

This, then, abridged and abbreviated, is the mechanism established by the Air Quality Act through which we will begin to control air pollution on a regional basis in the United States. We already have at our disposal enough technical know-how to achieve a significant degree of control of many of our most serious sources of pollution, and our most immediate need is to see that this technology is applied in adequate measure. This is a challenge which clearly calls for the development of appropriate control programs at all levels of government.

But it is also clear that we must improve both our fundamental knowledge of air pollution and our control technology, not only to better cope with today's air pollution problem, but to arm us against future problems.

The Air Quality Act also makes possible a greatly accelerated program of research in all our areas of ignorance. We will expand and refine our knowledge of the effects of air pollution; we will acquire more fundamental knowledge of how pollutants move about in the atmosphere, how they are transformed, and how they are removed from the atmosphere; we will develop better tools for measuring air pollution; and we will do whatever research is necessary to allow us to control those sources of pollution for which we now have no controls, or none that is really feasible. We have charted our course through these areas, and I would like to examine more specifically where this course will lead us.

First, we cannot hope to get very far very soon along this course without help from industry and other private organizations. We will, of course, be doing work in our own and other Government laboratories, but this will be only a small part of what has to be done. We will be working jointly with the academic community and private industry. But we must rely heavily on the work that the private sector can do.

As indicated earlier, we know that air pollution is dangerous, but this knowledge has been particularized very little. We do not know exactly how dangerous it is, we do not know exactly what fractions of it—or combinations of fractions—are responsible for what particular damage, and there are many other areas where our suspicions are inadequately supported by credible data.

We will therefore be contracting out many research projects designed to give us the sort of information about effects we so badly need. One large region which we have as yet scarcely touched is behavioral toxicology. We must learn how to relate ambient levels of carbon monoxide to degradation of response time and mental acuity. We must soon go farther than that. We must discover the relationship between exposure to the odors from a meat rendering plant—or a diesel bus—to feelings of malaise, irritability, and other symptoms which must at some date be factored into air quality standards.

Basic work is needed also on development of better tools to examine the effects of air pollution, such as increased understanding in certain areas relating to the human respiratory system. We must investigate in some detail the effects of pollutants and combinations of pollutants in the laboratory and develop relationships between the laboratory effects on animals and the effects of ambient pollutants on humans.

Much more data must be developed on synergism. The effects of pollutants on subjects with infectious diseases, on subjects with special sensitivities, and on subjects whose defenses against injury have been lowered in other ways must be more intensely and more broadly investigated.

In a widely different field, we need significantly greater economic studies.

We must be able to say how much damage to materials is caused by exposures to varying levels of pollution. And we must also conduct studies which will relate control expenditures to economic benefits.

We also have to gather a great deal of basic knowledge on the mechanics and chemistry of air pollution. Our knowledge of the life cycle of pollutants, for instance, is mostly suppositional. We do not fully understand the natural cleansing processes of the atmosphere, and we are forced to base some of our calculations for the transport and dispersion of pollutants on some rather shaky assumptions.

For most places in the country, we cannot even say, as precisely as we might like to, what the levels of all the important pollutants are at any given moment, nor how they vary from hour to hour, day to day, and season to season. We have this knowledge for only a handful of our large cities. In a few cities we have installed continuous air monitoring stations, and these stations monitor half a dozen of the most serious pollutants continuously. But we have only one such station in each of these cities—downtown—and our knowledge of pollution throughout the rest of the city is largely derivative. These stations are expensive. They require an air conditioned building, a supply of wet chemicals, and an operator. There is no good reason why such stations could not be designed at less cost. Surely when we can analyze the dust on the moon without sending a technician along to do the job, we should be able to analyze the dust we breathe on earth without one. What we need is a continuous monitor for the major pollutants, the size of a desk, needing no chemical supplies, easy to maintain, having telemetering capability—in other words, an inexpensive monitor that does not require an operator. Here is a specific task for science and industry.

We need instruments that will allow us to "map" pollutant concentrations and sources rapidly and cheaply from airborne platforms. By the time emission standards have been set by the States, control agencies will need the tools for checking compliance with the standards. These agencies should be equipped to measure remotely, without entering private property, the concentrations of stack emissions of sulfur oxides, nitrogen oxides, hydrocarbons, particulates, organics, and other pollutants.

The third area where scientific help is needed is in the development of control technology.

We have underway a comprehensive, multimillion dollar program for developing techniques and devices for controlling sulfur pollution. Nearly forty contracts have already been or will soon be let for various aspects of this program. Their price tags range from $5000 to $1.5 million. While the importance of sulfur pollution warrants the attention and expenditures involved in such an intensive program, there are other pollutants for which programs of a similar nature are required.

For example we are starting such a program for nitrogen oxides from stationary sources. It is anticipated that this program will result in changes to the design handbooks for all types of combustion units to allow minimum production of nitrogen oxides. In addition, other methods should be developed, especially for large and existing sources, that allow recovery of nitrogen as a useful by-product. With our Fiscal 68 funds we are supporting a comprehensive state-of-the-art and planning study in this area. This will permit bench and pilot studies to begin in Fiscal 69 for all significant sources of nitrogen oxides, and by the end of Fiscal 69 we expect that private research talent will be fully mobilized toward solutions, feasibility studies will be underway, mathematical models of heterogeneous combustion reactions will have been developed and partially verified, work will have begun on design and pilot testing of small and intermediate combustion units with minimum production of nitrogen oxides, and data analysis and conceptual designs of large boilers will have begun.

There is far more to be done than I have time to discuss in this presentation. Our methods of incineration must be improved. In fact, many existing control devices should be improved and made more economical. We expect to stimulate the research which will result in markedly cheaper and more effective electrostatic precipitators, inertial separators, filters, scrubbers, and catalytic combustion schemes. And beyond control devices, there is the enormous field of process modification. How far, for instance, can we control the pollution from rendering plants, foundries, smelters, paper mills and so forth by controlling temperature and other process variables? We must find out.

And so on and on. And I have not even mentioned motor vehicles. I could devote my entire presentation to motor vehicles. But here I will touch on the subject only very briefly. As you undoubtedly know, control of motor vehicle crankcase hydrocarbon emissions began in California with the installation of devices in 1961; the same devices were used nationally in 1963. Hydrocarbon and carbon monoxide emissions have been significantly reduced from new car exhaust in California since the introduction of 1966 models; and, under Federal standards, exhaust emissions have been controlled on new cars throughout the United States since the introduction of 1968 models. However, the increasing number of motor vehicles will offset the benefits of present controls, probably by the 1980's unless we can achieve a much higher degree of control. Engine modification will for the most part bring the automobile into line with the tighter standards we have proposed for 1970 model vehicles, but greater changes will be required to meet future needs. Changes in the composition of gasoline may be needed to reduce the photochemical reactivity of hydrocarbon emissions; still other changes may be needed if lead and other gasoline additives emitted to the air through vehicular exhaust are shown to be deleterious.

There are a multitude of problems to be solved before we can hope to begin to turn the tide against our common enemy in the air. Under the Air Quality Act, the Federal funds authorized for research and development are vastly expanded—with a total of $125 million earmarked for this purpose over the next two years. At the same time, the Act gives us statutory authority to help finance co-operative industry-Government research and development projects to bring about new and improved control technology. Thus, with industry's co-operation, the $125 million Federal expenditure can be multiplied into the kind of massive application of money and talents and resources which has long been necessary to close the technological gaps which hinder our struggle to achieve effective controls nationally.

The need for action, mutual understanding, and co-operation in controlling air pollution has never been so great or so urgent as it is today. But mutual understanding and co-operation without real effort on the part of those who are understanding each other and co-operating with each other has never accomplished anything. What we need more than mutual understanding and co-operation is strong effort by government at all levels—and by all of the private sector—to carry out the activities which are so clearly needed.

The air pollution control efforts of industry and of government at all levels in the United States have been judged inadequate by the Congress and by the public whom the Congress represents. We have no alternative, then, but to seek a fresh perspective and to think and plan along new lines. The public will turn a deaf ear to the old pleas that we must suffer the effects of pollution because we are too unsophisticated, technically, to conduct our business without reducing it. After all, the public logically thinks, we have satellites in orbit, and we will soon be visiting the moon.

There will always be the need for additional knowledge in our quest for the most equitable and the most efficient way to avoid inundation and suffocation in our wastes. Goals will be set and discarded. Criteria and standards will be set and revised. The war to keep man from spoiling his environment will never end. But we can and must reach a point where we can breathe the air about us without fear.

WATER POLLUTION

UNSOLVED ENGINEERING PROBLEMS IN WATER QUALITY MANAGEMENT

E. F. GLOYNA *The University of Texas at Austin*

ABSTRACT

There are many unsolved problems in water quality management. This paper considers some general water pollution characteristics and presents some specific examples of data. Attention is directed to engineering designs and waste treatment plant operations. Some topics covered include: available alternatives, influence of water reuse on long range planning, monitoring devices, nutrient removal, toxic accumulations, taste and odor control, disposal of refractory organics, problems associated with translation of laboratory data to usable designs, and training.

INTRODUCTION

The purpose of this keynote address is to examine the major technical and economic problems of water pollution and wastewater management alternatives, directing particular emphasis on the topics of the preceding papers.

Let us recognize that there are emerging conflicts in water use and because of the mammoth problems associated with pollution, engineers must be prophets of hope. However, the professional community in water resources today faces an era in which basic values must be analyzed more prudently than ever before. Engineers most assuredly will agree that "maximum beneficial use" can be realized only when the problems related to resource development are thoroughly understood, the basic parameters controlling the solutions to some of our environmental problems are clearly defined, the economic tradeoffs are acceptable to the body politic, and the basic water needs of human beings are satisfied.

The need to provide a suitable water supply is paramount. The people of North America use water in greater abundance and perhaps are less informed about the intrinsic values of useable water than any people in the world. In the formerly water-rich eastern part of the U.S.A., areas such as New York have sold water for $10 per 1000 gallons. Today cities in the U.S.A. receive an average revenue of 33c per 1000 gallons. Our society demands safe water in almost unlimited quantity. This growing mass of humanity at the same time wishes to see the arid lands bloom; the development of cheap power at the expense of hydroelectric dams, controlled thermal releases, etc.; the rerouting of rivers to make them navigable; water made aesthetically acceptable; and, last but not least, a water resource that may be called upon to provide a substantial source of the world's food supply.

While people do not generally recognize either the value or the cost of stream pollution there is an increasing cry for the governments to move in and do something, at least until this same citizenry faces the stark facts of increases in tax rates or product costs. Of course to some, taxes are a painless way of meeting the true costs.

Unfortunately it has been said that water resource engineers like Universities have become discipline oriented, whereas society is problem oriented, and as a result there is a basic incongruity between the needs of society and the ideas of the professional involved in water pollution.

Basically our water resource management problem can be likened after an old Chinese proverb:

"Give a man a fish and he will eat for a day; teach him to fish and he will eat for the rest of his days."

Or rephrased:

Give people the right to indiscriminant releases of wastes and they will profit for a while; show them how to equitably use their water resources and they will profit the rest of their days.

DEFINITION

Water Pollution might be defined as a discharge into water that imposes an external cost on subsequent users, or as a discharge that interferes with the optimum use of water resources.

CHARACTERISTICS OF THE PROBLEM

Pollution is the one aspect which establishes a technical link between various economic units. An essential element of the pollution problem is that the damages caused by waste disposal into water courses are in most instances external to the polluting unit.

1. Water pollution is usually discussed in much too narrow terms. The real problem is to see that water quality and quantity are managed in such a way as to maximize economic and social returns.
2. Waste disposal should be viewed and accepted as a legitimate economic activity to take its place alongside other possible uses of our water resources.
3. Technical aspects of handling water pollution are ahead of the economic-social-political aspects of water quality management; yet, the technical side of the question is not far enough advanced to provide sufficient or adequate answers.
4. The ultimate environmental polluters will be the consumers of industrial products. The business community needs to think more about the degradability and safety of its products in terms of final disposition.
5. The first step in minimizing the effects of wastes on streams and treatment plants is to reduce the volume of such wastes. This may be accomplished by: (a) classification of wastes; (b) conservation of waste-water; (c) changing production to decrease wastes; (d) reusing both industrial and municipal effluents for raw water supplies.
6. The man on the street generally regards pollution as something he can see and smell. Yet experts know that many pollutants that appear to be colorless and pleasant to be around may be highly destructive.

THE NATURE OF POLLUTION

Pollutants seem to fit into about eight general categories:

1. Infectious agents.
2. Oxygen-demanding wastes.
3. Plant nutrients.
4. Organic chemicals.
5. Inorganic chemical and mineral substances.

6. Sediments and other solids.
7. Radioactive materials.
8. Heat.

SOURCES AND EFFECTS OF INDUSTRIAL WASTEWATERS

Every industry produces liquid wastes. A classification of these wastes may be made by type of industry or by effect of the waste on the environment.

On an industrial basis the manufacture of a specific product by different factories will result in similar liquid waste materials. However, each plant within an industry will produce different quantities of wastes, and these will have different effects on water quality when placed into a specific unique receiving stream. Obviously, this classification gives no indication of interaction type effects produced by more than one industry within a selected area.

A classification based upon their effects in the receiving water body has more advantages for water quality studies than classification by industry. Notably, most of the analytical procedures record the effects of industrial wastes rather than the components, although the latter are of significance in certain instances.

MAJOR ENGINEERING PROBLEMS

A listing of some general problem areas must surely include the following:
1. Costly alternatives.
2. Estimating effects of return flows.
3. Data acquisition.
4. Nutrient removal.
5. Thermal pollution.
6. Toxic accumulations.
7. Tastes and odors control.
8. Disposal of refractory organics.
9. Translation of laboratory data into operational facilities.
10. Training people.
11. Others.

1. Costly Alternatives

The U.S. National Academy of Sciences suggests that there are only a few basic methods for waste management now available [1].
(a) Recovery and reuse—water, air, land and pollutant.
(b) Waste treatment—modification, removal and disposal of contaminant.
(c) Product modification.
(d) Process change.
(e) Elimination.
(f) Dispersion.
(g) Dilution.
(h) Detention.
(i) Diversion.
(j) Environmental treatment.
(k) Desensitization of pollution receptors such as vaccination.

2. Return Flows

With respect to return flows it is becoming increasingly clear that long-range water quality plans can be made only after return flows have been evaluated. As an example, of the 3.2 million acre-feet of freshwater withdrawn annually by municipal and industrial water users in Texas, approximately 60 % is returned directly to the surface waters of the state. Within the next 50 years, withdrawals may conceivably increase to 11 million acre-feet annually, and return flows may increase to about 6 million acre-feet per year [2]. Effective utilization of this increasing quantity of return flow will not be feasible unless a workable plan is developed for maintaining the quality of the surface waters into which the wastewater is released.

Table 1 shows average future effluent concentrations that will have to be maintained merely to maintain present receiving water quality, regardless of what the present quality may be. Any cleaning up of surface waters will require higher effluent qualities than those shown. In areas such as the Victoria Trading Area, Table 1, it does not appear that municipal effluents can be improved significantly by conventional biological treatment processes.

It is estimated that by 1980 enough phosphate (PO_4) will be discharged each year to add 1 mg/l to the average annual runoff of about 35 million acre-feet per year of all Texas streams. Much higher concentrations will prevail at the release points.

3. Data Acquisition

Pollution control requires objective and accurate data. There is a most serious and prevailing need for precise, reliable data that can be utilized for specifying the design of systems, performance, and management. The testing system must provide greater specificity and sensitivity, automatic analyses, digital data presentations, and automatic printout. Data must accurately depict the projected reaction rates, the present ecological environment, and the future changes in the aquatic system.

Today management is meeting its responsibility to the public and engineers are providing better designs; both must have more continuous data. Such data collection systems must realistically monitor each major pollutant source and provide the spacial and temporal basis for environmental predictions.

TABLE 1. PROJECTED EFFLUENT QUALITIES NECESSARY TO MAINTAIN PRESENT WASTE LOADS IN STREAMS
(mg/l)

	Texas State Total				Victoria Trading Area			
	1960	1980	2000	2020	1960	1980	2000	2020
Municipal								
B.O.D.	36	19	13	9	21	9	6	4
Suspended sol.	47	25	17	11	29	13	9	6
Total sol.	705	380	260	170	800	360	240	160
Chlorides	160	87	59	39	285	130	85	57
Nitrates	25	14	9	6	25	11	8	5
Phosphates	25	14	10	6	28	12	8	6
Industrial								
B.O.D.	180	87	65	47	41	18	13	9
Suspended sol.	400	192	145	105	130	57	42	30
Total sol.	5550	2660	2000	1450	3470	1520	1110	800
Chlorides	4625	2215	1650	1200	990	435	315	230
C.O.D.	620	300	220	165	400	180	130	95
Sulfates	1100	520	385	285	22	10	7	5

Specifically, flow, integrated waste loads, and certain pollutants must be monitored. The "sewage" yardsticks are not adequate for monitoring most industrial waste streams. Some promising automatic monitoring devices include the following meters:

magnetic flow
total oxygen demand
total organic carbon
dissolved oxygen
oxidation reduction potential
temperature
pH
conductivity.

4. Nutrient Removal

Nutrient removals, primarily nitrogen and phosphorus, must be accelerated as more waste streams find their way to the ever increasingly used waterways. Today the available data would indicate that it is possible to remove 90–95 % of the phosphates by chemical treatment at a cost of 5 cents (U.S.) per 1000 gallons. Nitrogen removal through digestion techniques is also possible.

The removal of these nutrients could easily cost billions of dollars. Yet, at this point there is not enough data available on how much of the nutrients must be removed to accomplish any desired effect on the aquatic environment.

More work must be done toward correlating primary productivity with increased waste loads. For example, the transport of ions in an aqueous environment is related to the total biological activity, and the magnitude of community metabolism may be used to describe community types. Communities undergoing eutrophication usually exhibit relatively high productivity. Organically enriched communities are usually characterized by relatively high productivity and respiration. Productivity/respiration (P/R) ratio is an index by which an aquatic community can be classified. When respiratory demands exceed oxygen production (P/R ratio of less than one), the community is said to be heterotrophic.

5. Thermal Pollution

The addition of excessive heat to a reservoir, stream or estuary may produce end results which are equivalent to organic pollution. Increased water temperatures may cause severe economic losses in power plant operations, high evaporative losses, and gross errors in estimating the assimilative capacity of a stream [3]. The latter problem is magnified because:

(a) increased heat lowers the assimilative capacity of a stream and heat hastens the rate of BOD exertion;
(b) organisms require more dissolved oxygen for existence as the temperature is increased;
(c) changes in temperature may significantly change the reproduction rate, as well as other activities of aquatic organisms;
(d) certain compounds may become more toxic to aquatic organisms as the temperature increases; and
(e) increases in temperature frequently result in decreases in species diversification and increases in select groups of organisms.

Approximately one gallon of water is evaporated for each 8800 BTU dissipated in a cooling tower or 0.61 gallons is evaporated for each kw-h produced [4]. In Texas between 49 and 58 % of the heat added to a reservoir results in evaporation [5].

6. Toxicity

Meaningful data are needed more today than ever before. However, we do not really know how to rapidly identify toxic compounds. The myriad of organisms which constitute the aquatic food chain represent an extremely complex problem. The destruction or partial inactivation of any part of the aquatic food chain leads to profound and adverse ecological effects. For example, recent studies of the effects of various organics on algal forms have shown that the efficiency of waste stabilization ponds can be reduced materially due to chlorophyll destruction by certain toxic compounds [6].

It is evident that the destructive characteristic of phenolic compounds to chlorophyll is a function of the substituent group as well as the relative substitution position. Introduction to phenol of any substituent group other than a hydroxyl group increases the destruction of chlorophyll. The effectiveness of the substituent group in raising this "toxicity" decreases accordingly: $-NO_2 > -Br > -Cl > -NH_2 > CH_3 > -OH$. The additional introduction of another substituted group generally further reduces the chlorophyll content. For example, among the chlorine-substituted phenols the degree of "toxicity" decreases in the order of: pentachlorophenols > trichlorophenols > dichlorophenols > monochlorophenols. This is the same case for methyl-substituted phenols since xylenols produce greater effects than cresols at concentrations above 100 mg/l. However, nitro-substituted and hydroxyl-substituted phenols do not follow this rule. *Para-* and *ortho-*substituted phenols generally demonstrated a higher "toxicity" than the *meta-*isomer, however halogen-substituted phenols were more destructive in *meta-*substitutions.

Among the five chlorine-substituted phenols, the relative order of photosynthetic suppression was found to be: 2,4,6-trichlorophenol > 2,4-dichlorophenol > *meta-*chlorophenol > *para-*chlorophenol > *ortho-*chlorophenol.

7. Taste and Odors

To the layman, taste and odor are probably the most graphic evidence of pollution. Many compounds in petrochemical wastes cause tastes and odors at very low concentrations with the synergistic effects of complex mixtures significantly magnifying these effects. A study utilizing m-cresol, n-butanol, pyridine, n-butyl-mercaptan, n-amyl acetate, acrylonitrile, 2-4 dichlorophenol, and acetophenone showed marked synergistic effects. A mixture containing each compound at 1/8 of its threshold value seems to produce a significant olfactory response. Binary mixtures of selected pairs of these compounds showed similar effects. Any or all of these chemicals might be found in a petrochemical effluent, and the significance of these results in taste and odor problems is apparent.

A study of a refinery wastewater has indicated that the neutral organic compounds (non-polar) consisting principally of aliphatic and aromatic hydrocarbons, are the primary sources of odor in the wastewater. The oxygenated and aromatic fractions of the neutral organic group may be the most odiferous. The odors seem to be a complex mixture of hydrocarbons, alcohols, aldehydes, ketones, esters and nitriles and the odors caused by this fraction cannot be attributed to any single compound. Many neutral organic compounds are commonly found in petrochemical wastes. Organic acids are also found in many petrochemical wastes, and many of these acids can cause tastes and odors in water. Alkyl benzene sulfonates can be detected by some people at concentrations below 1 mg/l.

8. Disposal of Refractory Organics

Wastes from petrochemical operations are derived primarily from by-product formation, incomplete reactions, mechanical and accidental losses, or substituted organics. Hydrocarbons are most common in condensates and caustic wastes from primary conversion processes. These wastes along with other industrial process wastes and domestic sewage contain increasing amounts of non-biodegradable COD.

Refinery waste recovery processes involve treatment of wastes rich in phenolic materials, sulfides, etc. The BOD, BOD_5-COD, and COD-TOC characterization of typical wastes are shown in Figs. 1, 2, and 3.

Notably a residual COD in either refinery or petrochemical waste effluents is always to be expected and this can create some potential reuse problems. In Fig. 4, the maximum COD and BOD removals are obtainable for a specific waste when the product of the average mixed liquor volatile solids (MLVSS or S_a) and detention exceeds 60,000. At a volatile suspended solids concentration of 2400 mg/l normally employed in activated sludge or extended aeration systems, a minimum detention time requirement of 20–30 hours is indicated for maximum organic removal. These data tend to demonstrate the problem associated with the residual components.

The degradable phenol in this waste was about 500 mg/l but the residual COD was due to complex refractory organics.

9. Translation of Data

The problem of estimating the predicted flow, oxygen requirements and biological sludge production for most refinery and petrochemical operations can be approximated closely in

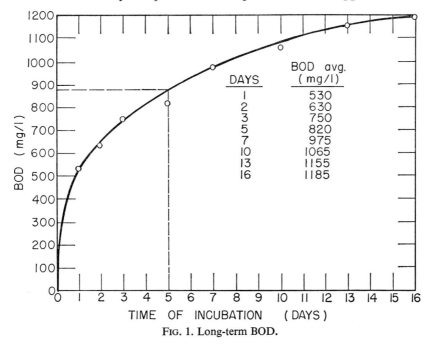

DAYS	BOD avg. (mg/l)
1	530
2	630
3	750
5	820
7	975
10	1065
13	1155
16	1185

FIG. 1. Long-term BOD.

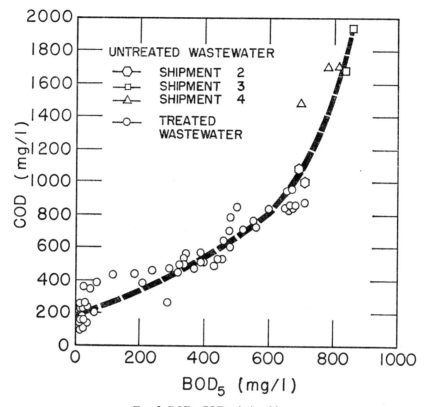

FIG. 2. BOD$_5$-COD relationship.

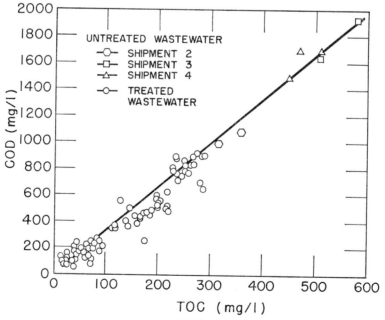

FIG. 3. TOC-COD relationship.

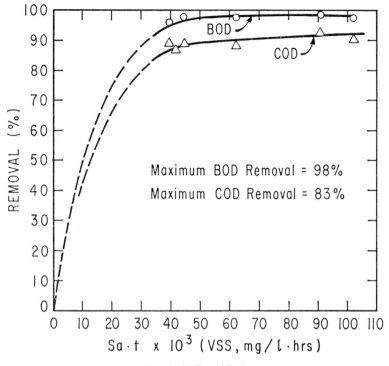

FIG. 4. COD residuals.

the laboratory but translation of these data to the field is still difficult. Some of this problem is due to the long time that elapses between the laboratory initiation and the time hardware actually becomes available. While it is recognized that the maintenance of steady state operations in a refinery waste treatment plant involves rigid control of in-plant processes, surface water runoffs, and waste treatment plant operations, it is also necessary to obtain useful reaction rates on which designs can be made.

For example the oxygen requirements for an aerated lagoon or extended aeration system can be determined by considering the following model:

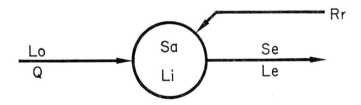

where

Lo = initial BOD or COD, mg/l
Li = aeration tank BOD or COD
Le = effluent BOD or COD ($Le = Li$ for completely mixed system)
Lr = mg/l of BOD, COD removed

37

Q = flow, liters/day
Sa = average mixed liquor volatile suspended solids in aeration tank
Se = average mixed liquor volatile suspended solids in effluent
     ($Sa = Se$ for completely mixed system)
t = detention time, days
Rr = oxygen uptake rate, $mgO_2/l/day$
V = volume of tank, liters
k' = chemical reaction demand coefficient

The total oxygen demand (RrV) includes the following:

1. Oxygen required for biological organic removal ($a'LrQ$).
2. Oxygen required for endogenous respiration (cells lyse and release soluble oxidizable organic compounds) ($b'SaV$).
3. Oxygen required for chemical oxidation of sulfides, sulfites, aldehydes, etc. ($k'Q$).

The mathematical expression for this demand is:

$$RrV = a'LrQ + b'SaV + k'Q$$

The constants a' and b' can be determined by rearranging the equation,

$$\frac{Rr}{Sa} = a' \frac{Lr}{Sa \cdot t} + b'$$

and $t = V/Q$ and $K'Q$ are calculated separately.

These constants as evaluated from typical refinery batch and continuous type studies (Fig. 5) show that discrepancies occur as a result of air stripping. Due to the nature of the test, the air stripping effects were most pronounced in the continuous units.

The oxygen transfer coefficient, α, is difficult to ascertain. A change in product or mode of operation may drastically change the oxygen transfer characteristics.

The problem of estimating sludge production, settling rates, and disposal characteristics also involves a number of variables. Again just as an example sludge production is normally based on the following equation:

$$\Delta S = aLr - b\,Sa$$

where ΔS = net increase in MLVSS, mg/l
    a = fraction of COD converted to new cells
    b = fraction/day of VSS oxidized
   Lr = BOD, COD removed, mg/l
   Sa = volatile suspended solids, mg/l

Figure 6 shows the difference in using batch and continuous data.

10. Training

The need to provide technically trained manpower at all levels of wastewater management is paramount. The U.S. Federal Water Pollution Control Administration noted at a recent congressional hearing that between now and 1972, state and local governments would need an additional 5400 scientists, and related engineers, professional personnel for water pollution control purposes, an additional 3900 technicians, and 10,000 trained sewage treatment plant operators.

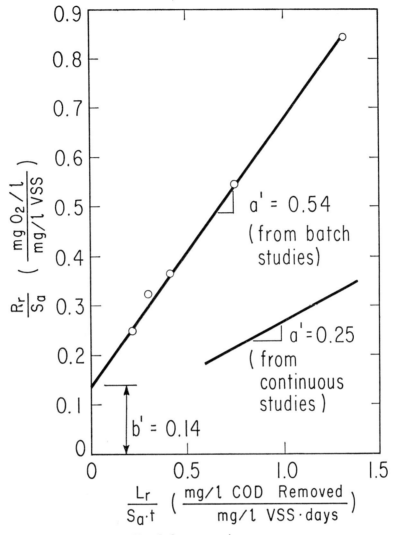

FIG. 5. Oxygen requirements.

In the past there was an orderly development of technology and training. Today there is a need for the specialist as soon as designs are developed. Consequently, training programs must provide an individual who is not only capable of translating the latest science and technology into operational units, but one who recognizes the constraints imposed on water resource management by society.

11. Others

Not least on the list of unsolved problems are those associated with urban runoff, animal feed lots, solids handling, solids-liquid separation, treatment of high volume, dilute concentration wastes, disposal of water treatment plant sludges, disposal of inorganic concentrates, etc.

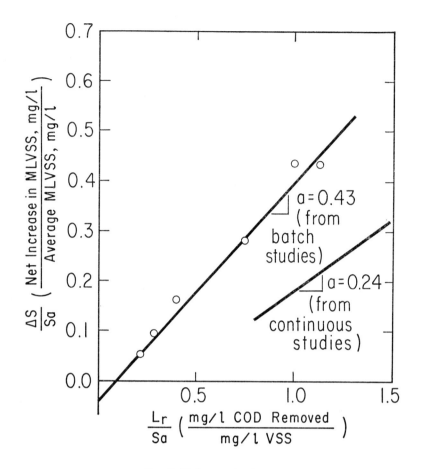

FIG. 6. Sludge production.

REFERENCES

1. SPILHOUS, A., Waste management and control, Publ. 1400 Nat'l. Acad. Sciences, Nat'l. Research Council, Washington D.C., 1966, p. 22.
2. WELLS, D. M. and GLOYNA, E. F., Estimating the effects of return flows, *Journal American Water Works Association*, **59**:7, presented at AWWA Annual Conference, Bal Harbour, Florida, May 1966, pp. 805–819.
3. KRENKEL, P. A., Notes on thermal pollution, Vanderbilt University, Nashville, Tennessee, 1968.
4. Steam electric plant factors, *Nat'l. Coal Assoc.*, **22**, Washington, D.C., 1963, pp. 16–17.
5. DREW, H. W., A projection of *per capita* water use for electric power generation in Texas, Report Prepared for the Texas Water Commission, May 15, 1965.
6. HUANG, H. and GLOYNA, E. F., Effects of toxic organics on photosynthetic reoxygenation, Parts I and II, *International Journal on Water Pollution*, in press, 1968.
7. GLOYNA, E. F. and FORD, D. L., Monograph on Petrochemical Waste Treatment. Unpublished Report, The University of Texas, 1968.
8. GLOYNA, E. F. and FORD, D. L., Petrochemical waste treatment studies, Unpublished Report, Center for Research in Water Resources, The University of Texas, Austin, Texas, 1968.
9. GLOYNA, E. F. and FORD, D. L., Refinery waste treatment studies, Unpublished Report, Center for Research in Water Resources, The University of Texas, Austin, Texas, 1968.

DISCUSSION

S. K. KRISHNASWAMI (*Department of National Health and Welfare, Edmonton*).

I do not know how disappointed Dr. J. B. Cragg is in our inability as engineers to meet his challenge to restore our total environment through pollution control efforts. I am afraid that all our efforts for the prevention, control, and abatement of pollution are directed only toward man's requirements of water quality and the promotion of his esthetic aspirations rather than toward the preservation of his total environment. I think we lack an organized effort to prevent, control, and abate pollution from the view points of global ecology that Dr. Cragg has referred to.

Our pollution control standards, objectives, and ideals are all based upon only man's requirements of water quality for the various uses of water such as agriculture, industry, municipal supply, recreation and aquatic food culture.

LIQUID WASTE IN THE PULP AND PAPER INDUSTRY

D. R. STANLEY *Stanley Associates Engineering Ltd., Edmonton*

ABSTRACT

Water pollution problems due to liquid waste from the pulp and paper industry and methods of treatment to alleviate these problems are described. A specific problem of stream pollution due to waste from a bleached Kraft pulp mill in Alberta is presented and the approach used in solving the problem outlined. Several methods of treatment were considered including activated sludge, trickling filters, aerated lagoons and anaerobic lagoons. The activated sludge process provided the most reliable method of alleviating the problem, but would have been very expensive. The aerated lagoon type of treatment was considered to have the best potential as a technically feasible and economic solution to the problem.

INTRODUCTION

Although most of these attending this conference are professional engineers, I assume that only a few are familiar with the technical aspects of pollution and probably fewer still with the problems of liquid waste in the pulp and paper industry. I propose first to deal generally with liquid wastes in the industry and then to describe the studies and methods of solution to a specific problem.

The pulp and paper industry is a very important one in Canada. This can be seen from the following quotation from a paper by Mr. Douglas Jones of the Canadian Pulp and Paper Association prepared in 1966 for the Pollution And Our Environment Conference in Montreal.

"The pulp and paper industry is today, and has been for many years, Canada's leading manufacturing industry. It leads all others in the value of its production, as well as in employment, wages paid, exports, and capital investment.

"The industry accounts for about one-sixth of Canada's export trade, and its operations have a profound effect, either direct or indirect, on virtually every element of the economy.

"Although the industry more than doubled during the past twenty years, it is currently engaged in the greatest expansion in its history, and its capital expenditures in 1965 totalled some $475 million. So it has been, and will continue to be, a key element in the nation's economic growth and development.

"The annual production of the industry is now valued at more than two billion dollars, or close to five per cent of Canada's gross national product. The Province of Quebec is the leading producer, accounting for 37 per cent of the national output. Ontario is second with 24 per cent, followed by British Columbia with 23 per cent, New Brunswick, Nova Scotia and Newfoundland with 14 per cent, and Alberta, Saskatchewan and Manitoba with 2 per cent."

The pulp and paper industry is a large user of water and the major pollution problems are due to the discharge of liquid wastes from pulp mills into streams where there is insufficient dilution. The adverse effects on a stream may include oxygen depletion, deposits of suspended matter, toxicity to fish, colour, and odour.

1. *Oxygen depletion* due to high BOD (Biochemical Oxygen Demand) in the plant effluents is the most common difficulty with pulp mill wastes. If the waste is discharged into a stream and there is not sufficient flow for dilution, the oxygen in the stream can be depleted to the point where fish are harmed or killed. If serious enough, the oxygen depletion can create "barriers" which block the passage of fish from one part of a stream to another.

A modern full bleached Kraft (sulfate) mill of 1000 tons/day capacity would discharge about 60 million gallons per day of waste and about 35,000 lb of BOD which is the equivalent BOD of sewage from a city of about 200,000 people. The quantity and characteristics of the waste will vary considerably with the design of the plant and process used. Mills using the sulfite process may discharge about the same volume of waste but the BOD may be many times higher.

2. *Deposits of suspended matter* from pulp mill waste can create a blanket on the bottom of a stream, making it incapable of sustaining bottom dwelling fish food organisms. The wastes contain a large amount of organic particulate matter which may come from the debarking operation and from fibre lost in the screening of pulp.

3. *Toxicity to fish* and their eggs can result from waste from bleached Kraft mills at dilutions of less than 20 to 1. For a sixty million gallon/day effluent such dilution would require a stream flow of $1 \cdot 2$ billion gallons/day or about 1800 cfs.

4. *Colour* is not too often a problem because receiving streams usually provide sufficient dilution or are already coloured, so that added colour may not be noticeable.

5. *Odour and taste problems* have arisen where it has been reported that fish taken from streams receiving waste from Kraft mills have a taste associated with the odour of the mill.

TREATMENT METHODS

Treatment of pulp and paper mill wastes can be accomplished by one or a combination of the following:

1. *Recovering methods.* These involve the use of "save-alls" either in closed or partly closed systems within the mills. The processes are based on filtration, sedimentation or flotation and provide waste treatment measures as well as conserving fibres and fillers.

2. *Sedimentation or flotation.* These methods may be used for part or all of the plant effluent to remove suspended matter.

3. *Chemical precipitation.* This method can be used to remove colloids and colour.

4. *Lagooning.* Lagooning can be employed to provide storage settling and some reduction in BOD.

5. *Biological treatment.* The use of biological treatment methods for reducing BOD in plant wastes is very common. Some colour reduction may also be accomplished at the same time. The activated sludge process, which is common in municipal sewage treatment, can be used but is expensive. Mechanically aerated lagoons are much more economical and quite effective although the degree of treatment may not be as high as can be obtained with the activated sludge process. Aerated lagoons pose some problems in cold climates but recent experience indicates that they can be used successfully even when temperatures are well below zero.

At the present time, the technology is available to provide satisfactory waste treatment for the pulp and paper industry but, as in most things, the problem is one of economics. In the early pulp mills, the loss of fibre was very high and as the cost of raw material increased, it became economical to reduce losses. This resulted in a considerable reduction in pollution load from plants.

Until about 10 years ago, the improved condition of effluents was largely due to capital expenditures that were made to effect economies in operation. However, in recent years, the industry has been faced with increasing expenditures on pollution control without any economic return. At one time little, if any, consideration was given to pollution problems when sites were being chosen and plants designed. Nowadays new mills make adequate provision for the control of water pollution. The Canadian Pulp and Paper Association estimates that each new mill in Canada spends 4 to 5% of its capital investment for control of air and water pollution.

There are situations in existing mills where, if it were necessary to provide a high degree of treatment, the capital cost of treatment could be as high as 10% of the value of the mill and the overall cost represent 4 to 5% of the sale price of the product. It is obvious that in such cases, the cost of waste treatment could be a major factor in the total costs of a plant even to the point of making a project uneconomical.

Significant progress has been made in the pulp and paper industry in pollution control. The paper industry is probably spending more to solve pollution problems than in any other industry. On the other hand, some of the worst problems of stream pollution have been caused by some of the old pulp and paper mills. The difficulty, of course, is to provide the necessary treatment without increasing the cost for the mills to the point where they will become uneconomic to operate. Thus there is a great need for developing more economical methods of pollution control. This can only be accomplished through the proper type of research on the method of pollution control and plant operation.

One type of treatment that is now being used but requires more study is aerated lagoons. Whereas there has been a considerable amount of experience with mechanically aerated lagoons during the past few years in different parts of the world, there has been little, if any, experience available on the design and operation of such facilities in the climates such as we experience in Alberta. It is proposed to describe in this paper a study that was conducted on the problem of waste treatment and disposal for the pulp mill of Northwest Pulp and Power Ltd. at Hinton, Alberta and to show how the use of laboratory testing and pilot plant operation led to the design of a full-scale treatment plant which utilized an aerated lagoon with surface aerators. This facility was put into operation in the fall of 1967 and has been operating successfully for about six months.

Investigations and studies included the following:

1. Quality and quantity surveys of the waste streams from the different parts of the mill.
2. Evaluation of the efficiency of the present treatment facilities.
3. Analysis of alternatives for adequate treatment of the waste from existing mill.
4. Preliminary design of proposed initial and ultimate treatment facilities with estimates of cost.
5. Laboratory studies of feasibility of anaerobic treatment and aerated lagoons under different temperature conditions, retention periods and nutrient additions.

6. Pilot plant studies to test the validity of the laboratory findings and to provide a basis for the design of full-scale facilities.

The Northwest Pulp and Power mill at Hinton, Alberta is located adjacent to the Athabasca River, about 180 miles west of Edmonton and has been in operation since 1957, producing more than 500 tons per day of bleached Kraft pulp.

Exclusive of in-plant solids recovery techniques, the only form of waste treatment utilized at the time of the study was the ponding of effluent in an 8 foot deep 21 acre lagoon. The pond received the entire mill general waste stream plus a flow of 0·4 mgd from the Town of Hinton. The total flow to the pond was 10 to 11 mgd and the theoretical detention period just over 5 days before sludge build-up. The layout of the plant and its relationship to the lagoon and the Athabasca River is shown in Fig. 1. Tests on the influent and effluent from the pond indicated that it acted simply as a settling basin removing suspended solids but did not provide any significant amount of biological reduction of the BOD. A schematic layout showing the relationship to the different processes in the plant and the waste collection and disposal facilities is shown in Fig. 2.

TREATMENT REQUIREMENTS

On the basis of Alberta Government requirements and tests on the waste, it appeared that it would be necessary to remove 60 % of the BOD from the total plant waste. Settling tests on the waste indicated what suspended solids and BOD removal could be expected from primary facilities and, as a result, it was estimated that 42,000 lb of the total BOD in the waste from the plant would have to be removed during the winter months by some secondary or biological process.

To pass the entire waste through treatment facilities would have required the addition of lime or caustic soda to increase the pH to about 7. The cost of lime for this purpose was estimated at about $400 per day. To avoid this high cost, a scheme was devised for by-passing a portion of the waste from the acid sewer directly to the river. It was felt that this would not have any ill effects on the river because of the relatively high buffer capacity in the river water at low flow periods.

With the remaining waste it was necessary to provide secondary facilities to remove a higher percentage of the BOD. Tests indicated that 77 % of the acid waste would have to be by-passed directly to the river to maintain a pH of 7 in the waste entering the biological facilities. On this basis, it was calculated that it would be necessary to remove 70 % of the BOD in the waste that was to be treated in the biological facilities.

METHODS OF TREATMENT

Four methods of secondary treatment were considered, namely: activated sludge, trickling filters, aerated lagoons and anaerobic lagoons. Estimates of capital and operating costs for each were made. On the basis of the cost per thousand gallons and cost per pound of BOD removed, the activated sludge process appeared to be about three times as expensive as an aerated lagoon. The anaerobic lagoon was the cheapest but we were not able to show in laboratory tests that any substantial BOD reduction could be obtained through the use of this method of treatment.

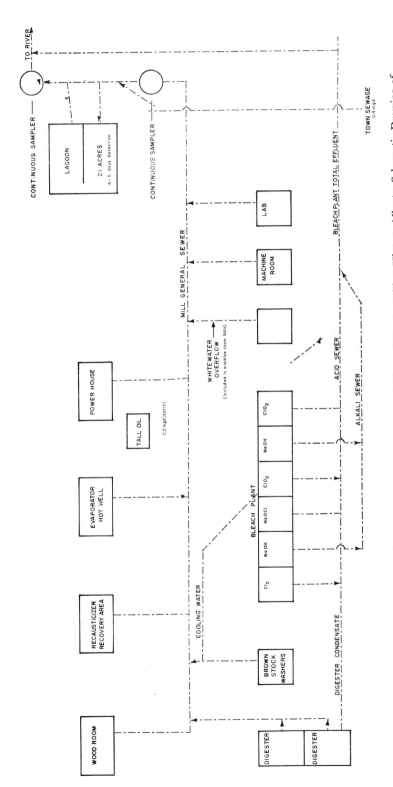

FIG. 2. North Western Pulp and Power Ltd waste treatment and disposal for the Mill at Hinton, Alberta. Schematic Drawing of existing waste collection and disposal facilities. (Stanley Associates Engineering Ltd.)

In each type of treatment considered, it was assumed that nutrients would have to be added. It appeared from the economic comparison of the methods that the aerated lagoons provided the most practical solution to the problem providing they could be designed and built to remove 70% of the BOD and could be operated efficiently under cold weather conditions.

Two methods of aeration were considered, namely the use of the surface aerators and the use of diffused air. Comparisons of the two types of aeration indicated that diffused air system would be much costlier than a system using surface aerators. The diffused air system has been employed in some municipal installations in Western Canada and operated under cold weather conditions but experience was limited and certain operating difficulties made it difficult to assess the long-range operating costs. Surface aerators, on the other hand, had been used quite extensively but in more moderate climates and, therefore, the basic problem was to assess whether or not such a system would be feasible under the cold weather conditions at Hinton.

Efforts were then concentrated on determining the feasibility of aerated lagoons using surface aerators and developing criteria which would allow the design of full-scale facilities. The limited experience indicated that surface aerators could be operated at low temperatures and that there was a reasonable probability that the efficiency of treatment would be high enough to meet requirements even when the temperature of the waste dropped due to cold weather.

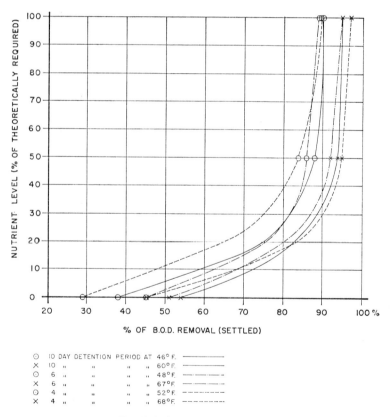

FIG. 3. Laboratory scale results.

Laboratory tests were therefore carried out at different temperatures, levels of nutrient addition, and detention periods to determine the effect on treatment efficiency of these parameters. Figure 3 shows the results of these tests and indicates the following:

1. Treatment efficiencies in excess of 80% BOD removal can be maintained with adequate nutrient, temperatures as low as 50°F. and detention times as low as 4 days.

2. Waste temperature is more significant in determining treatment efficiency than detention time.

3. Reducing nutrient to 50% of the theoretical requirement has very little effect on the efficiency. With reduction below the 50% level, a significant reduction in treatment efficiency becomes evident.

PILOT SCALE TESTS

Laboratory results were not considered reliable enough to use as a basis for designing a full-scale plant. Therefore, an existing-one acre pond was converted to a pilot scale facility to obtain additional data.

Laboratory scale work had indicated that a four-day detention period would provide almost as good treatment as six or ten days. It was therefore decided to test the pilot scale operation at a four-day detention time. The results of three tests are shown in Table 1.

TABLE 1. PILOT LAGOON TREATMENT EFFICIENCIES AT FOUR-DAY THEORETICAL DETENTION

Parameter	Trial 1	Trial 2	Trial 3
Flow	246 U.S. gpm	246 U.S. gpm	246 U.S. gpm
Period of record	12 days	12 days	6 days
Average waste temp.	48°F	47°F	58°F
Average air temp.	− 10°F	− 8°F	35°F
Nitrogen added	14·8 lb/day	18·8 lb/day	44·3 lb/day
Phosphorous added	1·3 lb/day	4·1 lb/day	8·9 lb/day
Average BOD$_5$(influent)	294 ppm	359 ppm	420 ppm
Average BOD$_5$(effluent)	122 ppm	108 ppm	105 ppm
% Efficiency	58·5	70	75
BOD (ultimate) removed	530 lb/day	770 lb/day	1020 lb/day
BOD : N : P	100 : 2·8 : 0·24	100 : 2·4 : 0·53	100 : 4·3 : 0·87

It should be noted that in Trial 1, due to a calculation error, the proportion of phosphorus to nitrogen was considerably lower than the theoretical proportions. The treatment efficiency for this trial is low, but it is difficult to conclude whether the concentration of phosphorus or of nitrogen is the more critical. The rate of nutrient addition for Trial 2 is about 1/2 of the theoretical ratio which is 100 : 5 : 1.

The higher efficiency noted in Trial 3 may have been due to a higher waste temperature of approximately 11°F or the use of more nutrient. On the basis of results from the laboratory scale tests, one would conclude that the difference in temperature of 10 or 11°F would have a greater effect on the efficiency than the difference in nutrient addition. The treatment efficiencies in the pilot scale tests seem to be approximately 10% less than those shown in Fig. 3 for the laboratory work.

One of the major concerns in utilizing surface aerated lagoons was the heat loss and consequent temperature drop expected when operating in very cold weather. Calculations of probable temperature drop were made and these were checked later against the experience with the pilot plant operation. The temperature drop observed was about 12°F, whereas the calculations indicated a temperature drop of more than double this figure. The most obvious reason for this appeared to be the formation of a layer of foam on the pond. This was 2 or 3 feet thick over most of the pond tapering to zero thickness in the immediate vicinity of the aerators. The foam seemed to solidify and provide a good insulation layer.

At no time was any ice accumulation observed on the aerator frame, motor, or float assembly. However, the waste temperature was quite high at all times, and probably much difficulty would be encountered with lower temperature wastes.

From the results of the laboratory and the pilot scale tests, it was concluded that the use of surface aerated lagoons for treating Kraft mill effluent in northern climates is feasible and economical where treatment efficiencies of 70% BOD removal are required. It was also concluded that further testing and experimenting with operation could develop more economical and efficient design and operating procedures.

FULL-SCALE TREATMENT FACILITIES

On the basis of the experiments carried out, a full-scale waste treatment facility was constructed and put into operation in the late fall of 1967. This included a clarifier for removal of suspended particulate matter and a lagoon with surface aerators. The facility has been operating for about 6 months over the winter of 1967–68.

For the first two months of operation, approximately 80% BOD removal was obtained in the aerated lagoon with a nutrient addition of approximately one-half of the theoretical requirement. This is a considerably better performance than experienced in the pilot plant operation. About 55% BOD removal was observed at a nutrient level of one-quarter the theoretical requirement.

The aerated lagoon was built by modifying the pond shown in Fig. 1. The north arm of this pond was deepened to more than twenty feet and twelve aerators placed in this section which provides three to four days' detention at the flow rate of 16 U.S. mgd. The waste then travels easterly in the north side of the pond where there are no aerators and thence to the outlet as shown in Fig. 1. Tests indicated that of the total BOD removed, 85% is removed in the first quarter of the north arm of the pond. If we assume no horizontal mixing in the pond, a retention period of one day should provide 85% of the BOD removal that can be obtained from a four-day detention period. Many more observations will have to be made to confirm this performance.

ACKNOWLEDGEMENTS

Laboratory and pilot plant data reported in this paper were previously published in a paper "Surface Aerated Lagoons in Northern Climates" by D. R. Stanley and W. K. Oldham, presented to the 1967 Conference of the Canadian Institute of Pollution Control. Data on the operation of the full-scale treatment facility was obtained from Mr. Graham Parker of North Western Pulp and Power Ltd. at Hinton.

DISCUSSION

S. K. KRISHNASWAMI (*Department of National Health and Welfare*), *Edmonton*

Your statement on color in your paper seems to me to be an oversimplification of the problem. Color is an important aesthetic consideration. Increases in color of receiving waters due to wastewater discharges from pulp mills should be controlled.

We do not know much about the effects of color-producing substances on stream biota. In Canada, surface waters may contain color up to about 120 units (Pt-Co scale), whereas the generally accepted standard for color in raw waters is 15 units. If the receiving water is already colored, it is all the more important that color of waste-waters should be controlled in order to conform to standards.

PETROCHEMICAL WASTE DISPOSAL

E. E. KUPCHANKO *Department of Health, Edmonton*

ABSTRACT

The complexities of the disposal of Petrochemical waste calls for considerable study and evaluation of problems peculiar to each operation. Water reuse is becoming increasingly important because of the added costs of waste treatment. Disposal of mercaptans, hydrogen sulfide, oil, caustic and organic wastes is often troublesome in the petroleum and petrochemical industry and several methods are available for their removal from waste waters. Deep well disposal appears to offer a practical and economical method of disposing of extremely objectionable waste materials. Preliminary evaluation of other methods of treatment such as adsorption and solvent extraction appear, in certain circumstances, to be feasible.

INTRODUCTION

The petroleum industry is one of the largest industries in Canada with net cash expenditures of over 1 billion dollars annually [1]. The value of petroleum products produced in Canada amounted to over 900 million dollars in 1966, with the production of over 300 million bbl of crude oil and natural gas products [2].

Products and by-products of petrochemical industry include kerosene, lubricants, gas oil, fuel oil, wax, asphalt, petroleum coke and other materials such as petrolatum and insecticides. Similarly, chemicals are being derived from petroleum products and natural gas in increasing amounts.

The continued high rate of industrial growth will accentuate the problems of adequate supplies of water and the disposal of domestic and industrial waste. Canada is well endowed with fresh water resources but these resources have been tapped at a rapidly increasing rate to provide fresh water at low cost. The strain upon the natural capabilities in an area undoubtedly will increase, reducing the effective supply of pure fresh water [3].

PETROCHEMICAL WASTES

Petrochemical and refinery wastes can be classified into two general groups; from chemically contaminated water, and oil contaminated water. The principal characteristics of these wastes largely depends upon processing methods practiced and upon the raw products processed.

The principal source of pollution from petroleum refineries and petrochemical plants is generally large volume wastes containing oils, suspended and dissolved solids, wax, sulfides, mercaptans, phenolic compounds and many other exotic compounds depending upon the processes used. The effects of these types of wastes have been documented to some extent in the literature [4, 5]. A complete listing of all the constituents and waste streams is extremely difficult; a few general classifications of waste constituents have been attempted [6, 7].

53

A nation-wide survey indicated that the net pollution load from petroleum refineries measured as Biochemical Oxygen Demand yielded an approximate industry average of 100 lbs. per 1000 bbl of crude processed. More recent work [8] provides a less general estimate of polluting load in terms of refinery capacity (Fig. 1).

1. Hydrocarbon or Oil Wastes

The source of the hydrocarbon wastes is usually from leaks and spills. Leakage from heat exchangers and pump glands into cooling water is of significance. Condensation of vapors into quench water will result in emulsion formation. Similarly, emulsions will be formed from condensed process streams in the presence of hydrocarbon vapors. Water washing of crude oil and other products, as a means of desalting and cleaning results in loss of oil. Other sources include water, which is incompletely separated from oil in storage tanks, and oil losses during chemical treatment. It has been suggested that oil from leaks and spills can amount to as much as 3% of the total crude oil treated [9]. One of the main difficulties in recovering oil is the formation of stable or quasi-stable emulsions [10].

2. Sulphur Compounds

Steam condensate in the reflux system may contain significant amounts of both hydrogen sulfide and mercaptans. These are discharged through process sewers to the separators, and then to the main sewer system. Some oxidation and volatilization of hydrogen sulfide

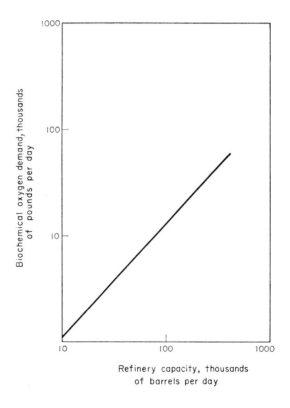

FIG. 1. Refinery waste requirements. (Copyrighted 1965, Gulf Publishing Co., Houston, Texas).

and low boiling mercaptans occur in the separators and sewers. Depending on the plant process and sewer water temperatures, the sulfide concentrations of the combined sewer system can be between 2 mg/l and 5 mg/l [11].

3. Alkaline Wastes

Alkalies are used in the petrochemical industry to purify various hydrocarbon streams. Sodium or potassium hydroxide solution removes sulfur compounds, converts them into disulfides, and extracts unwanted compounds (such as phenols and creosols). Sodium sulfide and other sodium salts are concentrated in alkaline solutions. Normally a treatment operation with caustic is followed by a water wash to remove entrained sodium hydroxide and therefore the water from such a process has a high pH. This complex of compounds in solution is a possible source of water pollution from the standpoint of toxicity, oxygen consumption, taste, odor and appearance.

4. Phenolic Wastes

Phenols and creosols are produced by the various cracking processes used in refinery operations. Most of these leave in the oil streams, by solution in water condensed from steam in reflux coolers, or by combination as sodium salts in the caustic solution. Phenolic wastes are among the most troublesome from a disposal standpoint [33].

5. Ammonia

Ammonia arises from two sources: ammonia added directly to process streams for the control of corrosion, and the breakdown of nitrogenous compounds occurring naturally in the feed. Much of the ammonia that reaches the process sewers escapes to the atmosphere. Not all of the nitrogen appears as ammonia. Some of it is combined and reported as basic nitrogen compounds which are not easily eliminated.

6. Miscellaneous Wastes

Chromate or phosphate corrosion inhibitors can create pollution problems unless a completely closed system is maintained. Tars, spent catalysts, acids and catalyst complexes are usually disposed of by burning, burying, neutralizing or by direct discharge into streams. The petrochemical industry discharges process water carrying compounds never found in natural waters or which do not exist in nature. Disposal of these wastes is not always simple.

TREATMENT

Before utilization of disposal techniques, an evaluation of the alternatives of waste recovery and utilization, and process recovery should be made to select treatment and discharges representing the best economic as well as technical choice of alternatives.

Petrochemical wastes wherever possible should be segregated:

(a) *Hydrocarbon free sewers:* Includes uncontaminated storm runoffs, boiler blowdowns, water treatment wastes, back wash waters, and cooling water blowdown. No treatment of these streams is required.

(b) *Contaminated storm water sewers:* These consist of contaminated surface water collected from drainage areas, process tankage and wash-down operations. Treatment facilities may be required.

(c) *Process water sewers:* Includes all wastes and condensates in direct contact with hydro-carbons such as at accumulators, knockout drums, and separators. Treatment facilities are required.

(d) *Sanitary sewers:* All domestic sewage generated requires sewage treatment facilities.

A large number of treatment processes are now available for specific wastes. A discussion of the more common petrochemical plant waste treatment practices is presented below.

1. Water Reuse

Higher costs of obtaining water and of its subsequent disposal have forced industrial firms to investigate the feasibility of water reuse. It has been estimated that the consumption of water by the average industry is approximately 2% of the intake [12]. Approximately one third of the intake volume is returned with the dissolved solids content approximately doubled; one third is contaminated with a wide variety of inorganic and organic chemicals originating in the process; and one third of the intake is lost to atmosphere or incorporated in the product [13].

Koenig [14] compares the current costs of various methods for disposal of waste water with costs of a number of reuse systems. For example, it appears that oxidation ponds are cheaper than any other processes for water reclamation.

One of the disadvantages of water reuse systems is the accumulation of dissolved solids. A stream concentrated with these pollutants may still require treatment if it cannot be utilized.

A central water and waste treatment facility should be considered when constructing a large chemical complex. This not only provides the advantage of sharing the service of a central waste treatment plant but offers the approach to water reuse by re-circulation [15].

Many petrochemical plants are pursuing the reuse concept to a greater extent. Reacting to local conditions such as unavailability of new water or a high cost of water supply as compared to waste disposal, industry can successfully utilize "water reuse" by application of present technology.

2. Removal of Oil or Floating Hydrocarbons

Primary oil and water separation is normally performed in gravity type separators or API separators. Research has provided design criteria for inlet systems, oil skimming and sludge removal [16]. Direct skimming utilizing the API separator is generally limited by the gravity of the feed. Oil-in-water emulsions, for example, will not undergo gravity separation. Salts of naphthenic and sulfonic acids as well as free acids will form emulsions and will clog gravity type separators. If chemicals or fine solids cause oil emulsions with a specific gravity approaching that of water, performance of a separator may be inadequate to meet local requirements. Normally an oil water separator should produce an effluent containing a minimum of 100 mg/l total oil. The addition of flocculating agents can reduce the oil content to 25–40 mg/l. The installation of parallel plates in an API separator has been found to reduce the effluent oil concentration by up to 60% compared with API separators of equal capacity and area [17]. These plates, dividing the separating tank into horizontal layers, function as collecting surfaces for oil globules and thus shorten the paths necessary to reach a collecting surface (Fig. 2a). The plates are installed in an inclined position in order to promote oil movement to the water surface and sludge movement to the bottom. Any slow separating oil can be precipitated by addition of an aqueous coagulating agent.

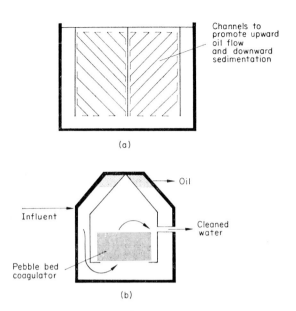

FIG. 2a. Cross-section of parallel plate interceptor [17].
FIG. 2b. Pebble bed oil coagulator [19].

In alkaline waste waters, sodium salts of naphthenic acid, sulfonic acid and fatty acids will act as stabilizers of emulsions. The most common type, the oil in water emulsion, carries a negative charge on the ionic protective layer and can be destroyed by cations. Salts such as $CaCl_2$, $FeCl_2$, $FeSO_4$, and $Al_2(SO_4)_3$ have been used to destroy emulsified wastes since the hydroxides of these metals are insoluble. Adjustment of pH may be necessary to obtain a satisfactory break of the emulsion [18].

A method of pebble bed coagulation for oil removal has been studied [19] and provides separation of almost any oil from an oily mixture short of a stable emulsion, provided that the specific gravity of the oil is not greater than $0 \cdot 98$. A general diagram of the arrangement is presented in Fig. 2b. Results of tests have indicated that the pressure drop across the bed was not excessive and inputs containing up to several thousand mg/l oil content yielded an effluent which reached a maximum of only 40 mg/l.

The air flotation process is becoming increasingly popular because of its demonstrated ability to substantially reduce the oil content of gravity effluents. Results of less than 10 mg/l oil in the effluent are indicative of what can be achieved when flotation is used in combination with chemical flocculation. Tests [20] have shown that the Chemical Oxygen Demand can be more effectively removed from waste waters by dissolved air flotation systems. Indications are that COD removal may be increased to as much as 92%.

A general survey of package flotation costs is presented in Fig. 3. Simonsen [21] has indicated that the total installation or construction costs of air flotation units ranged from $41 to $50 per gallon per minute through-put. The cost for converting an existing API separator was $15 per gallon per minute through-put. Comparison of these figures is also presented in Fig. 3. It is observed that flotation unit costs are relatively independent of influent oil concentrations.

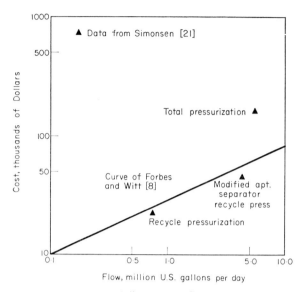

Fig. 3. Capital cost of dissolved air flotation units [8, 21].

3. Biological Treatment

Many petroleum wastes were originally thought to be toxic to biological systems, however aerobic bacterial strains acclimated to many chemical compounds have been developed. The biological systems for treatment of petrochemical wastes generally consist of activated sludge, trickling filters, oxidation ponds or aerated lagoons. Biological oxidation is now probably considered to be the ultimate procedure for the stabilization of organic waste waters. Many petrochemical wastes are deficient in nutrients and the addition of nitrogen and phosphorous compounds may be required for satisfactory biological treatment.

Activated sludge systems are normally used where a high degree of treatment is required, (Biochemical Oxygen Demand removals of over 90%). Completely mixed activated sludge systems are generally utilized for the treatment of petrochemical wastes due to the possibility of shock loads of toxic materials. An air flotation unit followed by an activated sludge unit will significantly remove as much as 3000 mg/l of phenolics through proper design of the activated sludge unit. A large holding pond can be utilized before the activated sludge unit to minimize the effect of shock loads of toxic material. Spills of spent caustic, doctor solution, and other chemicals if allowed to get to the activated sludge unit may completely destroy the organisms; also, the presence of sulfides can be damaging to normal sludge growth.

Harlow [23] reported that an activated sludge unit construction cost to treat petrochemical waste was approximately $120 per lb. of Biochemical Oxygen Demand treated per day. Data compiled by Forbes and Witt [8] shows that costs generally vary with through-put, and for large installations (0·1 to 10 mgd) installed costs of activated sludge units vary from $90 to $500 per lb of Biochemical Oxygen Demand treated per day. For smaller plants (less than 0·1 mgd) construction costs may be as high as $700 to $900 per lb of Biochemical Oxygen Demand treated per day (Fig. 4).

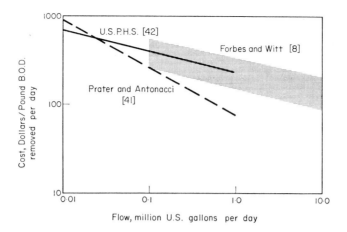

FIG. 4. Activated sludge equipment costs [8, 41, 42].

As shown in Fig. 5, construction costs for trickling filters are slightly lower than for activated sludge units. The use of plastic media, due to its light weight per unit volume, is becoming very popular, facilitating the use of relatively tall towers. The added advantage is a large surface area with ample void space.

Trickling filters are able to absorb shock loads due to toxic materials remarkably well, and will produce 80 to 90% reduction in Biochemical Oxygen Demand. Installations treating wastes containing benzene, toluene, xylene, hexane and methanol have been extremely successful [24] although usually a second tower or an oxidation pond is required for purifying the effluent where local requirements are quite stringent. Typical loadings reported are: 44 lb of phenol per day per 1000 ft^3, 236 lb Chemical Oxygen Demand per day per 1000 ft^3 [25], and 75 lb of Biochemical Oxygen Demand per day per 1000 ft^3 [26]. In some cases organic loadings of less than 20 lbs of Biochemical Oxygen Demand per day per 1000 ft^3 [27] have been advocated.

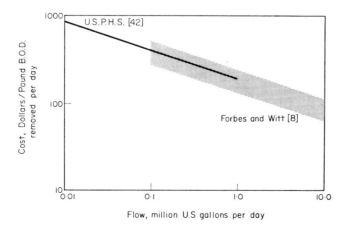

FIG. 5. Trickling filter equipment costs [8, 42].

59

Oxidation ponds are popular in areas where land is relatively inexpensive. When the volume of effluent is small the ponds are constructed to provide seven months to a year retention time. Thus, the disadvantage of variation of the quality of the effluent through seasonal changes is minimized.

Normally oxidation ponds larger than those used for domestic wastes are used to treat petrochemical waste. Several ponds are used in series to retain any floating hydrocarbons and to allow optimum retention of the organisms in the ponds. A typical loading for petrochemical waste in oxidation ponds is 20 lb Biochemical Oxygen Demand per acre per day. In some instances up to 60 days was required to produce acceptable phenol reductions [27].

The major advantages of oxidation ponds is their economical operation; although their main use is generally in effluent polishing.

The aerated lagoon allows higher organic loadings than standard oxidation ponds due to the great concentration of organisms. Several ponds are used in series to permit settling of microbial solids. In one installation, the Biochemical Oxygen Demand was reduced from 150 mg/l to 17 mg/l, in addition a 94% reduction of phenolics, 89% reduction in oils, 69% reduction in Chemical Oxygen Demand with almost a complete elimination of sulfides was achieved. The hydraulic residence time was reported to be 3·6 days [11]. The advantage of aerated lagoons is a high degree of waste stabilization, positive oxygen transfer and simplicity of operation.

4. Incineration

Incineration of combustible or semi-combustible wastes has been practiced in the petrochemical industry for a number of years. Sludge from chemical clarifiers, activated sludge units and separators can be incinerated. Normally these wastes are pumped to a sludge thickener and to a vacuum filter before being conveyed to an incinerator. The ash is collected at the bottom of the incinerator in small bins for easy disposal to a waste disposal area.

The major problem with incineration is to design an incinerator to handle a wide variety of wastes. Obviously any organic wastes which are incinerated cannot contribute to pollution of a stream and, if burned cleanly, avoids the problem of air pollution. Residues or sludges containing as much as 40% water can be incinerated [28].

Dilute liquid wastes, such as sour condensates, have been handled by injecting directly into existing burner fire boxes or high temperature stacks. Incinerator units have been installed with high excess air ratios and high refractory wall temperatures to handle burning rates as high as 9000 gallons per day. Ring type gas burners near the waste atomizer provide extra heat [29].

5. Stripping and Regeneration

The majority of installed sour water strippers employ steam as both a heating medium and as the stripping gas. Stripping steam (250°F, 8–32 SCF/gal) has been utilized, and units can be provided with or without overhead condensers (Fig. 6). The condensed steam is recycled or refluxed back to the stripper. Efficiencies of 96 to virtually 100% removal of hydrogen sulfide is possible. Mercaptans can also be stripped in a regeneration tower at 250°F using 40 lb steam. Hydrogen sulfide and any mercaptans flashed off are flared through a low pressure flare system. Detailed design criteria can be found in the literature [30].

A column has been designed [31] for the purification of sulfide bearing process waters by air oxidation. Oxidation of the sulfide takes place in the liquid phase and results in the formation of thiosulfate with approximately ten per cent being converted to sulfate.

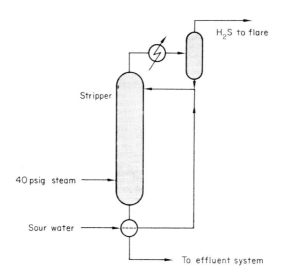

FIG. 6. Sour water stripper.

To prevent water pollution and to conserve caustic soda, spent alkali can be regenerated. There are many processes available for regeneration [32]: steam hydrolysis, use of nascent oxygen derived from electrolysis, air regeneration and the use of slaked lime. With steam hydrolysis it is possible to regenerate 90% of the caustic soda by converting mercaptans to disulfides which are relatively insoluble in the recovered caustic. Some refiners have followed the practice of regenerating spent alkali with hydrated lime, after incineration to carbonate and sulfate. In some remote areas this practice is necessary because long rail hauls make the use of fresh caustic uneconomical while lime is readily available. The use of lime regeneration is also practiced in areas where water quality restrictions forbid the discharge of alkali-bearing wastes.

6. Deep Well Disposal

Deep well disposal was initiated by the petroleum industry. The oil industry has been injecting brine into subsurface formations for many years. The storage available in underground formations is extremely large; for example, if two million gallons per day of liquid were pumped down an injection well for 100 years it would fill a 20 foot high cylinder to a radius of $4\cdot75$ miles [34]. It is therefore reasonable to assume that injection could be practiced well into the future in so far as the underground capacity is concerned, provided the waste is compatible with the formation. Several authors [35, 36] have listed conditions acceptable for disposal of wastes in injection wells. The waste should be highly toxic or otherwise objectionable and not readily treatable by conventional methods. Chemical and physical characteristics of the waste should be such, that there is reasonable assurance that the well will remain operative for a reasonable length of time. Waste waters should normally be pretreated to remove any suspended solids or entrained gases. Plugging can occur from; precipitation of alkaline earth, heavy metals, oxidation-reduction reaction products, polymerization, or other reactions. Where corrosive wastes are to be injected, corrosion resistant cement or plastic lined tubing should be used inside the casing.

Compatibility tests of the aquifer water and waste should always be run before deciding on disposal by injection. A mixture of the two are allowed to stand for approximately 24 hours at the temperature of the aquifer. The mixture is then considered compatible if precipitates are not observed.

Permeable formations such as sandstone, limestone and dolomites are the most often used for disposal. Many of the disposal wells operating in Alberta discharge into a very porous formation and the use of high pressure pumping facilities is not required.

Pretreatment of the waste is generally utilized to remove solids above a certain crucial quality and size. This generally consists of filtration, a typical flow diagram is presented in Fig. 7.

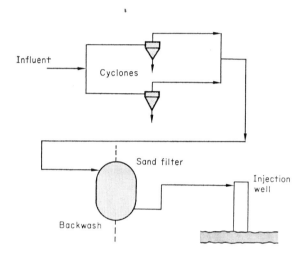

FIG. 7. Injection pre-treatment.

A cost comparison of injection wells made by the U.S. Public Health Service [37] is presented in Fig. 8. At volumes of 100,000 gallons per day, costs of disposal range from 40c to 80c per thousand U.S. gallons, depending on depth. A comparison of data from local sources is also given, and is in reasonable agreement with the U.S. Public Health Service data.

7. Chemical Oxidation

Chemical oxidation is effective to some extent for removal of phenolic constituents and odors from waste effluents. Chlorine dioxide chlorine, ozone and potassium permanganate have been employed with chlorine having the widest application. A comparison of oxidation by chlorine, chlorine dioxide and ozone was performed by Cleary and Kinney [38] and it appears that chlorine dioxide has an economic advantage over other oxidizing agents.

The problem with many petrochemical wastes is that the oxygen demand of the waste may be considerably higher than the constituents requiring removal, therefore large volumes of chemicals may be required for satisfactory treatment. Chemical oxidation is feasible where substances are resistant or toxic to biochemical action, or in situations where the addition of a relatively low dosage of chemical will react with specific constituents of a waste.

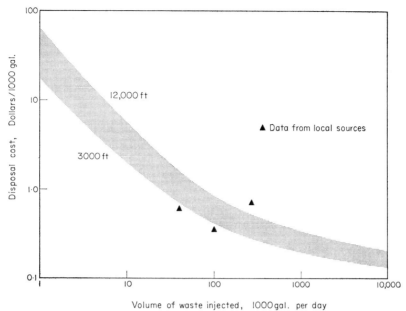

FIG. 8. Cost of injection to underground formations [37].

8. Adsorption

A great deal of fundamental ground work has been done in adsorption techniques and it appears that the use of adsorbents and adsorptive processes is the most promising of the currently known methods of waste treatment.

Activated carbon is presently the most widely used of all adsorbents. Adsorption in columns of fluidized media (carbon and alumina) generally showed better than 90% removal of organic matter to the selected break-through point [39]. Laboratory scale studies show that a two stage counter current adsorption process holds the most promise among adsorption processes evaluated and seems to be worthy of further development. Treatment costs were found to be 8c/1000 gal [40].

One of the problems with the use of activated carbon for adsorption is the difficulty in economically regenerating the media.

SUMMARY

The complex and diversified nature of petrochemical wastes requires study and consideration of the problems unique to each situation. Present-day technology can provide a solution to any specific pollution problems, however, present limitations are generally economic rather than technical.

The approach by industry in the past has been not to consider waste treatment as a major aspect of plant design. With the increasing use of water and the public demand for pollution control, it is essential that consideration be given to increasing the existing capabilities of pollution abatement.

The petrochemical industry can contribute to pollution abatement by evaluating the effect that the various contaminants discharged into the receiving waters will have on downstream water usage. The industry is also in the best position to provide new processes and equipment to achieve effective water pollution control.

REFERENCES

1. Canadian Petroleum Association, *Statistical Handbook*, 1966.
2. Statistics of Mineral Producing of Canada by Provinces, 1966.
3. Economic Council of Canada, *The Canadian Economy From the 1960's to the 1970's*, Fourth Annual Review, September 1967.
4. GLOYNA, E. F. and MALINA, Jr., J. F., Petrochemical effects on water, *Industrial Water and Wastes*, Part I, Sept.-Oct. 1962, pp. 134–138, Part II, Nov.-Dec. 1962, pp. 157–161, Part III, Jan.-Feb. 1963, pp. 14–22, Part IV, March-April 1963, pp. 22–25.
5. DOUGLAS, N. H. and IRWIN, W. H., Relative resistance of fish species to petroleum refinery wastes, *Industrial Water and Wastes*, Part I, Nov.-Dec. 1962, pp. 171–175, Part II, Jan.-Feb. 1963, pp. 23–27, Part III, March-April 1963, pp. 22–25.
6. WESTION, R. P. and HART, W. B., The water pollution abatement problems of the petroleum industry, *Water Works and Sewerage*, May 1941.
7. American Petroleum Institute, Manual on disposal of refinery wastes, *Chemical Wastes*, Vol. III, 1960, pp. 15–31.
8. FORBES, M. C. and WITT, P. A., Estimate cost of water disposal, *Hydrocarbon Processing and Petroleum Refiner*, 44:8, August 1965, p. 158.
9. NEMEROW, N. L., *Theories and Practices of Industrial Waste Treatment*, Addison-Wesley, 1963, p. 432.
10. HART, W. B., *Industrial Waste Disposal for Petroleum Refineries and Allied Plants*, Petroleum Processing Pub., Cleveland, Ohio, 1947.
11. LANKIN, J. C. and SORG, L. V., American oil cleans up wastes in aerated lagoons, *Hydrocarbon Processing and Petroleum Refiner*, Vol. 43, No. 5, 1964, pp. 133–136.
12. IIHENNY, W. F., Recovery of additional water from industrial waste water, *Chemical Engineering Progress*, Vol. 63, No. 676, June 1967.
13. MCGAUHEY, P. H., *Water Quality Management*, Sanitary Engineering Research Laboratory Publication, University of California, Berkeley 1966, pp. 1–5.
14. KOENIG, L., Reuse can be cheaper than disposal, American Institute of Chemical Engineering, Paper 16A, 61st Annual Meeting, Feb. 19–23, 1967.
15. EWING, R. C., Waste treatment plant designed for industrial complex, *Oil and Gas Journal*, 65, No. II, March 13, 1967, pp. 106–108.
16. American Petroleum Institute, *Manual on Disposal of Refinery Wastes*, 1960, Vol. I, pp. 17–38.
17. BRUNSMAN, J. J., CORNELISSEN, J. and ELERS, H., Improved oil separation gravity separators, *JWPCF*, Vol. 34, No. I, 1962, pp. 44–45.
18. BALDEN, A. R., Treatment of emulsifiable wastes prior to disposal, *Proceedings of Industrial Waste Conference*, Purdue University, 1961, pp. 22–25.
19. Anonymous, Oil pollution: a separation technique, *Engineering (Brit.)* 1962, p. 193.
20. PRATHER, B. V., Will air flotation remove the chemical oxygen demand of refinery waste water?, *Petroleum Refiner*, Vol. 40, No. 5, May 1961.
21. SIMONSEN, R. N., Remove oil by air flotation, *Hydrocarbon Processing and Petroleum Refiner*, Vol. 41, No. 5, May 1962, pp. 145–148.
22. ROSS, W. and SHEPPARD, A. A., Biological oxidation of petroleum phenolic waste waters, *Proc. 16th Ind. Waste Conf., Purdue University*, 1956, p. 106.
23. HARLOW, H. W., SHANNON. E. S. and SERCU, C. L., A petrochemical waste treatment system, *Proc. 16th Ind. Waste Conf., Purdue University*, 1962, pp. 156–166.
24. SHANNON, E. S., Experiences in handling and treating petrochemical plant wastes, 14th Oklahoma Ind. Waste Conf., Oklahoma State University, Nov. 20, 1964.
25. SMITH, R. M., Some systems for the biological oxidation of phenol bearing wastes, *Biotechnology and Bioengineering*, Vol. 5, 1963, pp. 275–286.
26. SAK, J., Plastic biological oxidation media for industrial waste treatment needs, 14th Ontario Industrial Waste Conf., June 1967, p. 187.
27. MCKINNEY, R., Biological treatment systems for refinery wastes, *Journal Water Pollution Control Federation*, Vol. 39, No. 3, March 1967, p. 346.
28. MILLS, ROSS, E., Process waste burner destroys liquid organic chemical wastes safely, *Water and Sewage Works*, Vol. III, No. 6, July 1964, pp. 337–340.
29. Anonymous, Huston orders cleanup: new techniques used, *Chemical Engineering*, Vol. 75, No. 6, March 11, 1968, p. 96.
30. BEYCHOK, M. R., *Aqueous Wastes from Petroleum and Petrochemical Plants*, John Wiley and Sons, 1967, pp. 178–179.
31. MARTIN, J. D. and LEVANAS, L. C., New column removes sulfide with air, *Hydrocarbon Processing and Petroleum Refinery*, 41:5, May 1962, pp. 149–153.

32. McRae, A. D., Disposal of alkaline wastes in the petrochemical industry, *Sewage and Industrial Wastes*, Vol. 31, No. 6, June 1959, p. 712.
33. Anonymous, Phenol removal from water, *Environmental Science and Technology*, Vol. 1, No. 1, Jan. 1967, p. 11.
34. Summary Report: Advanced Waste Treatment Research, U.S. Department of Health Education and Welfare, April 1965, Pub. AWTR-14, p. 99.
35. Warner, D. L., Deep well disposal of industrial wastes, *Chemical Engineering*, Vol. 72, No. 1, Jan. 4, 1965, p. 73.
36. Brown, R. W. and Spalding, C. W., Deep well disposal of spent hardwood pulping liquid, *Journal Water Pollution Control Federation*, Vol. 38, 1966, p. 1916.
37. Ultimate Disposal of Advanced Treatment Waste, AWTR-8, U.S. Department of Health Education and Welfare, p. 69.
38. Cleary, F. and Kinney, J. E., Findings from a co-operative study of phenol waste treatment, *Proc. 6th Ind. Waste Conf. of Purdue University*, 1951, p. 1581.
39. Federal Water Pollution Control Administration, Adsorption of biochemically resistant materials from solution 2, Pub. AWTR-16, March 1966.
40. Daries, D. S. and Kaplan, R. A., Removal of refractory organics from waste water with powdered activated carbon, *Journal Water Pollution Control Federation*, Vol. 38, No. 3, March 1966, p. 442.
41. Prater, R. H. and Antonacci, W., Find packaged sewage plants costs, *Hydrocarbon Processing and Petroleum Refiner*, Vol. 42, No. 2, February 1963, p. 147.
42. U.S. Public Health Service, Modern sewage treatment plants—how much do they cost?, U.S. Department of Health, Education and Welfare, Bulletin No. 1229.

DISCUSSION

W. Martin (*Western Co-operative Fertilizers Ltd., Calgary*):

Does the Provincial Government monitor the rivers of Alberta for concentrations of sulphates and chlorides? Also, are limits set on the amount of these materials that can be introduced per unit time or are these contaminants not of a serious enough nature to justify limit setting? Where have deep wells been drilled in the southern part of Alberta for use in accepting plant effluents? Also, into what formation were these wells?

Author's Reply

The water pollution control section, Environmental Health Services Division, monitors the major rivers in the Province generally on a monthly basis and more often in some cases. Sulfates and chlorides are among the constituents that are analyzed on a routine basis. All industries discharging waste materials into a lake or stream must have a permit from the Provincial Board of Health. The effluent permit restricts the various chemical constituents added to surface waters and normally these are set in relation to the assimilative capacity of the stream. Chlorides and sulfates are undesirable because they increase the total solids of the receiving water. These may either settle out or render the water unsuitable in some other way. Effluent requirements of 1500 mg/l maximum are generally advocated, however, consideration must be given to the volume of waste in relation to the receiving water.

Many of the natural gas processing plants have deep well injection facilities to dispose of the formation water that enters with the natural gas. In the oil industry the water flood program is used extensively for increased production.

There are several formations suitable for deep well injection and further information can be obtained by contacting the Oil and Gas Conservation Board.

POLLUTION FROM MUNICIPAL SOURCES

P. D. LAWSON   *Reid, Crowther and Partners Ltd., Calgary*
K. J. BRISBIN   *Underwood McLellan and Associates Ltd., Calgary*

ABSTRACT

Treatment of waste water has consisted of decomposing the non-stable constituents but it is now becoming a requirement to remove the stabilized end products from the effluents. The nature of pollution and its sources are reviewed followed by a brief description of sewage treatment processes. Several examples of waste water treatment requirements are discussed in relationship to the environmental requirements. The desirability of national, provincial and regional approaches to pollution control is examined. Lastly, the ultimate disposal of pollutional matter is discussed in relationship to natural cycles of decay and synthesis and of the newer chemicals which are not biodegradable.

INTRODUCTION

From the inception of community living, the disposal of man's wastes has been a problem. Conditions in the Middle Ages, with piles of filth and refuse in the streets became more and more intolerable until the introduction of waterborne removal in sewers around 1800. These sewerage systems were the first major stage of pollution control and enabled cities to grow to larger sizes and, in conjunction with a pure water supply, were basically responsible for the disappearance of most diseases in Western civilization.

The early sewers, and some of our present ones, discharged untreated sewage into the nearest river or lake. As the cities grew, the river's capacity for self purification was exceeded so that their condition presented intolerable conditions to the citizens of the towns on their banks. Towards the end of the 19th century the second stage of combating pollution commenced with the design of early sewage treatment plants. In Britain a Royal Commission on sewage disposal commenced work in 1898 and published ten reports in the ensuing seventeen years which dealt with all aspects of pollution and the treatment of sewage.

Since the First World War, advances have been rapid and the number of sewage treatment plants has increased greatly. Unfortunately, the construction of such plants has hardly kept up with the growth in the amount of pollution discharged from our cities. However, it is probably true to say that in 1968 we have reached a point where the sewage from most towns and cities in North America is given some form of treatment before discharge.

Figure 1, taken from statistics quoted by Dr. Okun [1] shows the tremendous growth of the urban population in the U.S.A.

All forms of sewage treatment to date have consisted essentially of decomposing the pollutional matter in the sewage to stable end products which are then discharged with the effluent into the rivers and lakes. The effects of this disposal of treated sewage have only become apparent in the last two decades. The end products of sewage treatment are stable and do not in themselves degrade the receiving stream, but their effect is that of adding large amounts of fertilizer to the water which enables heavy and rapid growths of plant material

67

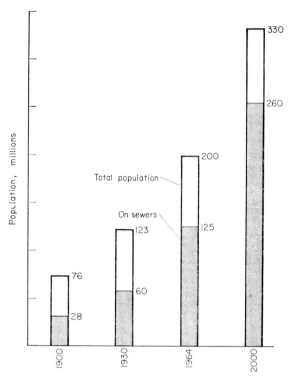

FIG. 1. Population of U.S.A. at various times showing sewer usage.

to take place. These in turn die and cause pollution. The discharge of these nutrients has so enriched many of our lakes that the amount of plant and animal life therein has become a severe problem. All lakes undergo this process of enrichment or eutrophication but the discharge of man-made pollution has greatly accelerated the process. We thus stand on the threshold of the third major stage in the control of pollution, that is the removal of these nutrients from sewage effluents. The magnitude of this task should not be underestimated. For example, the removal of half the dissolved solids from the sewage effluent of the City of Calgary would require the disposal for each and every day of approximately 100 tons of dry solids or 400,000 gallons per day of brine solution (assuming 5% solution). This amounts to the astronomical figure of 35,000 tons of dry solids or 150,000,000 gallons of brine solution per year.

At present we avoid this disposal problem by discharging these dissolved inert solids in our sewage effluents. The results can be seen in Lake Erie but if we are to talk about cleaning up Lake Erie we should be aware of the magnitude of the task as shown by the above figures. Clearly it is not practicable to remove all dissolved solids from our effluents—we must learn more about eutrophication so that we can selectively remove those solids which are the major causes of the problem.

TYPES AND VOLUMES OF POLLUTANTS

Before examining the amount of municipal pollutants released to receiving waters in Canada, it is necessary to define "Pollution". Most people would define pollution differently and in terms of what they themselves find objectionable. The best definition of pollution is, in our opinion, "Any change in the quality of water which renders it unsuitable for its intended use". This definition of course, begs the question, as a further definition of "intended use" is required. However, any definition of pollution must take into account the intended use, as pollution is not in any way a single item or a single cause, nor does it have a single cure. Rather, it is a whole family of related effects.

There is no such thing as an unpolluted stream. The streams cascading from the Rocky Mountains are already polluted by natural agencies such as glacier silt, dissolved limestone and natural run-off from the catchment area. A stream of completely pure water would be useless for most purposes as it would be completely lifeless and would not support fish life —a little pollution is a good thing.

To the man in the street, the word "Pollution" conjures up a vision of a stream covered with odoriferous floating solids—he is mostly concerned with aesthetic values in pollution.

To the fisherman, pollution consists largely of oxygen depletion in the streams, resulting in the death of fish, but it may also be industrial pollution which is only evident when it causes taste in the fish.

To the naturalist, pollution is exemplified by any sudden change in the biological life in the stream, such as an algae bloom or loss of one species of fish.

The most obvious form of pollution is aesthetic pollution caused by floating scum or foam, large solids caught on the sides of the banks, or sludge banks. Such pollution can be readily eliminated and should be mandatory for all discharges.

The second main type of pollution is that of the discharge of substances which absorb the dissolved oxygen from the stream as they decompose. Municipal wastes are major offenders in this regard with the organic waste being measured by the B.O.D. test.

The discharge of suspended or settleable solid matter is the third class of pollutant, and this imparts turbidity to the stream and reduces natural re-aeration. However, such pollution should not be confused with naturally occurring turbidity such as occurs in glacier-fed streams or in streams with muddy banks such as the Red River in Winnipeg.

The discharge of refractory organics has now become a major concern. Such organic compounds are those which do not occur naturally, and which are often resistant to biochemical decomposition. They include such things as herbicides, and insecticides which may persist for many miles in a stream or even indefinitely. The whole world is now polluted with DDT and virtually no person or animal, including the Eskimo or the Antarctic Penguin is now free of this pollutant. This particular type of pollution has given rise to many "scares" in the popular press, and indeed far too little is known of their effects, especially long-term effects. Perhaps more importantly for the future is the fact that our present technology in sewage treatment and water treatment is ill-equipped to deal with minute traces of these harmful organic compounds.

To examine and control these pollutants requires a study of the magnitude of the problem, and the effect of the pollutants on the downstream user. Figure 2 shows the approximate quantities of primary pollutants from municipal sources throughout Canada. Of these items, the first two—BOD and suspended solids—are readily removed in conventional sewage treatment plants. The remaining items require further treatment as discussed later on. Even though we achieve 90% removal of B.O.D. and suspended solids by secondary sewage treatment methods, the remaining 10% still represents a very sizeable pollution load. To remove this remaining pollution, and to remove the phosphates, refractory organics, etc., requires a new technology and a considerable expense. Realizing this, it is necessary to decide for what purposes we wish to use our rivers.

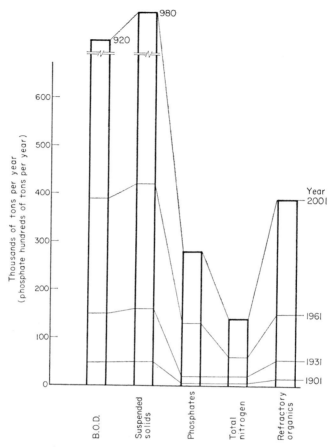

FIG. 2. Relative quantities of primary pollutants from municipal sources throughout Canada.

It is at this point that problems arise in logical analysis and rational solutions. What is the value per mile of a river with 10 parts per million dissolved oxygen compared with a river with 5 parts per million or 2 parts per million oxygen?

What is the benefit of providing further treatment to sewage effluent and treated storm water overflows in Metropolitan Toronto so that swimming may take place in Lake Ontario in this location as compared with the cost of providing either open or covered swimming pools along the lake front?

These and many similar questions are complex problems which require the skills of the Sociologist, the Planner, the Economist and the Engineer to arrive at a solution.

METHODS OF SEWAGE TREATMENT

The Sanitary Engineer has a wide choice of sewage treatment processes available to him which permit construction of treatment works capable of giving an effluent of almost any desired purity.

While there is need for research to improve treatment processes, it cannot be said that lack of technology is holding up the necessary treatment of sewage. The problem before us is the *allocation of sufficient funds* to provide the required degree of treatment. The Sanitary Engineer has sufficient know-how to treat almost any waste, to any desired purity, although improved processes are always required to reduce costs.

A modern sewage treatment plant usually consists of three stages. The first of these, known as primary treatment, consists of screening, grit removal and sedimentation whereby the settleable pollutant matter is removed. This is essentially mechanical, and will remove approximately one-third of the pollution.

The second stage of the plant (secondary treatment) consists of controlled decomposition of the colloidal and dissolved solids by bacterial means.

Secondary treatment will remove approximately 90% of the B.O.D. which is the standard reached by most plants. Tertiary treatment will remove a further 5 to 10% of the B.O.D. by microstraining of the effluent, filtration on sand beds or detention in oxidation ponds.

The third stage consists of treatment of the sludge derived from the first two stages. This sludge disposal is usually a costly part of the process and is often not appreciated by the layman but contains most of the problems for the Sanitary Engineer.

Nutrient removal, which may be required in the future to form a fourth stage will consist of removing phosphorous and nitrogenous compounds from the waste waters, in excess of the 25% removed in conventional secondary treatment. Some of the methods for nutrient removal being investigated include:

1. Precipitation by lime.
2. Coagulation with alum.
3. A proprietary process known as "pep".
4. Phytoplankton—i.e. the maturing of algae growth with subsequent harvesting of the algal mass.

These various processes are in their infancy at this time.

The capital cost of a primary treatment plant will vary from $10·00 to $30·00 *per capita* depending upon the size and location of the plant. A complete treatment plant will cost in the order of $30·00 to $50·00 *per capita*, while the addition of tertiary treatment will cost an additional $10·00. Such figures, when applied to a population of 500,000 result in costs of $5,000,000 for a primary plant, $15,000,000 for a secondary plant and up to $20,000,000 when incorporating tertiary treatment.

The figures are approximate and serve only to indicate the relative value of the costs involved. These costs may seem high, but if we place them on the basis of annual cost, including capital repayment and operating costs, we have a cost of $15·00 to $20·00 per year for the average household. This is a small sum in comparison with some of the other items on which we spend our money. On Fig. 3, we have shown the relative costs for a telephone, for annual spending on expressways and other items including our favorite— the family automobile.

Looked at in this light our spending on sewage treatment is small. This is mainly because water pollution has not been recognized as a personal problem in the past—it does not affect us personally unless we live downstream from a sewage outfall or boat or fish in the river. While we may feel that spending on sewage treatment is large, we should consider which the items on the chart are the most necessary and which are really luxuries.

With increasing leisure and the trend towards greater recreational use of water resources, water pollution confronts and concerns us all. Advanced treatment methods can ensure that pollution does not get worse, and we must be prepared to make the necessary expenditures.

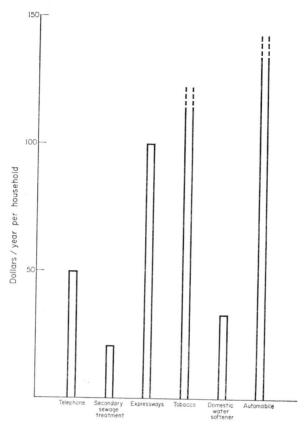

FIG. 3. Comparison of annual costs of secondary sewage treatment facilities and other household expenses.

EXAMPLES OF MUNICIPAL POLLUTION SITUATIONS

The different problems facing cities vary widely with the characteristics of the receiving body to which they discharge and with the uses made of the stream.

The City of Calgary discharges its sewage to the Bow River which has a long-term average discharge of 3240 c.f.s. and a normal minimum flow of 1800 c.f.s. This minimum flow occurs in winter when long stretches of the river are ice covered and no natural re-aeration can take place. Against these figures the discharge of sewage from the city at present amounts to 75 c.f.s. giving a dilution of 24 to 1 based on minimum flow. Surveys by the Province have determined that the maximum assimilative capacity of the Bow River at Calgary is 54,000 lb of B.O.D. per day while maintaining a minimum dissolved oxygen content of 5 parts per million. Of this amount 14,000 has been allocated to direct industrial discharges to the River and the remaining 40,000 lb of B.O.D. has been allocated to municipal discharges from the City.

This allowance of 40,000 lb of B.O.D. is fixed and requires increasing degrees of treatment as the city grows. For instance, discharges of raw sewage would not exceed this limit if the city population had remained less than 160,000. With the provision of primary treatment in the 1950's, the limit was not exceeded until the population reached 230,000. Secondary treatment is now being provided and will enable discharges to be held below the limit until the city population reaches 1,500,000, estimated for the year 2020.

The Bow River reaches Calgary in a virtually unpolluted state and as it is a relatively shallow, rapid and clear stream the effects of stabilized nutrients in the discharge of treated sewage are quite evident. There are considerable algae and weed growths downstream from the City and these create considerable problems at night in the summer when low dissolved oxygen levels are recorded.

The Bow River is a good fishing river but at present there is a problem with regard to the taste of the fish, probably due more to industrial discharges than to the discharge from the municipal sewage plant.

Thus the problems at Calgary are an amalgam of oxygen depletion due to municipal sewage discharges, weed growth due to nutrient discharges and taste problems in the fish. Of these the first is being attended to by the enlargement of the sewage treatment plant.

The City of Edmonton is located on the North Saskatchewan River which has an average discharge of 7570 c.f.s. and an average minimum flow of 2000 c.f.s. These flows required Edmonton to institute secondary sewage treatment in 1958 but this secondary treatment is required only during the winter months. In the summer months, due to the melting snows from the mountains, the river flow is generally in excess of 8000 c.f.s. At such a time the Edmonton sewage plant reverts to primary treatment only and the river is capable of assimilating the effluent while maintaining the dissolved oxygen. The North Saskatchewan River is a relatively turbid stream so that the effects of nutrient discharges to this river have been minimal, unlike Calgary.

The City of Kelowna, B.C. is located on Lake Okanagan. This lake is some 70 miles long, but the flow through the lake is relatively small having an average discharge of 500 c.f.s. and normal minimum flows in the order of 100 c.f.s. With warm summer temperatures, a considerable agricultural area draining into the lake, plus the towns of Vernon and Kelowna, with a combined population of 30,000 the natural eutrophication process is accelerating in Lake Okanagan.

As this lake is a valuable recreational asset, eutrophication could detract from its value and the Province is actively studying the problems of discharging highly treated sewage into this lake. The discharge of B.O.D. as such does not present a problem but the nutrients do. Consequently attention is being given to the use of the treated effluents from the sewage treatment plants for irrigation of the surrounding agriculture lands so as to reduce or eliminate the discharge of treated sewage effluent into the lake.

Turning now to the town of Banff, sewage from Banff is discharged in an untreated form into the Bow River. Plans have been on file for some time for construction of a sewage treatment plant, but the need for this plant has not yet become sufficiently urgent to warrant funds being set aside for its construction. The flow of the Bow River at Banff has a normal minimum of 200 c.f.s. in the winter and a normal flow in excess of 2000 c.f.s. during the holiday months in summer. The winter population of Banff is some 3000 persons, the summer population is much higher but fortunately, so is the flow in the river. With considerable turbulence and re-aeration in the river and with two hydro-electric impoundments before the City of Calgary, the discharge has no apparent deleterious effect on the river when it reaches Calgary.

The different situation of these four municipalities demonstrates that a uniform requirement for treatment and discharge cannot be formulated on a country-wide basis but that each individual case must be investigated.

PHILOSOPHY OF TREATMENT

It is suggested that a rational economic and social basis for determining the desired use and quality of our rivers is at present one of the main things that is lacking in determining what degree of treatment is required. Take the case of the City of Calgary. The downstream users of the river consist of the small town of Bassano, 90 miles downstream with a population of 800; the City of Medicine Hat, 200 miles downstream with a population of 25,000; and lastly the City of Saskatoon, 530 miles downstream with a population of 130,000. On the basis of drinking qualities alone it would be more economical to provide the necessary degree of treatment to the drinking water at Bassano and Medicine Hat rather than having the City of Calgary providing complete sewage treatment.

However, the river is also used for irrigation, for fishing and is a recreational asset. For these reasons there is ample justification for requiring Calgary to provide sewage treatment. The degree of sewage treatment required is at present based upon the criteria for fish life that the dissolved oxygen should not drop below 5 parts per million. To many people the weed growth is also objectionable.

With the increased growth of cities and the pressure on existing recreational needs it is probable that the use of our rivers for recreational purposes will steadily increase and as such the demand for ever cleaner rivers will increase.

As previously discussed, the removal of nutrients will give rise to considerable problems in the disposal of the resultant materials and these, combined with ever increasing volume of garbage, will result in increases in our solid waste disposal problem.

As the disposal of waste products passes from one point of disposal to another, the problems become more local, i.e. the problem of air pollution is inescapable for any of us, the problem of water pollution is of concern only to those who are situated close to the river downstream from the source of pollution, and land pollution (i.e. disposal of waste to land) becomes a problem only to those in the immediate vicinity of the disposal point.

In the past the philosophy has been that a river or lake could always be used to take away the liquid wastes from the municipalities on its banks. This concept is now changing but it is an inescapable fact that the liquid volume must ultimately be discharged to the receiving stream. The question is the degree of treatment required before it can be accepted into that stream. Pollution cannot be shut off or eliminated, it can only be controlled and ameliorated.

We must accept that each person living in the city will continue to produce every day his waste. These mixed with water must be disposed of and the word "disposed" is used advisedly instead of the word "treatment" which now describes our present sewage plants. The liquid portion will have to continue to discharge to a water course but the solid pollutional matter will be removed and disposed of either by incineration—in which case the ultimate disposal is to the air—by flushing down the river after a varying degree of treatment—in which case the ultimate disposal is to a lake or the ocean, or lastly it can be disposed of to the land.

ENVIRONMENTAL MANAGEMENT

Because of the inter-action of various forms of pollution it is desirable to consider them in terms of an integrated or systems approach for complete environmental management. The economic benefits of treating sewage by a city to a higher degree of purification may be compared with the increased cost of water treatment and taste problems for the downstream municipality. Spray irrigation of sewage effluents has an effect upon the land as fertilizer and insecticide run-off from the land affects the river. Lastly, the disposal of refuse or sewage sludge by burning has an effect on air pollution.

For these reasons therefore, the concept of an overall environmental management unit is based upon the logical unit of a river and its drainage basin has considerable appeal.

In Britain, the entire country is divided into 27 areas, each under a River Authority. These authorities have jurisdiction over one or more rivers and are empowered to licence abstractions from the river and discharges to ground water. Lastly, they are charged with making overall surveys of the river and predicting future conditions and abstractions for 20 years into the future.

In Canada, pollution control is a provincial matter and fortunately, there are relatively few rivers which cross provincial boundaries.

The authors believe that the self-purification capacity of a river should be used in order that our resources be developed as resources. However, in view of future increases in pollution, it is most desirable that the maximum self-purification of the river should not be used but that rather some considerable margin for future development should be left.

Our present disposal methods for municipal pollution provide for the ultimate flushing of the pollution out to the sea and away from our environment. This use of the sea as the ultimate disposal point raises the possibility of future problems. It is understood that concern is already being expressed regarding the condition of the ocean off New York and New Jersey in view of the large and ever-increasing amounts of sludges from treatment plants which are being barged to sea in that area. This problem will be of particular concern with regards to the refractory chemicals which, dispersed throughout the oceans, reaches us through the food chain from plankton to fish to ourselves.

The whole of nature is based upon the forces in balance and on circles of synthesis, death and decay followed by re-use.

Man's effect on his environment in the past has been largely confined to the modifications of these interacting circular activities. However, within the last 2 or 3 decades, with the tremendous growth of the chemical industry, we have begun the construction of linear activities wherein there is no death and decay. Insecticides and herbicides fall into these categories.

The ultimate accumulative effect of these linear activities requires study and investigating. Allied to this, a study of means of decomposing these chemical compounds must also be undertaken.

Few of us face the fact that our present sewage and water treatment plants are not equipped to deal with small quantities of these non-destructible organic chemicals. Here is a field requiring research and development.

CONCLUSIONS

Pollution from municipal sources is one of the most important sources of pollution and it is a source which is constantly growing as the population of our urban centres increases. Unfortunately, the receiving bodies do not increase in size and as waste water discharges increase the treatment must be to a constantly increasing standard.

Detergents in municipal waste water have been of great benefit to the profession of sanitary engineering. Their obvious presence in our water courses and in sewer discharges have focused the attention of the public upon pollution. Whereas 20 years ago there were "no votes" in sewage treatment and money was hard to find, pollution control has now become one of our foremost popular demands.

The sanitary engineering profession for years has been used to being low man on the municipal totem pole and has been used to getting by with minimum expenditures to achieve the minimum results which were just acceptable to the regulatory authority. Within the last decade, however, the general population has become aware of and wishes to overcome pollution. We believe that the public is at this time willing to pay the costs of better sewage treatment.

The sanitary engineering profession and those connected with it, having for years been ahead of the populace are now behind it. It is necessary that our profession lift up its eyes from the present position of what is the minimum we can get by with to what is economically feasible and desirable. Let us catch up with public opinion and propose to treat our sewage to a high degree of purification.

REFERENCE

1. OKUN, D. A., Future of water quality management, *Journal of the Institute of Water Pollution Control*, Part 2, 1968.

DISCUSSION

S. K. KRISHNASWAMI (*Department of National Health and Welfare*), *Edmonton:*

I think it is almost a myth that "tertiary treatment" of municipal sewage will eliminate eutrophication of fresh water bodies. Eutrophication is a natural and irreversible process that will take place regardless of whether or not we add nutrients through waste water discharges. The only important consideration is that waste water discharges accelerate the rate of eutrophication. It is very unlikely that treatment of sewage would produce an effluent having a specific electrolytic conductance of less than say 30 μMhos/cm (25 deg C).

Besides phosphates and nitrates, there may be other growth stimulating factors, such as zinc, iron, molybdenum, etc., which are not easily removed by tertiary treatment processes. Even at phosphate and nitrate concentrations of less than 0·1 and 0·01 mg/l respectively, "blooms" of photosynthetic organisms can still occur if other essential stimulants are present. Therefore, it is important to evaluate in detail just exactly what factors are involved in a particular condition of eutrophy before tertiary treatment is recommended.

AUTHOR'S REPLY

I agree completely with Mr. Krishnaswami's statement. We should distinguish between tertiary treatment, which is a "polishing" process to reduce further the B.O.D. and suspended solids remaining after normal secondary treatment, and nutrient removal. The latter is different from tertiary treatment in that it calls for the removal of stable inorganic and organic compounds from the stabilized sewage effluent.

I agree that eutrophication of lakes has always had a place in nature but man's activities have greatly increased the rate of enrichment so that we have created problems which did not exist before. The eutrophication problem is, as you say, very complex and little understood. Much work will have to be done before we can even begin to understand it.

AIR POLLUTION AND URBAN WASTE

FUNDAMENTAL CONCEPTS OF ATMOSPHERIC POLLUTION

A. T. ROSSANO, Jr. *University of Washington*

ABSTRACT

Atmospheric pollution is one of the fastest growing environmental problems of our modern technological society. Factors of population expansion, industrial growth, and urbanization have contributed significantly to the accelerated rate of degradation of the atmosphere in metropolitan areas within recent years. Under adverse meteorological conditions emissions from various contaminant sources tend to concentrate in the atmosphere. The resulting lowering of air quality can lead to adverse effects on susceptible receptors.

Several alternative approaches to emission control are available as immediate steps toward the abatement of air pollution sources. For the long-term solution, implementation of a comprehensive air resource management program is a rational approach. The objective of such a plan is the optimum utilization of the atmosphere for disposal of gaseous wastes and the promotion of man's health and well-being.

INTRODUCTION

It is axiomatic that the more advanced a civilization becomes the more complex are the problems related to man's environment, namely congestion, crime, housing, noise, etc. Of recent years it has become increasingly obvious that the improper disposal of solid, liquid and gaseous wastes is creating a burgeoning problem of environmental pollution. [1] The resulting alteration of man's natural environment has reached the point where the environment itself is now beginning to exert untoward effects on man.

Up until a few decades ago public health and sanitary engineering authorities were concerned with contamination of water and food by bacteriological organisms, particularly those which inhabit the gastro-intestinal tract of man. Today public health authorities are not only concerned with the prevention of water- and food-borne typhoid, cholera and dysentery but also with asthma, emphysema and chronic bronchitis, which are airborne diseases.

HISTORICAL BACKGROUND

Historically air pollution is not a new phenomenon. *Natural* forms of air pollution such as volcanic eruptions were known and feared by pre-historic man.

Man-made pollution probably dates back to the early cave man who discovered fire. Though he soon realized that this was an invaluable source of energy for keeping warm and cooking food, from time to time he undoubtedly was forced to flee from his cave coughing and choking from the noxious smoke and gases produced by his primitive fire.

Many other historical references to air pollution can be found in Roman and English history. The introduction of so-called "sea-coals" in 13th-century England created mounting complaints of the nuisance from smoke and gases. This gave rise to the first smoke

79

control regulations which were so strictly enforced that at times the death penalty was evoked.

John Evelyn, the famous English naturalist, was so provoked by the severe air pollution in London that in 1661 he wrote his now famous paper entitled "Fumifugium, or the Inconvenience of the Aer and Smoak of London Dissipated". In this remarkable treatise he not only described the nature and sources of air pollution in London, but also recommended control measures, such as relocation of offending industries in remote areas, and planting of trees and shrubs for green belts.

In the early nineteen hundreds Dr. Des Voeux, an English physician, coined the term "smog" to describe the offensive combination of smoke and fog which he concluded was the cause of respiratory distress among his patients. As London grew larger the smog problem worsened until 1952 when a very severe episode resulted in the death of 4000 persons and an untold number of illnesses.

In the United States the problem of smoke was clearly manifest during the early history of the developing industrial centers of the East and Midwest. St. Louis and Cincinnati were among the first cities to develop smoke abatement programs. The widespread adoption of smoke prevention regulations and improved fuel burning technology and equipment gradually brought the problem under a tolerable degree of control.

As the national economy slowly switched from coal to petroleum as a major source of energy conversion the quality of the atmospheric environment took a turn for the worse. While the smoke pollution problem was subsiding a new and perhaps worse form of air pollution began to emerge. Instead of smoke, soot, and flyash, this new species of pollution was characterized by such exotic substances as oxidants, peroxides, ozonides and various hydrocarbon reaction products. This was first encountered in Los Angeles in the early 1940's and has gradually worsened in spite of heroic control efforts.

In many ways this new type of smog, more correctly referred to as photochemical air pollution, is worse than the old problem of coal smoke in that it is not thoroughly understood, is more difficult to control, and has graver health implications because of its widespread distribution throughout the populated areas of this country.

FACTORS RESPONSIBLE FOR THE BURGEONING AIR POLLUTION PROBLEM

While as mentioned previously, air pollution is not a new phenomenon, it is now apparent that it is one of our most rapidly growing environmental problems. What are the factors contributing to this rather recent trend towards deterioration of the air environment in the United States? There are three major underlying factors which serve to explain this condition.

1. Population Growth

The upward trends in population growth in the United States since World War II have indeed been impressive. More people mean more manufactured goods and services. This in turn leads to the second factor.

2. Expansion in Industry and Technology

The growth of industrial activity in the same period, has likewise been remarkable in terms of expansion of existing plant capacity, and the increase in number of new manufacturing establishments. In addition, there has been the introduction of a great number of new processes, methods and products.

3. Social Changes

Two important social changes occurred during this same period, and serve to accelerate the trend of burgeoning air pollution.

(a) **Urbanization.** The unrelenting movement of people from rural sections to urban centers has led to the rapid growth of cities into large metropolitan complexes. On the East Coast the expansion of the metropolitan areas of Boston, New York, Philadelphia, Baltimore, and Washington D.C. has resulted in the virtual fusion of the entire region into one large megalopolis. There no longer exist the open and sparsely populated spaces between these cities that existed twenty or more years ago. Within a few years over 3/4 of the nations population will reside in less than 10% of the land area.

(b) **Standard of living.** The other social factor which indirectly contributed to the intensification of air pollution over relatively recent years has been the rising standard of living which has prevailed during this period. Large segments of population have been economically able to enjoy a better life including higher quality of nutrition, housing, transportation and a variety of labor-saving devices. Few families today are without a television set, refrigeration, automatic washing machines and clothes dryer, etc. The vast majority of these conveniences require electric power, and this in part accounts for the fact that the demand for electric power in the United States doubles every ten years. Most of this power is generated by thermal power plants burning coal or oil. Since the combustion of these fuels produces large volumes of contaminant emissions the potential for air pollution from this source is rapidly increasing.

The motor vehicle, on which practically every American family is highly dependent, likewise is another major source of pollutants which are emitted largely from the internal combustion engine.

The combined impact of population growth, expansion in industry and technology, and social changes operating in our contemporary society, can be regarded as the compounding factors which have resulted in serious degradation of the urban air environment in relatively recent years. In certain metropolitan areas such as New York, Los Angeles, Philadelphia, Chicago, and St. Louis, this trend has already reached alarming proportions. In those areas the rate of pollution very frequently exceeds the capacity of the atmosphere to purify itself by natural processes of dilution and dispersion. During these periods severe air pollution occurs and is clearly manifested by eye-irritation, reduced visibility, and other adverse effects.

Air pollution defined. Air pollution means the presence in the out-door atmosphere of one or more contaminants, such as dust, fume, gas, mist, odor, smoke, or vapor, in quantities, of characteristics, and of duration such as to be injurious to human, plant or animal life or to property, or which unreasonably interfere with man's comfortable enjoyment of life and possessions.

Upon closer examination of some of the underlying facts concerning the nature, causes, and effects of community air pollution, it becomes increasingly obvious that it represents a most complex environmental phenomenon. Moreover, air pollution as we know from personal experience, is a constantly changing condition. Skies laden with heavy air pollution can be quickly transformed to clear, blue skies within hours by a sudden change in the weather such as results from the passage of a weather front. It is obvious therefore that we are dealing with a dynamic problem. As complex as the phenomenon may be, it can be easily and graphically depicted by means of a simplified systems analysis approach. Figure 1 represents such a systems diagram.

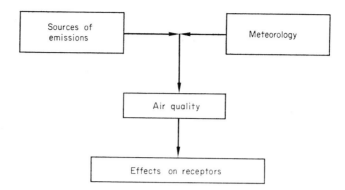

FIG. 1. Dynamics of air pollution.

It can be inferred that the mere presence of sources of emissions does not necessarily constitute air pollution. However, it is possible for unfavorable meteorological factors to interact with the emission factor to create undesirable air quality. If this quality deteriorates sufficiently the atmospheric environment begins to exert adverse effects on man and his environment. The degree of inconvenience, damage or illness produced depends on the particular receptor involved and the degree of exposure.

4. Meteorology and Topography

The ability of the atmosphere to adsorb pollutants depends on meteorological factors, principally wind speed, vertical temperature profile and solar radiation. The role of meteorology in air pollution is very well reviewed by Dr. Munn's [2] excellent paper on this subject. In his paper the author describes the diffusion process by which contaminants are carried downstream from the source and diluted. Two methods are discussed for relating air pollution levels to meteorological variables. One of these is an empirical method involving multivariate analysis yielding frequency distribution data. The other is urban modeling based on source inventory, and mathematical models of turbulent flow. The latter method leads to the derivation of air quality patterns for the area.

The paper by Professors Longley and Hage [2] discusses the so-called heat island effect in urban areas, and its relation to the dispersion of pollutants. Two models are described. Using one of these the authors conclude that pollutants tend to become uniformly distributed throughout the vertical.

In the other model it is postulated that the city-country temperature differences are the result of the relatively lower rates of radiative heat loss within the city. This leads to the prediction that pollutants tend to stratify in the vertical. Data from Edmonton and Calgary support the view that the latter model is more appropriate.

Solar radiation is an important factor in air pollution since it provides the energy needed in the reaction which occurs between oxides of nitrogen and hydrocarbons to produce photochemical smog of the Los Angeles type.

Local topography is another important consideration as valley structure tends to confine and channel air pollutants.

5. Effects of Air Pollution

It has been said, quite appropriately, that air pollution means many things to many people.

The housewife is concerned about the soiling effects.

The physician worries about his patients who may be suffering from cardio-pulmonary disease, and the additional physiological stress posed by breathing polluted air.

The farmer thinks about the possible economic loss from damage to his crops and live-stock exposed to potentially toxic dusts and gases.

Residents in areas having panoramic views become irate when man-made smoke and haze obliterate their beautiful vistas.

Almost everyone reacts unfavorably to obnoxious odors or eye-irritating smog.

Health effect. No discussion of air pollution effects would be complete without mention of the public health implications. I shall not comment on this subject since the comprehensive paper by Dr. de Villiers [2] treats this matter in great detail. The author concludes that there exists sufficient evidence to indicate that urban atmospheres affect health adversely by contributing to excess death rates, increased illness and earlier initiation of chronic respiratory diseases.

GUIDELINES TO AIR POLLUTION PREVENTION AND CONTROL

1. Technical Approach

A rational approach to the prevention and control of air pollution can be made on two fronts. The first of these is the technical approach. Fortunately, there currently exist satisfactory solutions to the control of the vast majority of air pollution sources. Presented below are five guidelines or principles of engineering control:

(a) Substitution of fuels or raw materials having a lower potential for pollution. [Example: in areas where SO_2 from fuel burning is a problem, it can be controlled by the use of coal or oil having a lower sulfur content, or switching to natural gas.]

(b) Modification of a process to minimize pollutant emissions. [Example: reduction of smoke through improved firing and combustion practices.]

In the fine paper by Dr. Murray [2] he suggests a number of ways in which odorous emissions from kraft pulping operations can be reduced. He states, "The problem of the recovery furnace is a problem of good operation and combustion control within the furnace design capacity." The paper contains data which vividly demonstrates the reduction of hydrogen sulfide emissions by keeping the liquor throughput of the furnace below a critical rate. A corresponding and dramatic reduction of hydrogen sulfide can be accomplished by maintaining the oxygen in the flue gas at about 3%. Dr. Murray also points out that black liquor oxidation can very substantially reduce H_2S emissions from the direct contact evaporators.

(c) The use of gas and particle collectors such as filters, scrubbers, and precipitators to reduce pollutant emission rates. Example: the use of bag filters in cement plants not only reduces dust emissions to well below acceptable levels, but also recovers a valuable product and increases profits.

The removal of sulfur oxides from flue gases permits recovery of sulfur which at today's market prices not only pays for the pollution control process but frequently returns a profit.

(d) The use of tall stacks to dilute and disperse pollutants. Chimneys provide some degree of protection from air pollution in those cases where there may be no other recourse. Frequently no alternative control methods exist, as in the case with oxides of nitrogen from large-scale combustion. Stacks in this instance may be the only choice. Considerable attention is being given to the effectiveness of stacks in dispersing pollution. The fine paper by Colley and Aziz [2] discusses the mathematical equations describing the laminar flow of air downwind from an exhaust. The authors develop a mathematical diffusion model and solve the equations by means of an electronic computer. The paper contains remarkable computer printouts illustrating transient and steady state concentration profiles for several atmospheric conditions. The results of this study indicate the great potential for predicting air concentrations downwind of elevated point sources. This technique could be a very valuable tool to the stack designer.

The aerodynamic downwash of stack gases resulting from the flow of air around nearby buildings and structures is undesirable because of the hazard from exposure of persons and vegetation to high concentrations of pollutants. Methods are not available at present for predicting the flow of gases under these conditions. Wind tunnel tests simulating the complex situation can yield reliable results.

The paper by Professors Lord and Leutheusser [2] describe wind modelling tests of stack exhaust gases. The theoretical basis and experimental procedures and facilities are discussed. An oil smoke aerosol is emitted from a scale model stack situated in a wind tunnel provided with an observation window. Photographs illustrate the flow patterns of the smoke plume as it leaves the point of discharge and flows over surrounding structures. This wind tunnel approach enables the designer to determine the proper height of stacks to minimize the downwash phenomenon.

(e) Regulation of processes in accordance with meteorological predictions. In some cases it is possible to minimize air pollution and optimize operating costs, for example, by turning on an SO_2 scrubber only when adverse weather conditions are anticipated; or the plant can switch from oil to gas under these conditions. Where it is feasible the plant could elect to greatly reduce its production rate when poor atmospheric dispersion conditions are predicted.

2. Air Resource Management

These five engineering approaches to air pollution control represent constructive steps for dealing with air pollution problems for the present and near future.

In the long run we shall need more efficient and economic measures. A more fruitful approach would be to regard the atmosphere as a natural resource which is not only vital but also limited. In this context the goal and objectives are not confined to the narrow concept of air pollution *reduction*, but to the broader concept of *air resource management* [3].

Air Resource Management can be described as a comprehensive program for optimizing the use of the natural air resource in a manner consistent with the various immediate and long-range needs of mankind.

The prime, specific objectives should be:

1. The proper utilization of the atmosphere for the ultimate disposal of airborne wastes and residues, and
2. The conservation of air quality at the level necessary for the preservation and promotion of man's health and well-being.

It must be recognized that the air in urban areas most probably will never again be "country fresh." The best one can hope for in the future is a compromise representing the optimum choice, considering what is technically feasible, legally permissible, economically attainable, and socially acceptable to the majority of people. Ultimately, decisions will have to be made by the individual communities on a social basis, through the elected officials. The challenge now confronting us, as engineers, is to provide satisfactory alternative choices for the decision makers.

While the derivation of these choices is an exquisitely difficult task, newly developed techniques of systems analysis using mathematical diffusion models and electronic computers appear very promising. Future sophisticated models will include not only emission and meteorological data inputs but also economic, social and legal considerations.

In their paper on solid waste disposal, MacLaren and Sexsmith [2] describe how the systems analysis approach can be applied to the solution of a most complex socio-economic and engineering problem. The various significant parameters are integrated into a plan designed to derive an optimum scheme. Essential considerations include environmental quality objectives, technical and financial feasibility, public acceptance, by-product recovery and efficiency. A similar analysis could be applied to derive "best choice" decisions in comprehensive and long-range air resource management planning.

The matter of planning for pollution control is likewise discussed in an excellent paper by Mr. Perks [2]. He states that the modern urban planner is rapidly adopting more dynamic approaches in the form of economic and systems analyses. The author warns that since pollution frequently has a subjective meaning effective planners must include a greater effort to evaluate *social perception* of environmental pollution. Standards based on technological and economical feasibility alone are inadequate since they may ignore health and cultural aspects which may be of greater concern to the public. The author concludes with the thought that rational planning can lead to optimum solutions only if it is acceptable to the general public, in terms of ecological, cultural and economic factors.

FUTURE OUTLOOK

1. Jurisdiction

The solution of a complex, multifaceted and geographically wide-spread problem such as air pollution will require the closest possible partnership between Federal, regional and state authorities. While the area-wide approach is sound, planning, enforcement and surveillence should be done on a local level. The role of the Federal government should be principally that of providing leadership, making policy, and rendering technical and financial assistance. The task of establishing air quality criteria can best be accomplished by the federal government because of its larger financial and scientific resources. The regional authorities should move quickly to adopt standards which are consistent with the criteria and goals set forth by the central government. However, where local conditions indicate that stricter standards are necessary or desirable, the local authorities should have the freedom to adopt tighter regulations. Basically the national government should assume local enforcement only in these areas which refuse to act, or are not reasonably capable of doing so.

2. Responsibilities

In the very fine paper by Mr. Baugh on Management Views of Pollution Control he points out that responsibilities go beyond government. The public and industry likewise have very important roles to play.

Mr. Baugh states that industry has a real obligation to prevent pollution, of industrial origin, which may threaten future generations. Industry can assume its obligation by (1)

M.A.H.E.—D

recognizing that pollution is not socially acceptable, and (2) co-operating with regulatory agencies by helping them to set standards and then comply with them. The author then makes a very important point: the time to prevent pollution is on the drawing boards. New plants should be designed initially to minimize pollution. Lastly, he implies that industry is in a strategic position to bring about the technological improvements and process changes which will be acceptable from the standpoint of business economics as well as environmental problems.

Mr. Baugh's paper reflects a most enlightened and, I may add, encouraging viewpoint on the part of industry.

3. Prevention

It is traditional in environmental pollution experience to take constructive action only after considerable damage has been demonstrated. As Professor Cragg [2] so ably discussed, if we postpone positive steps any longer we risk irreparable damage. There is also the probability that a triggering effect or chain-reaction could dramatically catapult the ecological pollution problem beyond manageable proportions.

Our goal must be to *prevent* pollution. Funds and efforts expended early in the game could yield far more satisfactory and economical solutions than waiting until the roof falls in.

As mentioned previously, the technology and knowledge to abate most pollution problems already exists. We must overcome this reluctance to apply them. Moreover, there are many attractive prospects for converting pollution into profits. A recent paper in the *Journal of the APCA* [4] described how the Basic Oxygen Furnace has cut the time for steel making from about 10 hours in the open hearth furnace to only 35 minutes per heat. Hoods and gas cleaning, however, are necessary to collect the added gases and particulates generated in this process. These controls recover carbon monoxide, a valuable fuel, and iron oxide which together are worth 40c/ton of steel produced. In addition the CO can be used as a raw material for producing petrochemicals for synthesizing ammonia, methanol, acetic acid, aldehydes, ketones, alcohols and other products.

At the current price of sulfur of about $45/ton, desulfurization of residual oils, and removal of sulfur dioxide from flue gases appear quite attractive economically. Obviously more research is needed to find ways of recovery and recycling wastes as useful by-products. This approach could be a very great stimulant for controlling air pollution. Industry should take a leadership role in this area of research and development.

4. Manpower

The need for additional trained specialists for the future research, teaching, and enforcement activities is rapidly outstripping the supply. If this trend continues we shall face a manpower crisis.

Personnel trained at all levels of specialization—professional and sub-professional—are in great demand. A rigorous recruitment program is needed to enlarge the number of qualified candidates enrolled in air pollution specialist training programs at universities. An increase in federal and private funds for training stipends would serve as a strong stimulant to bright young men entering college or graduate schools.

Continuing education programs in air pollution could help in training mature professionals interested in switching into this field.

CONCLUSION

Air pollution is rapidly becoming a serious environmental problem. Continued population growth, industrial and technological expansion and urbanization in the developing areas of western U.S. and Canada will lead to worsening of the problem. Strong steps should be taken to protect the natural air resources while there is still the opportunity. Air pollution is no respector of political boundaries, consequently air pollution control on a regional basis is a necessity. Enforcement should be on a local or regional basis, however, the technical and financial resources of the federal government will be required. I look to the development of a strong, constructive partnership between Federal and State, or provincial, governments for developing acceptable regional air quality standards and control programs.

Stronger efforts should be made to apply the air pollution control technologies that are already available. Research and demonstrations, supported by the government and the private sector, should be accelerated in order to find more efficient and feasible techniques for the most difficult problems.

The pool of trained specialists will have to be greatly augmented to implement the expanding efforts in research, control technology and enforcement. The university should take the leadership in this regard. The responsibility for air pollution control rests with all of us—government, industry, and the general public. We all breathe air.

Let us resolve to take advantage of the experience of less fortunate areas of the world. It is not yet too late to take the vigorous and realistic steps to protect our vital air resource for the benefit and enjoyment of ourselves, our children, and their children.

REFERENCES

1. ROSSANO, A. T., Jr., Air pollution principles. Presented at the Annual Meeting of the Pacific Northwest International Section ot the Air Pollution Control Association, Seattle, Washington, November 3–4, 1966.
2. Various papers presented at the Banff Conference on Pollution.
3. ROSSANO, A. T., Jr., The community air pollution survey. *Air Pollution*, Chapter 31, Volume II, Academic Press, New York, 1968.
4. MYERS, R. L., Opportunities for the industrial scientist—engineering in air pollution research, *Journal of the APCA*, Vol. 17, No. 12, December 1967.

METEOROLOGY AND AIR POLLUTION

R. E. MUNN *Meteorological Service of Canada, Toronto*

ABSTRACT

Air pollution meteorology is described qualitatively, including some of the assumptions made in the prediction models. The major variables are the wind and turbulence, which transport and dilute pollutants respectively. The wind flow results from the combined effect of continental-scale weather patterns and meso-scale valley, slope or lake-breeze circulations. The latter can sometimes create high pollution potential when regional winds are light; on the other hand, local breezes may prevent stagnation conditions. Turbulence is dependent on the roughness of the ground, the speed of the wind and atmospheric buoyancy forces. Day-time convection is favourable for dilution while night-time inversions inhibit dispersion. Aerodynamic downwash behind buildings can cause locally high concentrations. For a tall chimney, the exit velocity and excess temperature are important in determining the initial rise of the plume, and subsequent ground-level concentrations. Finally, there is a brief discussion of mixing depths, urban modelling of pollution, and empirical methods of relating air quality to meteorological factors.

INTRODUCTION

Complete elimination of the sources of air pollution is not possible at the present time or for many years to come. The atmosphere is therefore being used as a giant sewer, having a very large but not infinite capacity to dilute contaminants to tolerable levels. It follows that intelligent exploitation of this natural resource can only be made if the meteorological processes are understood. For example, the amount of SO_2 emitted from a tall chimney is not *per se* a criterion for control programs; the important variable is the ground-level concentration, which is a function of meteorological factors as well as of source strength.

It is intuitively evident that the transport and diffusion of air pollution depends on the turbulent wind, and it is easy to describe the dependence qualitatively. The quantitative prediction of air quality at any point in space and time, on the other hand, has been called a "mathematical extravaganza". Too often the emphasis is placed on a textbook equation without serious consideration being given to the physical assumptions underlying the model. All diffusion equations are cast in terms of some ideal flow conditions that are rarely, if ever, fully realized in the atmosphere. It is fortuitous, therefore, if a prediction is verified with an accuracy of more than an order-of-magnitude.

This paper describes the qualitative aspects of air pollution meteorology and discusses the basis for the physical models of diffusion. More extensive treatments have been given elsewhere [1, 2].

SOURCE STRENGTH AND THE EFFECT OF WIND SPEED

When pollution is emitted from a chimney, the smoke or gas is carried forward and stretched by the wind. The effect is illustrated in Fig. 1 [3]; stronger winds produce more stretching and dilution. This is why diffusion equations include the wind speed $\bar{u}$ as one variable.

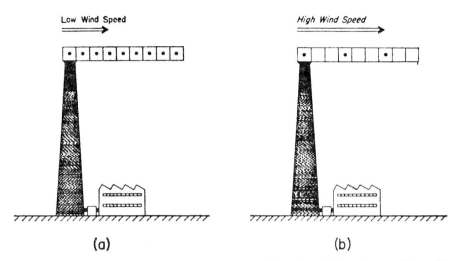

FIG. 1. The effect of wind speed in stretching and diluting pollution from a chimney [3].

In this connection, the source strength Q of pollution must be specified in terms of *mass per unit time*, not *volume per unit time*. The diffusion equations assume a point source; initial dilution of the pollution in the chimney has little effect on the downwind ground-level concentration E, except indirectly in influencing the exit velocity or gas temperature; turbulent mixing in the atmosphere is so vigorous that smoke particles soon forget that they had an initial separation in the chimney.

The grouping $\bar{u}E/Q$ is often found. This process of combining variables is called *normalization* of the diffusion equation, and permits cases with different source strengths Q and/or wind speeds $\bar{u}$ to be considered together, i.e. the analysis is simplified by elimination of two variables.

It is important to note that all the diffusion models fail when the wind is calm.

ATMOSPHERIC TRANSPORT

As part of the 1966 Cleaner Air Week program in Toronto, school children released helium-filled balloons designed to travel at a constant height of about 2000 ft above the ground. Tags were attached, and many of these were returned by mail to the Cleaner Air Week committee. The extreme travel distances are shown in Table 1 [4].

When winds were light on October 18th, no balloons were found at greater distances than 90 miles. During stronger flows, however, the balloons (and presumably Toronto pollution also) travelled far beyond county, provincial and national boundaries in 24 hours, although dilution of pollutants would be greater than on October 18th.

Petterson [5] has recently studied the plume emitted from the Brookhaven nuclear reactor on Long Island. On a day when winds were westerly, aircraft sampling for argon-41 indicated that the plume still retained its identity at distances of 200 miles from the source. These examples illustrate the importance of global transport, a subject of increasing interest and concern. For example, traces of DDT have been found recently in Antarctic snow-cores while in Greenland, the lead concentrations in snow have increased tenfold since 1850 [6].

TABLE 1. EXTREME LOCATIONS OF BALLOON TAGS RETURNED TO TORONTO, OCTOBER 17–21, 1966 [4]

Date	Place where balloon found	Travel distance of balloon	Wind in Toronto area		
			Surface	2000′	4000′
Oct. 17	Megantic, Quebec	450 miles	SW9	W19	W17
Oct. 18	Uxbridge, Ont.	90 miles	SE9	S9	NW5
Oct. 19	Barry's Bay, Ont.	135 miles	NW13	E6	S9
Oct. 20	Wilmington, Deleware	350 miles	NW16	NW11	NW19
Oct. 21	Springfield, Vermont	350 miles	S15	SW13	SW30

On a lesser but still large scale, transport of significant amounts of pollution from city to city is not impossible on occasion; the "megalopolous" along the Atlantic seaboard from Boston to Washington is one area where air resource management on a regional scale is desirable.

Local wind circulations are often important in the transport of pollution. Lake and sea-breezes, valley and slope winds frequently cause a rather regular diurnal ebb and flow of pollution (at Denver, Col., Crow [7], for example), when regional winds are weak. Even a city can create its own local wind circulation as a result of the heat-island that develops in the built-up area. Johnstown, Pa. is an example of the interaction between an urban and a valley flow; the normal down-valley drainage wind at night reverses its direction just downstream from the industrial heat-island complex [8]. These patterns are not easily modelled by diffusion equations and only recently are beginning to receive the attention they deserve.

DIFFUSION OF PASSIVE POLLUTION FROM A POINT SOURCE

Not only is a plume carried downstream and stretched by the wind, it also expands. This is called a diffusion process and it usually contributes substantially to dilution rates.

Point-source diffusion is termed the one-particle problem; a single "tagged" element is followed, the experiment is repeated many times, and the statistical properties of particle positions are studied. Volume-source diffusion from an initial large cloud or cluster, on the other hand, is called the two-particle problem; the relative distance between two "tagged" elements is followed, and the experiment is repeated many times. A city is supposed to consist of a large number of point sources, the effect of which is additive; the expansion of a radioactive cloud in the stratosphere is a volume-source problem.

Only the one-particle problem will be considered in this paper. A plume of smoke from a point source at any downwind distance x is characterized by its height above the ground, and by its cross-wind and vertical dimensions in the y and z axes, respectively. These latter quantities may be specified in terms of the visible outline, using photography, for example, or more generally in terms of the standard deviations s_y and s_z of the frequency distributions of particles or molecules of gas. The quantities s_y and s_z have dimensions of length and increase with increasing x as the plume expands downwind. Although experimental values may be obtained and fitted to empirical equations, a fundamental objective of diffusion research is to seek "universal" relationships for s_y and s_z. The models are based on the belief that s_y is determined in some way by wind direction fluctuations, while a record of the vertical component of turbulence contains sufficient information to predict the vertical spread s_z of the plume. The nature of the relationships may be explained qualitatively as follows.

Large eddies of air move the plume from side to side causing "meander" but not producing any expansion. Small turbulent fluctuations, on the other hand, are relatively inefficient in the diffusion process. It is eddies of the same scale as the plume that contribute most. As downwind distance and plume width increase, therefore, it is necessary to include the effect of larger and larger eddies in the analysis, i.e. to use a band-pass filter that shifts to lower and lower turbulence frequencies.

Usually the sampling time is not instantaneous. If a 10-minute average concentration is of interest, the meandering of the plume can no longer be neglected; analogous to increasing the exposure time in a photograph, the outline will be larger but the contrast will not be as sharp. The range of wind fluctuations of importance must therefore be increased to include periods comparable to the sampling time.

These rather simple ideas are the basis for diffusion models. The complexity of the problem is reduced initially by assuming:

(a) A continuous point source that creates no obstruction to the wind, releasing weightless particles (or an inert gas) at a constant rate.

(b) A steady wind, i.e. one that shows no trend during the period of travel and sampling (stationarity).

(c) A homogenous field of turbulence.

(d) The absence of buoyancy influences, i.e. a neutral temperature lapse rate condition.

This physical abstraction cannot be studied in the real world, largely because of the presence of an underlying surface which suppresses the vertical component of turbulence near the ground and causes a vertical gradient in wind (wind shear). Nevertheless, considerable attention has been given to the model. The fundamental assumption is that turbulence is a random or stochastic process. Although the trajectory of a single particle cannot be predicted, the positional probabilities for a large number of replications of the experiment can be specified. Unfortunately, these probabilities are for the *Lagrangian* reference frame, one that moves along with the speed of a typical fluid element, whereas the practical interest is in diffusion in a fixed *Eulerian* reference frame. The relationship between the two kinds of statistics has been the subject of much speculation and controversy but little experimentation. Hay and Pasquill [9] have made an empirical assumption that seems reasonable: that the ratio of the scales of Lagrangian–Eulerian turbulence is approximately constant. For an elevated point source and a uniform underlying surface, then, the lateral and vertical diffusion of a stream of weightless particles can be estimated from the lateral and vertical fluctuations of the wind at a point when the correct band-pass filter is used [10]. It should be noted that an earlier assumption by Sutton [11] about Lagrangian–Eulerian relationships is indefensible.

Even for this very simplified model, it would be a mistake to believe that there is a unique value of the concentration at any given downwind position in a single experiment. Because of the random nature of turbulence, the concentration at a point fluctuates from moment to moment. If E is the instantaneous and $\bar{E}$ the mean value at some centre-line position, Csanady [12] suggests that the probability P of E being equal to or less than $\bar{E}$ is given by,

$$P = 1 - \exp\left(-E/\bar{E}\right)$$

Because of the time lag of sensors, an instantaneous concentration is not usually obtained. As the smoothing time for E increases, its variability decreases; nevertheless, a 3-min value of E occasionally may be much greater than the 1-hr average value $\bar{E}$ at the same position in the flow.

The effect of the underlying surface is usually omitted from the models except to provide for perfect reflection from the ground. Diffusion in shear flow is being studied in many parts of the world but few practical results are available yet. It does seem, however, that changes of wind direction are more significant than of wind speed. The assumption of perfect reflection is also being questioned. The percentage loss of the plume to the ground is uncertain but may not always be negligible.

Atmospheric buoyancy changes the character of the turbulent fluctuations and therefore its effect can be included readily in the models. During strong temperature inversions at night, however, the flow often tends to be intermittent (short bursts of turbulence separated by periods of steady wind); the assumption of a stationary time series then fails and the models are inapplicable. In general, diffusion rates are greater in the daytime when there is positive buoyancy and are less at night.

In design studies, there is often no climatological record available for the proposed site. Pasquill [10] has therefore developed a simplified classification of diffusion for open country based on climatic records of surface wind and sunshine or cloudiness obtained from a nearby weather observing station. Bryant [13] has estimated the frequency of occurrence of each class, for example, for 8 locations in England and Wales. Nomograms then permit order-of-magnitude estimates of ground-level concentrations.

PLUME RISE

Pollution from a chimney often has an exit velocity and temperature excess, which produces buoyant rise. The height at which the plume is supposed to level off and become passive is called the *effective plume height*. This is an important quantity in diffusion calculations. A large number of formulae have been proposed, so many in fact that an international committee met in the Netherlands in November 1967 to try to reach agreement on a standard formula, but without success.

The best practical advice is to use two or three of the formulae in order to establish a probable upper and lower limit for plume rise. The downwind ground-level concentrations must then be specified in terms of a range of values.

AERODYNAMIC EFFECTS

When a strong wind passes around a bluff obstacle, the flow separates and a turbulent wake (cavity) forms in the lee of the obstruction. Smoke released from a short chimney on a square building may be caught in the cavity. The geometry of the building and the angle of attack of the wind are important. Wind-tunnel scale modelling is often used to study the problem, but there are an increasing number of atmospheric investigations [14, 15].

One modelling problem that arises is that although a satisfactory solution may be obtained, the construction of an adjacent tall building a few years hence may substantially alter the flow characteristics. The owner of the original structure may then be faced with a pollution problem through no fault of his own.

EMPIRICAL METHODS

Multivariate analysis and contingency tables are frequently used to relate air quality to several meteorological factors. However, the data do not often meet the significance-test requirements for random unbiased statistical samples. For instance, a regression between pollution concentrations and wind speed is biased because the lighter winds are more likely to occur at night. Prestratification of samples according to season and time of day is a help but does not eliminate interactions completely.

In many provinces, plans for a new chimney or for zoning changes to permit an "industrial park" must be submitted to pollution control officials for approval. A question that has never been fully resolved is whether the design should be based on average or extreme weather conditions. With a prevailing southwesterly wind, for example, the most serious pollution situations may nevertheless be associated with easterly winds. Should new industry then be encouraged to locate in the western or the eastern suburbs of a city?

For a fixed point at a given distance from a point Q, the ratio E/Q is a random variable and an estimate of its entire frequency distribution is presumably of interest. Hydrologists design flood-control projects in terms of *return periods*, and Barry [16] has suggested a similar approach to air pollution engineering. Extreme-value theory may perhaps be used to estimate the probability of various threshold values being exceeded, including thresholds higher than any observed values in the period of record. Barry believes that sites may possibly be "calibrated" in terms of these frequency distributions. Experimental verification from a number of "typical" locations is required to confirm the speculation.

URBAN MODELLING

A city is a collection of point sources. In order to obtain an integrated picture of the ground-level concentrations of pollution, it is first necessary to develop a source inventory, city block by city block. Curiously enough, little attention has been given to this in Canada, with the notable exception of studies by the Alberta Health Department.

The turbulence in a built-up area is complex. Nevertheless, some patterns can be identified, as shown for example in Fig. 2 [17]; isopleths are drawn of the standard deviations of wind direction fluctuations as obtained from a number of wind vanes in Fort Wayne, Indiana; it can be seen that the air is more turbulent in the centre of the city.

When an adequate source inventory is available, a simplified model of turbulent flow can be used to derive the patterns of air quality; however, a large computer is required to complete the calculations in a reasonable length of time. The results to date have been encouraging. Where the predictions have been tested with data from a network of sampling stations, the spatial gradients are correct within order-of-magnitude accuracy, although the absolute values may be in error [18, 19].

An important refinement is the inclusion of *mixing-depth*, the layer of air which is stirred from below and through which the pollution becomes well mixed. The top of this layer is sometimes clearly visible when flying over a city. The mixing is greater in the afternoon than at night and depends partly on continental-scale weather processes [20]. Pollution potential forecasts are issued daily in the United States for areas predicted to have a period of settled anticyclonic weather, weak horizontal ventilation and small mixing depths. The emphasis is on stagnation conditions, i.e. situations when the diffusion models fail for lack of a well-defined wind direction.

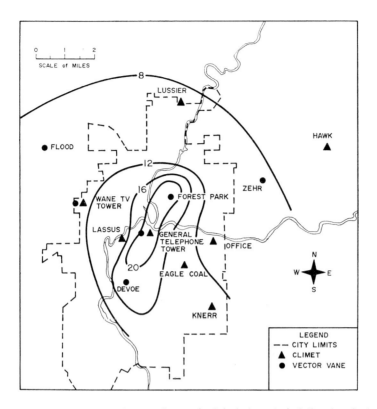

FIG. 2. Fort Wayne, Indiana. Isopleths of the standard deviation of wind direction (in degrees) on a selection of days when northwest winds were blowing [17].

CONCLUSIONS

A qualitative review of air pollution meteorology has been given. Despite many uncertainties, the models often seem to yield reasonable values, i.e. ground-level concentrations rarely exceed provincial control thresholds if a meteorological analysis has been included in the chimney design. This is probably due to an inherent safety factor. The models permit fluctuations of wind direction about a mean. More often than not, however, the wind direction gradually shifts during the day, causing the plume centre-line to rotate. A 30-degree veer in an hour or so spreads the pollution over a wider arc than if the direction were steady, thus reducing the predicted peak ground-level concentrations. Only in a narrow canyon is the pollution trajectory constrained by geometry.

Because the dilution capacity of the atmosphere is not unlimited and because of the trend towards taller and taller chimneys, the air pollution meteorologist is directing more of his attention towards large-scale weather processes. Many problems remain to be solved, admittedly, but progress is encouraging.

REFERENCES

1. PASQUILL, F., *Atmospheric Diffusion*, Van Nostrand, Toronto, 1962, 297 pp.
2. MUNN, R. E., *Descriptive Micrometeorology*, Academic Press, New York, 1966, 245 pp.
3. GIFFORD, F., Meteorology in relation to reactor hazards and site evaluation. In *Proc. Sixth Lasagna Conf.*, Vol. II, pp. 7–17, 1959.
4. STEWART, I. M., GODSON, W. L. and MUNN, R. E., The Toronto 1966 Cleaner Air Program balloon experiment. Internal report available from Met. Service of Canada, Toronto, 1966.
5. PETTERSON, K. R., Continuous point-source plume behaviour out to 160 miles, *J. Appl. Meterorol.*, **7**, 217–226, 1968.
6. MUROZUMI, M., CHOW, T. J. and PATTERSON, C. C., Changes in concentrations of common lead in north polar snows with time. Preprint 67–69. Air Poll. Control Assoc. Annual Meeting, Cleveland (1967).
7. CROW, L. W., Airflow related to Denver air pollution. *J. Air Poll. Control Assoc.* **14**, 56–59, 1964.
8. SMITH, D., A study of air pollution in Johnstown, Pa. M.Sc. thesis, Air Environment Centre, Penn. State Univ., 1967.
9. HAY, J. S. and PASQUILL, F., Diffusion from a continuous source in relation to the spectrum and scale of turbulence. *Adv. Geophys.* **6**, 345–365, 1959.
10. PASQUILL, F., The estimation ot the dispersion of windborne material. *Meteorol. Mag.* **90**, 33–49, 1961
11. SUTTON, G. I., A theory of eddy diffusion in the atmosphere. *Proc. Roy. Soc. London A.* **135**, 143–165, 1932.
12. CSANADY, G. T., Concentration fluctuations in turbulent diffusion. *J. Atmosph. Sc.* **24**, 21–28, 1967.
13. BRYANT, P., Methods of estimation of the dispersion of windborne material and data to assist in their application. AHSB (RP) R42, U.K. Atomic Energy Authority, H.M. Stationery Office, 1964, 18 pp.
14. MUNN, R. E. and COLE, A. F. W., Turbulence and diffusion in the wake of a building. *Atmos. Env.* **1**, 33–43, 1967.
15. RUMMERFIELD, P. S., CHOLAK, J. and KEREIAKES, J., Estimation of local diffusion of pollutants from a chimney: a prototype study employing an activated tracer. *Am. Ind. Hyg. J.* **28**, 366–371, 1967.
16. BARRY, P. J., A new approach to the problems of atmospheric dispersal of stack effluents. CRL-94, AECL, Chalk River, Ontario, 1967.
17. GRAHAM, I. R., An analysis of turbulence statistics at Fort Wayne, Indiana. *J. Appl. Meteorol.* **7**, 90–93, 1968.
18. TURNER, D. B., A diffusion model for an urban area. *J. Appl. Meteorol.* **3**, 83–91, 1964.
19. MILLER, M. E. and HOLZWORTH, G. C., An atmospheric diffusion model for metropolitan areas. *J. Air Poll. Control Assoc.* **17**, 46–50, 1967.
20. HOLZWORTH, G. C., Mixing depths, wind speeds and air pollution potential for selected locations in the United States. *J. Appl. Meteorol.* **6**, 1039–1044, 1967.

DISCUSSION

W. MARTIN (*Western Co-operative Fertilizers Ltd., Calgary*)

How does the atmosphere cleanse itself of the various pollutants which are continually introduced? Also, is there a concentrating effect occurring in the atmosphere of pollutants which are not scrubbed out of the atmosphere?

AUTHOR'S REPLY

The lower part of the atmosphere, called the troposphere, extends up to 30,000 feet or so. This is the region of clouds and precipitation. Rain is a very efficient cleanser and on the average, the half-life of pollutants in the troposphere is about 7 days.

The situation is very different in the stratosphere, the upper part of the atmosphere where there are no clouds and a semi-permanent temperature inversion. The only way that pollution can escape seems to be by "leakage" down through the jet stream. As a result, the half-life of stratospheric pollutants is more than a year.

O. JOHNSON (*Defense Research Establishment Suffield, Ralston*):

A considerable proportion of the research in meteorology at the Defence Research Establishment involves a study of the structure of turbulence in the lowest 100 metres of the atmosphere and the eddy diffusion in this layer from surface and elevated sources. Since the rate of diffusion depends on the intensity of turbulence, a knowledge of the structure of turbulence gives a measure of the diffusive power of the atmosphere.

We have a 92 metre tower which is located on a large area of gently rolling prairie. This tower is instrumented for measurements of turbulence at three levels and the vertical profiles of wind velocity and temperature. A moderate amount of data from this tower has been accumulated for southwest to west winds, mainly in chinook conditions, and it is planned to extend these measurements to cover a variety of synoptic conditions. The objective is to obtain sufficient data to relate the intensity of turbulence to the synoptic situation. This might make it possible to predict, very roughly, the rate of diffusion which should be helpful for predicting the level of air pollution.

VENTILATION AND MIXING IN ALBERTA CITIES

K. D. HAGE and R. W. LONGLEY *University of Alberta*

ABSTRACT

Two distinct urban heat island models that postulate strong vertical mixing of pollutants over an urban heat source in one case, and incompletely mixed pollutants in slightly stable air over the city in the second case, are compared with observations in Edmonton, Alberta. Local wind observations and preliminary vertical temperature gradient measurements in central Edmonton seem to support the view that vertical mixing is incomplete even in periods of large city-country temperature differences. In these circumstances effluent release heights and buoyancy as well as atmospheric properties may be important in determining vertical profiles of pollutants and their concentrations. It is suggested that air pollution climatology studies for the plains of Alberta should be concerned particularly with the relatively infrequent but important periods of poor ventilation.

INTRODUCTION

The concentration of pollutants in the air is the ratio of pollutant mass to the volume of air containing the mass. From the point of view of air pollution assessment and control perhaps the most important meteorological considerations are those that determine the location of particular masses of pollutants as a function of time and those that determine the volume of air through which the pollutants are distributed. Both considerations involve some degree of averaging in space and time and, to be meaningful, the degree of averaging must be related to air quality criteria. Long exposure to low concentrations may be as detrimental as the more obvious brief exposures to large concentrations. Except for localized sources of highly toxic, corrosive, or otherwise damaging pollutants the most acute air pollution problems that we are aware of have developed over urban areas with concentrated and persistent output of a wide variety of gases and particles that range from nuisances to serious hazards to health and property.

Under normal circumstances the atmospheric volume over an urban area is an open system with rapid exchange of air through the sides and top of the volume. Even under such favorable conditions, however, pollutant dosages can be large due to long exposures of residents and property to persistent low concentrations from a multitude of sources. In addition, because of local sheltering in basin and valley regions, and because of particular combinations of meteorological conditions the air exchange rate over a city can be strongly suppressed at times resulting in critical local accumulations of pollution.

The meteorological conditions that favour small air exchange rates are well known, namely, light winds throughout the volume of interest and weak vertical mixing through the top of the volume. Extensive wind profile measurements and some vertical mixing data are available for many rural locations in many parts of the world. Less well known, however, are the effects that cities may have both on the mean winds and on the intensity and depth

99

of vertical mixing. Urban heat islands are well documented in terms of low-level temperature measurements at fixed points and temperature traverses but important questions remain. Does the city generate its own time-dependent or steady air circulation with rising air over the centre and descending air around the periphery when the mean winds are light? Does the city create its own mixing layer because of its importance as a heat source? If so, does the mixed layer increase ventilation in the city by downward mixing of higher wind speeds from above? To what extent can results obtained elsewhere be applied to Alberta cities that have a relatively long period of persistent snow cover and low sun angles in winter, a relatively dry continental climate, and low density urban populations?

Two parameters—the mixing depth and the mean wind speed through the mixed layer—have been proposed by Holzworth [1] as key indices for the development of an urban air pollution potential climatology in the United States. The concept of a mixed layer is based on the principle that heat supplied at the earth's surface by the sun or by an artificial source such as a city results in vigorous vertical mixing of the air and its properties including pollution loads through a layer the thickness of which depends on the heating rate at the surface and the vertical temperature distribution of the ambient air. One consequence of vigorous vertical mixing of heat without condensation is that potential temperatures are constant with height, i.e., a dry adiabatic lapse rate is established. Mixing depths can be several kilometers or more on sunny afternoons in midsummer and the associated vertical mixing causes rapid dilution of polluted air. On calm clear nights studies have shown that the air over cities is much less stable than over surrounding rural areas (Duckworth and Sandberg [2], De Marrais [3]). Summers [4] postulated the development of a mixed layer over a city under such conditions and found quantitative support for his calculations in heat output and pollution observations for Montreal.

Among other things the mixed-layer model implies (a) that urban-rural surface temperature differences can be used together with the rural vertical temperature distribution (available from radiosonde observations near many cities) to estimate the mixing depth and (b) that average pollution concentrations are more or less constant with height from the effective height of the city heat source to the top of the mixed layer. Within a fixed low layer over the city one would expect increasing frequencies of dry adiabatic lapse rates with increasing urban heat island intensities.

On the other hand, if the urban heat island is the result of relatively less radiative cooling at night over the city than over nearby rural areas the implications are somewhat different. In these circumstances increasing frequencies of radiative equilibrium (isothermal) vertical temperature gradients would be expected with increasing urban heat island intensities and pollutants would tend to be stratified rather than thoroughly mixed. Source release heights and the buoyancy of emissions would be important factors in establishing the heights of layers of various pollutants. Furthermore, the lowest strata of pollutants would usually contribute most to concentrations in the lowest 50 ft of air occupied by most people and property.

The two models described above are limiting cases and it is likely that actual pollution distributions conform to mixing rates somewhere between the two extremes in many cities. Local studies are needed to establish the ventilation and mixing characteristics of the atmosphere over Alberta cities. Preliminary results of one such study are described in the following sections.

In 1967 the Department of Health of the Government of Alberta undertook detailed surface measurements of the urban heat islands and of the vertical temperature gradients within the cities of Edmonton and Calgary. Installation and maintenance of instruments was carried out by Geoscience Research Associates Ltd. under contract to the Department of Health. In Edmonton electrical resistance bulb thermometers (Bristol Model 66 A 12064) were installed at 3 levels (17 m, 57 m, and 112 m) on the C N Towers building at 104 Avenue and 100 A Street. The lowest and highest were mounted on 8 ft booms projected from building ledges on the north face. The thermometers were aspirated and shielded from direct solar radiation. The intermediate-level thermometer was exposed within an air intake vent that opened on the east face of the building. Data collection on a continuous basis was initiated June 1, 1967. Periodic calibration checks have shown no evidence of drift and indicate that the temperature differences were accurate to within $\pm 0 \cdot 1°F$. The absolute accuracy and representativeness of the measurements can be determined only by means of independent observations. Plans are underway to obtain such observations by means of a mobile tethered balloon sounding system. In Calgary, aspirated and shielded resistance bulb thermometers were mounted on a special 300 ft tower located at Bonnybrook Road and 42nd Avenue. Data collection was initiated in Calgary in late March 1968.

Seven bimetal thermographs mounted in wind-ventilated white metal containers were distributed at surface sites in Calgary and Edmonton and continuous temperature records commenced in late December, 1967 and early January 1968.

Conventional hourly meteorological observations were obtained for Calgary International Airport about $4 \cdot 5$ miles north northeast of the city centre and within the city limits, for Edmonton Industrial Airport about $2 \cdot 5$ miles northwest of the city centre, and for Edmonton International Airport 20 miles south of the city centre and 15 miles south of the city limits. In addition, hourly wind data were obtained from an anemometer mounted on a 6 m mast on top of the Henry Marshall Tory building (63 m above ground) at the University of Alberta about $1 \cdot 5$ miles southwest of the Edmonton city centre.

Preliminary analyses of some of the hourly wind and temperature data referred to above and of the C N Towers building temperature measurements in July and December 1967 are described in the following section.

ANALYSIS OF WINDS AND TEMPERATURES

The normal (30 year averages) surface winds at Calgary International Airport and Edmonton Industrial Airport are comparable in magnitude (9 to 10 mph) and show summer minima and spring maxima. The winter minimum in December and January at Edmonton, and at most observing stations of northern Alberta, however, is not evident in the wind speed data for Calgary.

Durations of persistent light winds in summer and winter are summarized for Calgary International Airport in Fig. 1. In five years of hourly wind observations (1963–1967) for the months of July, August, and September, the longest periods were 55, 33, and 16 hours for consecutive wind speeds less than or equal to 9, 6, and 3 mph, respectively. Corresponding extreme durations in the months of December, January, and February were 119, 70, and 30 hours. The average durations of the longest light wind period in an individual month varied between 45 and 65% of the extremes. If these results are representative of all years

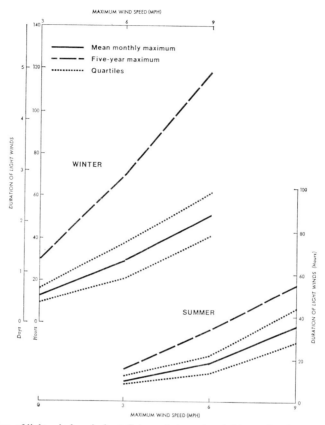

FIG. 1. Duration of light wind periods at Calgary International Airport in winter (Dec., Jan., and Feb.) and in summer (July, Aug. and Sept.) based on hourly wind data for 5 years.

then on the average one period of 50 consecutive hours with wind speeds below 10 mph can be expected in each winter month with one period of about 120 hours' duration once in five winters. Terrain variations such as those found within Calgary can strongly influence surface winds and it is possible that the airport observations are not representative of the city as a whole.

Analogous data for Edmonton Industrial Airport are shown in Fig. 2. Extreme durations of consecutive hourly wind speeds less than or equal to 9, 6, and 3 mph in July, August, and September, were 91, 46, and 14 hours, respectively. In December, January, and February the corresponding extremes were 147, 90, and 20 hours. Once again, if it is assumed that these results are representative of all years, one period of about 100 hours of consecutive wind speeds below 10 mph can be expected on the average in each winter month with one period of about 150 hours in five winters. The durations of persistent light winds were quite comparable at the two locations and many times shorter than those that would be expected in basins and valleys.

The most favourable meteorological condition for the accumulation of pollutants over an isolated urban area would be a combination of persistent light winds and persistent weak vertical mixing. Suitable vertical temperature gradient observations that could provide a basis for estimating the intensity of vertical mixing over Edmonton and Calgary are not

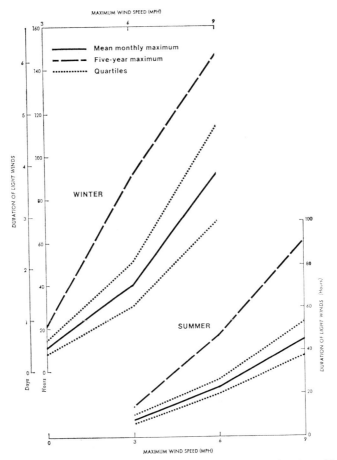

FIG. 2. Duration of light wind periods at Edmonton Industrial Airport in winter (Dec., Jan., and Feb.) and in summer (July, Aug. and Sept.) based on hourly wind data for 5 years.

available for time periods of more than a few months and it is not possible at present to derive conditional frequencies for simultaneous occurrence of light winds and weak mixing. Local radiosonde observations are not very suitable because of their coarse resolution of temperature profiles near the earth's surface and because of their low sampling frequency (once per 12 hours).

Before proceeding to a discussion of the vertical temperature gradient measurements that are now available from the C N Towers building in central Edmonton it is necessary to examine the accuracy of these observations. The exposure of the thermometers near the walls of a large building not far from other large buildings is such that one can legitimately question whether or not the observations are truly representative of ambient air temperatures. Occasional spurious or unrepresentative readings caused by bubbles or plumes of warm air from nearby heat sources cannot be avoided in a city. However, gross errors of this kind can be identified and allowed for by examining frequency distributions of the temperatures and temperature differences. Systematic errors due to radiation effects, instrumental errors, persistent local warm or cold air currents, etc., are likely to be much more difficult to identify and much more harmful to analyses and interpretations of the data.

The mean hourly temperatures at Edmonton Industrial Airport (XD), Edmonton International Airport (EG), and the lowest level (17 m) on the C N Towers building are compared in Fig. 3 for all hours of the day in July and December 1967. Because of vigorous vertical and horizontal mixing these temperatures should be nearly equal in midday hours in July. The upper curves in Fig. 3 lend credence to the observations because they show differences of less than $1 \cdot 0°F$ between XD and the C N Towers during the 5-hour period from 1300 to 1700 MST in July. The urban heat island effect is evident in the nighttime and early morning temperatures. In December (lower curves in Fig. 3) the C N Towers temperatures at 17 m were higher at all hours than those at XD and EG and the average urban heat island effect was less intense. Independent evidence of weak vertical mixing in midday hours of winter will be shown later in this section. The occurrence of higher maximum temperatures later in the day as one approaches the city centre from a rural area can be accounted for if the outgoing long-wave radiation from the city is attenuated more strongly than the incoming solar short-wave radiation. Under such conditions the time of balance between outgoing and incoming radiation, i.e. the time of maximum temperature, will be later in the city than in the country and slightly higher maximum temperatures will occur particularly on light wind days. The reduction in intensity of solar radiation by the urban atmosphere has been measured in eastern Canada by East [5] and Emslie [6] but less is known

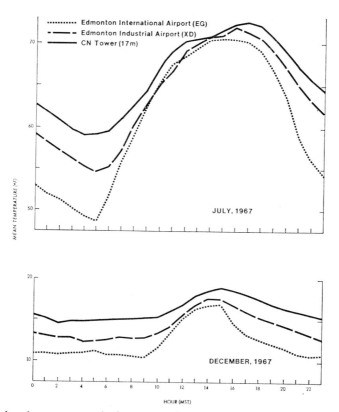

FIG. 3. Mean hourly temperatures in downtown Edmonton (CN Tower) compared with temperatures observed at urban (XD) and rural (EG) airports.

regarding the attentuation of long-wave radiation. It should be noted that the urban heat island intensity as measured by the XD–EG or C N Towers–EG temperature differences is sometimes offset especially in winter by the prevailing north-south large-scale temperature gradient. Peripheral rural temperature observations on the east and west sides of Edmonton are needed for a more accurate estimate of the average heat island intensity.

Hourly frequency distributions of the vertical temperature differences between 17 m and 112 m on the C N Towers building in July 1967 are shown in Table 1. All data were grouped in equal classes of size $0 \cdot 9°F$ and converted to units of °C per 100 m. A pronounced diurnal variation with frequent superadiabatic gradients in the daytime is evident in the distributions. The model gradient was between $-1 \cdot 0°C$ $(100 \text{ m})^{-1}$ (adiabatic) and $-0 \cdot 5°C$ $(100 \text{ m})^{-1}$. The frequency distributions for December 1967 are given in Table 2. The mean vertical gradients were smallest in daytime hours but there was no evidence of frequent excursions to superadiabatic values characteristic of the daytime hours of July. The modal gradient in December was near $-0 \cdot 5°C$ $(100 \text{ m})^{-1}$.

Frequency distributions of the temperature differences T_3-T_1 (112 m–17 m) and T_2-T_1 (57 m–17 m) for daylight hours only in July and December are shown in Table 3. In July the most frequent value of T_3-T_1 corresponded to the adiabatic gradient. However, the lowest layer showed a pronounced frequency maximum at $+0 \cdot 1°C$ $(100 \text{ m})^{-1}$ with large scatter. In December the modal value of T_3-T_1 was $-0 \cdot 5°C$ $(100 \text{ m})^{-1}$ and once again the modal gradient for the lowest layer was 2 classes larger at $+0 \cdot 6°C$ $(100 \text{ m})^{-1}$. The most reasonable explanation for these differences between the two layers appears to be that the observations T_2 at the middle level were in error by a small but systematic amount. The differences are not consistent with either (a) a radiative equilibrium hypothesis that would result in a preference for isothermal temperature gradients for the layer from 17 m to 57 m or (b) errors due to radiation from the air intake duct walls surrounding the temperature element at 57 m. A constant reduction of T_2 by an amount $0 \cdot 7°F$ would result in equal modal gradients for both layers in Table 3. However, attempts to identify and isolate an error of this magnitude have been unsuccessful to date. It is expected that the Calgary tower temperature gradient measurements and independent measurements by means of a tethered balloon in Edmonton will shed more light on the problem.

The frequency distributions of the temperature difference T_2-T_1 for the lowest layer (57 m–17 m) for all hours in July and December, adjusted by $0 \cdot 7°F$ in accordance with the preceding discussion, are shown in Tables 4 and 5. Table 4 (July 1967) shows that adiabatic gradients were preferred at all hours and that rather large superadiabatic gradients were measured occasionally during daytime hours. The mean vertical temperature gradients were between those reported by Best, *et al.* [7] for the layers 1 m to 15 m and 47 m to 107 m (Rye, Sussex, England) in midday hours of July. The mean gradients for the two layers (112 m–17 m, Table 1, and 57 m–17 m, Table 4) were consistent with the development of an "unstable sublayer" [8] below an adiabatic intermediate layer. Perhaps the most surprising result was the indication in Table 5 that slightly stable gradients were preferred at *all* hours in December even in the lowest layer. The absence of scattered superadiabatic gradients supports the view that low-level vertical mixing was appreciably dampened even over the city in December.

Hourly mean vertical temperature differences T_3-T_1 (112 m–17 m) on the C N Towers building are illustrated in Fig. 4. The average gradients were stable at all hours in December and at all nighttime hours in July. Superadiabatic gradients were found in the later morning hours of July followed by near-neutral gradients in the afternoon. The July curve suggests

TABLE 3. FREQUENCY DISTRIBUTION (PER CENT) OF VERTICAL TEMPERATURE GRADIENTS BETWEEN 17 m AND 112 m ($T_3 - T_1$) AND BETWEEN 17 m AND 57 m ($T_2 - T_1$) ON THE CN TOWERS BUILDING IN DAYTIME HOURS OF JULY, 1967 (1000–1500 MST)

Temperature gradient °C(100m)$^{-1}$	July 1967		December 1967	
	$T_3 - T_1$	$T_2 - T_1$	$T_3 - T_1$	$T_2 - T_1$
9·4				
		1		
− 8·4		1		
		1		
− 7·3		1		
		1		
− 6·3		2		
		2		
− 5·2		2		
		3		
− 4·2	< 1	2		
	2	3		
− 3·1	4	2		
	7	2		
− 2·0	7	3		
	14	3	1	
Adiabatic	30	5	16	1
	23	5	31	3
+ 0·1	8	29	17	12
	3	8	16	25
+ 1·1	1	4	11	20
		6	5	14
+ 2·2	< 1	2	2	12
		1	1	5
+ 3·2	< 1	4		3
		1	1	3
+ 4·3	< 1	2		1
		1		
+ 5·3		1		
		1		1
+ 6·4		1		
		1		1
+ 7·4		< 1		
		< 1		
+ 8·5		< 1		
+ 9·5				1
No. of hours	361	360	186	185

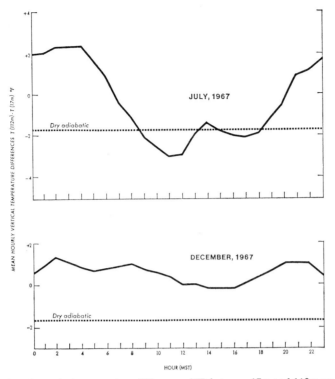

FIG. 4. Mean hourly vertical temperature differences (°F) between 17m and 112m on the CN Tower building in central Edmonton.

that convective mixing through deep layers commenced just before noon on the average and persisted through the afternoon until about 6 p.m. in July.

Diurnal changes in wind speed at low altitudes can be used as a relative measure of the intensity of vertical mixing of momentum because of the normal increase of wind speed with height. Intensification of vertical mixing results in higher wind speeds at low altitudes and a drop in speeds at higher altitudes. At intermediate heights the initial drop in speed may be followed by an increase as the mixed layer increases in depth. The diurnal changes of wind speeds and temperatures based on 5 years of July and December data for Edmonton Industrial Airport (XD) are shown in Fig. 5. Similar data for Calgary International Airport (YC) are shown in Fig. 6. At both locations the July data indicated intense vertical mixing in daytime hours. In December a diurnal variation of small amplitude was evident in Edmonton data (lower curves of Fig. 5) but not in Calgary data (lower curves of Fig. 6). Diurnal variations of wind speed at three sites in and near Edmonton are compared in Fig. 7. Three summer months (July, August, and September) and three winter months (December, January, and February) were combined in preparing Fig. 7 because data were available only for 2 years for the University site. The development of a deep mixed layer after 0900 MST in the summer months was reflected by the abrupt increase in wind speed at 63 m after that time (upper curves, Fig. 7). The winter variations in wind speed over the city consisted of a small maximum in the early afternoon at 13 m (XD) and a simultaneous minimum at 63 m. No systematic diurnal variation was observed at the rural site (EG).

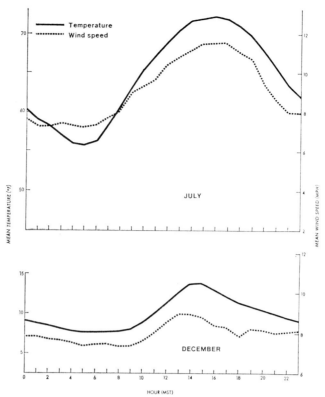

FIG. 5. Mean hourly temperatures and wind speeds at Edmonton Industrial Airport based on 5 years' data for July and December.

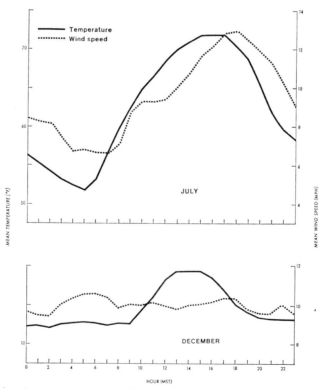

FIG. 6. Mean hourly temperatures and wind speeds at Calgary International Airport based on 5 years' data for July and December.

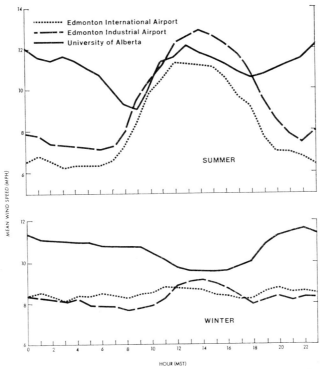

FIG. 7. Mean hourly wind speeds at 63m (University of Alberta) and 13·5m (Edmonton Industrial Airport) compared with those at 10m (Edmonton International Airport) in summer (July, Aug., and Sept.) and winter (Dec., Jan., and Feb.).

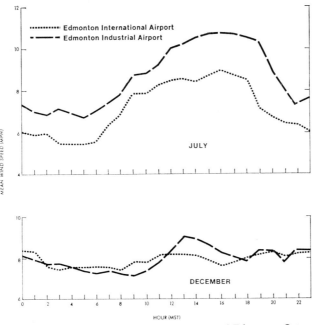

FIG. 8. Mean hourly winds at Edmonton Industrial Airport and Edmonton International Airport based on 3 years' data for July and December.

109

The wind data show a small urban enhancement of vertical mixing in midday hours in the winter and a larger urban enhancement of mixing at all hours in the summer. The latter effect resulted in mean winds at XD about 10% higher than those at EG. Unfortunately, even though the mean speeds at the two airports were almost identical in winter months the apparent difference in summer may have been a local effect due to differences in anemometer exposure. The Industrial Airport anemometer was mounted on the roof of the terminal building and its readings may be influenced by local wakes and eddies. The average vertical wind speed shear was larger over the city at night in summer than in winter in accord with what would be expected from the vertical temperature gradients in Fig. 4.

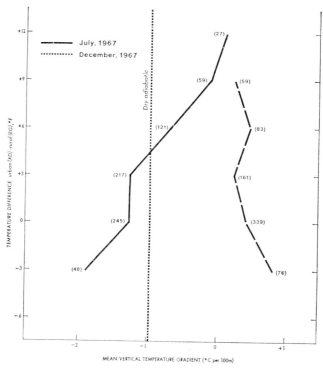

FIG. 9. Mean vertical temperature gradients between 17m and 57m on the CN Tower building in central Edmonton as functions of urban-rural temperature differences in July and December 1967. (Number of observations in parentheses).

Urban and rural diurnal wind speed variations based on July and December observations for the last 3 years for which data were available for EG are shown in Fig. 8. In general the curves were similar to those shown in Fig. 7 and suggest either more intense vertical mixing or mixing through a deeper layer over the city at all hours in the summer.

Figure 9 shows the mean vertical temperature gradients for the layer from 17 m to 57 m on the C N Towers building in central Edmonton as a function of the urban-rural surface temperature differences. It was assumed that the XD–EG temperature differences provided a valid relative measure of the urban heat island intensity. In all cases the temperature at 57 m was reduced by $0 \cdot 7°F$ below the observed values. The average gradients in December were all stable and independent of urban-rural temperature differences with the exception possibly of increased stability associated with occurrences of higher temperatures at EG (rural) than at XD (urban). In July, however, the average vertical temperature gradient in the layer 17 m to 57 m increased systematically towards greater stability with increased urban heat island intensities. In other words, the stability of a low layer of air over the city increased as the urban-rural temperature difference increased rather than showing a preference for neutral stability as would be expected in a well-mixed layer. If the temperature adjustment of $0\cdot7°F$ was not applied to the 57 m observation both curves in Fig. 9 would be displaced to the right, i.e., to greater stability but the general trends of the curves would be unchanged.

SUMMARY

Preliminary analyses of hourly wind observations in and near the cities of Edmonton and Calgary show that, while the average wind speeds at 10 m are relatively strong (8 to 11 mph in all months), periods of persistent light winds of a few days' duration are not uncommon, particularly in winter. Such periods are less frequent in summer because of intensive vertical mixing that results in a pronounced daytime wind speed maximum. The surface winds at Calgary and Edmonton International Airports showed no evidence of increased vertical mixing during the daytime in December.

A comparison of the mean hourly temperatures at 17 m on the CN Towers building in Edmonton with concurrent mean temperatures at two Edmonton airports and an analysis of the frequency distributions of the vertical temperature gradients between 17 m and 112 m showed no evidence of systematic errors in the Tower measurements. The measurements at 57 m appeared to be too high by about $0\cdot7°F$ but, to date, this suggestion has not been substantiated by instrument error checks. Independent measurements of vertical temperature gradients on the Calgary tower and by means of a portable tethered balloon sounding system in Edmonton should clarify the problem.

Two simplified models of the development of urban heat islands were considered in the analyses of wind and temperature data. In the "mixed layer" model the city acts as a heat source creating its own mixed layer characterized by an adiabatic lapse rate and a more or less uniform vertical distribution of pollution. In the radiation model the city experiences less radiative heat loss than the country but the vertical temperature gradients immediately above the surface are not necessarily adiabatic and pollution may be more or less layered at heights that depend on emission heights and buoyancy. Vertical temperature gradient measurements on the C N Towers building in central Edmonton showed a preference for (a) slightly stable lapse rates at all hours in December for both layers 17 m to 57 m and 17 m to 112 m, and (b) increased stability (17 m to 57 m) with increased urban heat island intensity in July. These results suggest that some tendency for stratification of pollution may exist even within the lowest few hundred feet over Edmonton on clear, calm nights in summer and at all hours of light wind days in winter. If such a tendency exists it will affect both pollution concentrations and the composition of pollution at particular heights within the city.

Surface and upper-level winds in and near Edmonton provided some evidence of urban enhancement of vertical mixing in midday hours of December and at all hours in July. Such enhancement should be accompanied by relatively stronger winds over the city than over nearby rural areas at the same low altitude with possible consequences involving organized urban-rural air circulations.

K. D. HAGE and R. W. LONGLEY

The development of a sound basis for modelling pollution concentrations as functions of space and time over Alberta cities requires an extension of the analysis described above. Pollution measurements that are now available for Edmonton and Calgary should be analyzed for evidence of incomplete vertical mixing. Preliminary calculations show low correlations between smoke density measurements at neighbouring samplers in both cities but more calculations are needed before any conclusions can be made. The analyses of temperature data should be extended to include thermograph data in both cities and the Calgary tower data that are now becoming available. The correlation between persistent light winds and stable vertical temperature gradients in winter should be investigated because if the correlation is high it may be unnecessary to have simultaneous measurements of both parameters to obtain conditional probabilities of combinations of light winds and weak vertical mixing. Additional tests of the absolute accuracy and representativeness of the vertical temperature profiles are urgently needed if generalizations are to be made from these data.

ACKNOWLEDGEMENTS

Much of the data used to produce the figures in this paper was supplied by the Division of Environmental Health Services, Government of Alberta.

REFERENCES

1. HOLZWORTH, G. C., Mixing depths, wind speeds, and air pollution potential for selected locations in the United States, *J. Appl. Meteor.*, **6**, No. 6, 1967, pp. 1039–1044.
2. DUCKWORTH, F. S. and SANDBERG, J. S., The effect of cities upon horizontal and vertical temperature gradients. *Bull. Amer. Meteor. Soc.*, **35**, No. 5, 1954, pp. 198–207.
3. DEMARRAIS, G. A., Vertical temperature difference observed over an urban area. *Bull. Amer. Meteor. Soc.*, **42**, No. 8, 1961, pp. 548–554.
4. SUMMERS, P. W., An urban heat island model; its role in air pollution problems, with applications to Montreal. *Proc. First Canadian Conference on Micrometeorology*, Part II, Toronto, 1967, pp. 435–436.
5. EAST, C., Comparaison du rayonnement solaire en ville et a la campagne. *Cahièrs de Géographie de Qüebec*, No. 25, 1968, pp. 81–89.
6. EMSLIE, J. H., The reduction of solar radiation by atmospheric pollution at Toronto, Canada. Meteor. Branch, Dept. of Transport CIR 4094, TEC 535, 1964, 10 pp.
7. BEST, A. D., KNIGHTING, E., PEDLOW, R. H. and STORMOUTH, K., Temperature and humidity gradients in the first 100 m over southeast England. *Geophys. Mem.*, No. 89, 1952, 11 pp.
8. GEIGER, R., *The Climate near the Ground*. Harvard Univ. Press (Translated from the fourth German edition, 1961), 1965, p. 78.

DISCUSSION

J. LUKACS (*Western Research and Development Ltd., Calgary*):

In view of the difficulties of mathematical modelling and as a consequence the difficulty of predicting ground level concentrations as pointed out by Dr. Munn would it not be important to measure source emission and ground level concentrations of different pollutants at the same time when observations of meteorological conditions are carried out. I feel that if this was done this data then could be used at a later date to improve the mathematical models and hopefully we could predict ground level concentrations with somewhat more certainty.

AUTHOR'S REPLY

The current state-of-the-art in urban air pollution modelling is such that experimental tests and evaluations of the performance of each model are essential. Because such models usually consist of a superposition of a multitude of individual point and area sources the testing can be done in two stages. First, the modelled ground-level concentrations from a single source are tested against past or new observations from controlled experiments with a single source. Second, low-level concentrations predicted by the integrated model must be tested against measurements of at least a few specific pollutants in an urban environment. A major obstacle in the way of such testing is the collection of data needed to establish an emission inventory for the specific pollutants that are selected. However, it can be done— a regional inventory of oxides of sulfur, oxides of nitrogen, carbon monoxide, hydrocarbons, and suspended particulates was compiled recently for the state of Connecticut.

WIND-TUNNEL MODELLING OF STACK GAS DISCHARGE

G. R. LORD and H. J. LEUTHEUSSER *University of Toronto*

ABSTRACT

The similitude requirements for model tests of gaseous discharge from chimneys and stacks are stated. Laboratory facilities required for such tests are described and experimental techniques are discussed.

INTRODUCTION

There is little that can be done at present to reduce the amount of gaseous pollutants which, by the very nature of combustion and other technical processes, must be released into the atmosphere. In most of these cases the only feasible solution to the problem of air pollution control is to take advantage of the natural dispersion potential of the atmosphere by discharging waste gases at as high an elevation above ground level as possible. However, the height of the required chimneys or stacks cannot be chosen at will since it is subject to engineering, economical, esthetic as well as air pollution considerations. As a consequence, the problem reduces usually to one of establishing the minimum height which will just prevent the undiluted stack effluents from becoming entrained in the system of large-scale eddies which is created by the flow of air about buildings and structures. The process which may force stack gases prematurely to the ground is termed "aerodynamic downwash". It may result in extremely high levels of pollution concentrations and, hence, it constitutes a real hazard to health, vegetation and the operation of air-breathing equipment.

The complexity of the edding motion downwind, i.e., in the wake, of buildings and structures is, however, such that the interaction between stack plume and wake cannot readily be analyzed. Simple wind-tunnel tests, on the other hand, permit detailed duplication of even the most complex prototype conditions. From such studies reliable conclusions can be drawn on the steps necessary to reduce the incidence of aerodynamic downwash.

Wind-tunnel modelling of stack-gas discharge was apparently first undertaken by Sherlock and Stalker [1] in 1934. Following their lead many other investigators have been working in this field and have published results of their investigations. Of the large number of technical papers available on the subject the first account of the applicable similitude requirements, by Strom and Halitsky [2], and the survey report on meteorological and engineering effects on the rise of stack plumes, by Moses, Carson and Strom [3], deserve special mention.

With the growing need for control of air pollution, wind-tunnel studies will very likely assume an ever-increasing role in the design of chimneys and stacks. Believing strongly in the soundness of the experimental approach to the solution of the complex flow problems involved, the writers attempt in the following to provide a guide-line for the preparation and the execution of such tests.

SIMILITUDE CONSIDERATIONS

1. The General Model Law for Gaseous Plumes

The applicable similitude parameters for modelling of gaseous stack plumes subjected to cross-wind and building wake interactions are most conveniently deduced from dimensional considerations. In particular, for a buoyant plume developing in the earth boundary layer the significant physical variables involved in the process (cf. Fig. 1, top) combine to the following functional relationship between non-dimensional parameters which, together, constitute the appropriate model law in its most general form, i.e.

$$f_1 (x/L, z/L, \delta/L, k/\delta, V_G/V_W, VL\rho/\mu, \rho V^2/\Delta\gamma L) = 0 \tag{1}$$

In this equation, x and z are any set of coordinates defining a point of the plume; δ is the thickness of the boundary layer, k is a measure of the absolute roughness of the surrounding

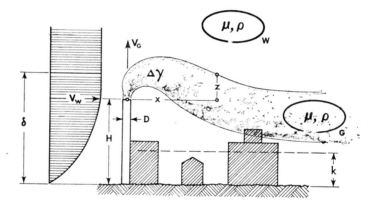

BUOYANT PLUME SUBJECTED TO AERODYNAMIC DOWNWASH.

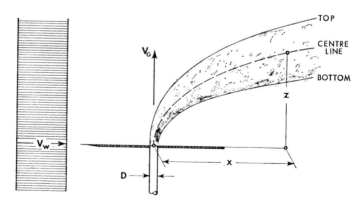

NON-BUOYANT PLUME SUBJECTED TO CROSS-WIND.

FIG. 1. Definition diagrams.

terrain; V is a characteristic velocity such as wind velocity V_W or gas exit velocity V_G; L is a characteristic length such as stack diameter D or stack height H; ρ and μ are the fluid properties of density and dynamic viscosity, respectively; and Δ_γ is the difference in specific weight between stack gas and ambient air. Subscripts G and W refer to stack gas and wind, respectively.

The general model law of equation (1) states that all of the seven parameters appearing therein must be mutually equal in any set of geometrically similar situations in order to assure dynamic similarity of the corresponding flow fields. Expressed differently, equation (1) implies that the geometric configuration (i.e., x/L and z/L) of a particular gas plume is a function of (i) the relative terrain roughness k/δ, (ii) the degree of boundary-layer immersion of the source point δ/H, (iii) the velocity ratio $R = V_G/V_W$, (iv) a suitably defined Reynolds number $R_N = VL\rho/\mu$, and (v) a suitably defined Froude number $F_N = V/(L\Delta\gamma/\rho)^{1/2}$.

2. Verification

Like any other functional relationship derived with the aid of dimensional arguments, the validity of equation (1) must be confirmed by observations of the physical phenomenon which it is supposed to describe. In particular, measurements may show that certain of the parameters appearing therein are insignificant, thereby simplifying the problem of its realization in actual applications.

The results of exploratory experiments by the second writer with non-buoyant gaseous jets discharged cross-wise into a turbulent smooth-plate boundary layer and subjected to wake interaction seem to indicate that aerodynamic downwash of gas plumes is not markedly affected by the degree of boundary-layer immersion of the source point and, hence, by the relative roughness of the upwind terrain.* Similarly, all available experimental evidence suggests that Reynolds number is not a significant similitude parameter in this case. To be sure, viscosity controls the dissipation of turbulent energy, but this process takes place in eddies which are much smaller than those which govern the configuration of the plume. The size of the large eddies, on the other hand, is determined by the phenomenon of flow separation. Since most buildings and structures are essentially angular in shape, the lines of separation are fixed and, hence, the large-scale eddy pattern ought to be independent of Reynolds number.

This leaves as similitude parameters proper only velocity ratio and Froude number. It is interesting to note that many of the large number of available descriptions of plume-rise pattern can be expressed in terms of only these two independent variables. A good example of this is the algebraically simple equation by Briggs [5] which seems to fit very well many field observations of rising plumes irrespective of relative roughness, boundary layer immersion and Reynolds number. Rewritten in the present nomenclature this formula is

$$z/DR = 1 \cdot 26 \, (x/DR)^{0 \cdot 67} \, (F_N)^{-0 \cdot 67} \qquad (2)$$

where z and x refer to the center line of the plume, and the Froude number is defined as $F_N = V_W/(D\Delta\gamma/\rho_G)^{1/2}$. An obvious shortcoming of equation (2) is that it does not account for the momentum rise of non-buoyant plumes for which, with $F_N = \infty$, it predicts $z = 0$. It would appear from this that the momentum rise, determined by the velocity ratio, is mainly responsible for the initial lift of the plume while the thermal rise of the plume,

---

* These two similitude parameters are, however, very significant in model tests of wind loading on buildings and structures [4].

117

reflected in the Froude number and effective over much of its longitudinal travel, becomes quickly the predominant rise component in the absence of downwash effects.

A detailed study of the momentum rise of non-buoyant plumes in the absence of wake intersection was performed by Pratte and Baines [6]. The physical circumstances of these tests are schematically explained by the bottom diagram of Fig. 1 which indicates that the results, reproduced in Fig. 2, pertain to a submerged fluid jet emitted from a quasi point-source into a uniform non-turbulent cross-wind. The particular choice of the plotting coordinates employed in Fig. 2 is suggested by equation (1) which with $L = D$, neglecting the non-applicable parameters and employing the principle of manipulation, can also be written as

$$f_2 \left(x/DR, \, z/DR, \, R, \, R_N \right) = 0 \qquad (3)$$

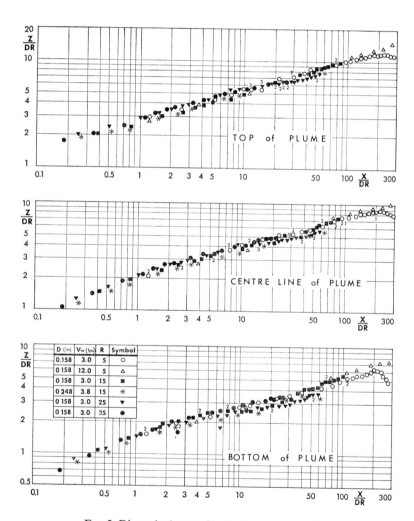

FIG. 2. Dimensionless profile of plume in cross-wind.

(a) $V_G = V_W = 5$ fps.

(b) $V_G = V_W = 20$ fps.

FIG. 3. Non-buoyant plume subjected to cross-wind and wake interactions, $R = 1$.

(a) $V_G = 20$ fps., $V_W = 5$ fps.

(b) $V_G = 40$ fps., $V_W = 10$ fps.

FIG. 4. Non-buoyant plume subjected to cross-wind and wake interactions, $R = 4$

The results clearly show that the plume configuration is a function only of velocity ratio and not of Reynolds number. Moreover, they indicate that there exists a universal non-dimensional plume profile, i.e.

$$f_3 (x/DR, z/DR) = 0 \qquad (4)$$

which describes all non-buoyant plumes subjected to interaction by a uniform non-turbulent cross-wind irrespective of velocity ratio. The algebraic form of equation (4) for the center-line of the plume is given by Pratte and Baines as

$$z/DR = 1 \cdot 76 \, (x/DR)^{0 \cdot 28} \qquad (5)$$

which is remarkably similar to equation (2) for the case of buoyant plumes developing in natural wind fields.

Photographic evidence of an equivalent wind-tunnel test-series by the writers for non-buoyant plumes subjected, however, to both cross-wind and wake interactions is presented in Figs. 3 and 4. In particular, the two pictures of Fig. 3 show plumes at a velocity ratio equal to unity but at actual velocities of, respectively, 5 and 20 feet per second. Similarly, the two pictures of Fig. 4 show plumes for the same geometric situation as in Fig. 3 but at a velocity ratio equal to 4 and for actual wind velocities of, respectively, 5 and 10 feet per second. It will be observed that in each of the two cases of velocity ratio portrayed, the plume configuration is sensibly independent of the magnitude of the actual velocity and, hence, of the Reynolds number. Indeed, the major difference between the two photographs of each series is an increasingly blurry appearance due to the lengthening of relative exposure time with increasing operating speed. On the other hand, the plume configuration is very much a function of the velocity ratio since, obviously, dispersion by wake interaction decreases markedly with increasing velocity ratio. Thus, while denying the existence of a simple universal relation for the plume profile of the form of equation (4) above, the findings confirm as the appropriate model law in this instance, i.e., non-buoyant plume subjected to both cross-wind and wake interactions, the following relation

$$f_4 (x/L, z/L, R) = 0 \qquad (6)$$

3. The Model Law for Gaseous Plumes Subject to Aerodynamic Downwash

From the foregoing arguments it can be concluded that for tests of buoyant plumes which are subjected to both cross-wind and wake interactions, the state of turbulence of the oncoming wind (reflected by the parameters of relative roughness and degree of boundary-layer immersion, respectively) may, in first approximation, be considered negligible in comparison to the large-scale eddy motion which is responsible for the aerodynamic downwash process. Since also the Reynolds number is apparently not a significant parameter in these cases, the appropriate model law for downwash tests becomes simply

$$f_5 (x/L, z/L, R, F_N) = 0 \qquad (7)$$

Although equation (7) is already much less complex than the general model law of equation (1), the occurrence in it of the Froude number (where applicable) leads to great practical difficulties in its application. Strictly speaking, Froude number equality for a thermal plume in a prototype and its geometrically similar model calls also for similitude of the temperature and density characteristics of the ambient atmospheres. More important still, the requirement for identical Froude numbers links automatically the prototype (P) to model

(M) velocity scale to the corresponding linear length scale and to the scale of relative density difference. In particular, with the Froude number defined as in equation (2) the ratio of wind velocities is

$$(V_W{}^2)_r = L_r \, e_r \tag{8}$$

where subscript r designates a prototype-to-model ratio and $e = (\rho_W/\rho_G) - 1$, is the relative density difference between plume and surrounding air. From the requirement for identical velocity ratios follows

$$(V_G)_r = (V_W)_r \tag{9}$$

which, together with equation (8), yields the scale equation for the prototype-model system under consideration, i.e.

$$V_r{}^2 = L_r \, e_r \tag{10}$$

The restrictive implications of equation (10) become clear when one considers that the linear length scale L_r is largely determined by the dimensions of the available wind tunnel (e.g., L_r is typically about 200 : 1 for an 8-foot wide test section), and that the most suitable tunnel velocity, i.e. $(V_W)_M$, for visual observation of model plumes is about 5 feet per second. This leaves the relative density difference for the model e_M as the only dependent variable, and it must be adjusted in accordance with equation (10) for any particular set of specified prototype operating conditions, i.e. $(V_W)_P$, $(V_G)_P$ and e_p.

4. The Approximate Model Law for Downwash Tests

The great experimental difficulties implied by the requirement for variable model-gas density renders equation (7) unsuitable for routine testing purposes involving a large number of operating conditions. Disregarding the Froude number on the other hand, not only removes most of the practical difficulties but it can also make model predictions more conservative. In view of the many inponderables involved in the modelling of atmospheric processes, neglect of the buoyant rise of plumes in designing chimneys and stacks against downwash thus may provide a desirable factor of safety.

Adoption of an incomplete similitude law, i.e.

$$f_6 \, (x/L, \, z/L, \, R) = 0 \tag{11}$$

in lieu of equation (7) for the modelling of buoyant gas plumes entails, however, the question of what to use as the appropriate model velocity ratio R_M. In other words, neglect of the Froude number leaves it up to the experimenter to decide upon the degree of correction by which he may wish to apply to R_M in order to approximate buoyancy by momentum effects.

Inspection of equations (2) and (5) suggests that the profile of a pure momentum plume, i.e. one for which $F_N = \infty$, can never be identical to that of a buoyant plume. The closest approximation possible may be a local identity of non-dimensional plume rise z/D at some critical non-dimensional distance x/D downwind of the stack. Thus, considering equation (5) as representative of model conditions and equation (2) as representative of the prototype, the model velocity ratio R_M for a non-buoyant model plume having the same relative rise at some specified plume in the prototype is

$$R_M = 0 \cdot 63 \, (R_P)^{0 \cdot 46} \, (F_N)^{-0 \cdot 93} \, (x/D)^{0 \cdot 54} \tag{12a}$$

or, roughly

$$R_M = (R_P \, x/D)^{0.5}/1.5 \, F_N \tag{12b}$$

where F_N is defined as in equation (2).

Another choice for the model velocity ration could be to put simply

$$R_M = R_P. \tag{13}$$

However, this would very likely lead to an overestimation of the performance of the buoyant prototype plume since the momentum of a "cold" and, hence, denser jet is greater than that of a "hot" one discharging at the same velocity.

The most conservative assumption for the model velocity ratio, and the one generally preferred by the writers, is based upon an equivalent non-buoyant prototype plume discharging at the temperature of the ambient air but having the same initial momentum as the actual prototype plume, i.e., for which, with A = stack cross-section area,

$$(A\rho_G \, V_G{}^2)_{P\text{-actual}} = (A\rho_G V_G{}^2)_{P\text{-ambient}} \tag{14}$$

Assuming perfect gas behaviour and identical thermodynamic properties for both gas and air, this assumption yields as the applicable model velocity ratio in this instance

$$R_M = R_P \, (T_W/T_G)_P{}^{0.5} \tag{15}$$

where T stands for absolute temperature.

EXPERIMENTAL FACILITIES

The design of chimneys and stacks against downwash with the aid of model tests performed in accordance with equation (11) can be accomplished in practically any wind tunnel of reasonable size. However, since the required tunnel velocity and, hence, the power demand are quite small, it may be feasible to construct at modest expense a special "micro-meteorological" wind tunnel offering a longer and larger test section than normally found in aerodynamic tunnels, thereby facilitating model construction and plume observation.

In the following a description is given of the experimental facilities which are employed for downwash tests in the Fluid Mechanics Laboratories of the Department of Mechanical Engineering, University of Toronto. The photograph of Fig. 5 shows a close-up of a typical model installation and of the ancillary equipment.

1. Wind Tunnel

The tunnel is of the open-return type and has a test section 8 feet wide, 4 feet high and 36 feet long. The test section is fully glazed on one side for a length of 24 feet and contains a number of observation windows in its ceiling. Several doors permit easy access to the tunnel from either side.

At its upstream end the tunnel comprises a honey-comb followed by a 16-foot wide, 8-foot high and 10-foot long stilling chamber equipped with smoothing screens and followed by a gradual contraction to the cross-section of the test-section. At the downstream end of the test section the tunnel consists of a gradual transition to circular cross-section, a 66-inch vane axial fan and, finally, a short diffuser. The outlet of the diffuser can be blocked thus forcing the air, and, particularly, any aerosol admixture through an exhaust duct to the outside of the building. The fan is belt-driven by a magnetic variable speed transmission which is close-coupled to a 60-horsepower electric motor running at a constant speed of 1770 r.p.m.

The maximum air speed realizable in the tunnel is about 60 feet per second, but downwash tests are usually performed at only 5 feet per second. The tunnel velocity is determined with a pitot-static tube, strategically arranged upwind of the model to be tested and connected to a sensitive micro-manometer mounted outside of the tunnel.

2. Smoke Generator

Effluents of model stacks are represented by a dense oil-aerosol produced in a commercially manufactured smoke generator. In this device a light detergent-free mineral oil is entrained by a jet of carbon-dioxide and forced, under controllable pressure, through a heating element and, subsequently, through a fine nozzle. Upon ejection, the gas jet expands and mixes with air, thereby forming the aerosol.

Metering of the volumetric rate of effluent discharge is accomplished with the aid of a set of carefully calibrated constriction-type flow meters of different orifice diameters and, hence, sensitivities. The meters are mounted interchangeably in a neoprene line connecting the smoke generator with the model stack, and the flow-dependent pressure-head differential across the orifices is determined from the readings of a manometer.

Irrespective of the particular choice made for controlling R_M, i.e., with anyone of the equations (12), (13), or (15), the assumption of the model law of equation (11) calls for neutrally buoyant model plumes developing in an isothermal wind-tunnel atmosphere. A typical result of a buoyancy test of an oil-aerosol jet is depicted in Fig. 6. The plume, injected horizontally cross-wise and, hence, without vertical momentum into the empty wind tunnel, is obviously horizontal over the whole of the visible extent of the test section and thereby justifies the assumption of neutral buoyancy for the particular model effluent used in this instance.

3. Stack Traversing Gear

Continuous change of the height of model stacks is made possible by the use of a motor-driven variable-speed traversing gear. The stack motion is remotely controllable from a carry-around switch box and can be adjusted to any value between zero and about 1·5 inch per second for both upward and downward travel.

EXPERIMENTAL TECHNIQUES

1. Model Construction

The extent of the prototype area to be included in the model of a particular stack installation depends on the effects the surroundings are estimated to have on the downwash phenomenon. Thus, in the case of an isolated complex, of say, a thermal-electric power plant, only the plant proper, i.e. the immediate surroundings of the stack or stacks, would probably have to be reproduced in order to encompass all of the significant downwash-contributing factors. On the other hand, for a plant located within a built-up industrial region, a much larger surrounding area, possibly up to a mile or more in diameter, may have to be considered.

The choice of the physical extent of the region to be reproduced determines the applicable linear length scale of the model which may range from 1 : 100 to 1 : 300. A large model scale, i.e. a large model-to-prototype length ratio, facilitates model construction and plume

FIG. 5. Close-up of a typical model installation and of ancillary equipment.

FIG. 6. Buoyancy test of an oil-aerosil used as model effluent.

(a) $H = 25$ feet

(b) $H - 83$ feet

Fig. 7. Effects on plume due to varying stack height.

observation but may also lead to distorting blockage effects if the development of the air flow about the model is significantly restricted by the proximity of the surrounding walls of the wind tunnel.

Models should include all prototype features of significant dimensions. However, reproduction in very much simplified detail, i.e. in the form of blocks, cylinders and spheres is usually sufficient, and most model components can thus conveniently be manufactured out of wood. In order to fix the various buildings and structures in their proper relative positions, they may be mounted on an integral model base. Because of the considerable size of some models, only portions thereof may at any one time be accommodated in the wind tunnel. To this end the model may have to be sectioned into strips of test-section width and of alignment corresponding to selected wind directions.

Models of stacks are best machined out of brass tubing. They should be of sufficient length to permit continuous variation of the stack height over a wide range of elevations. The model stacks are passed through holes in the model base and the floor of the test section to the outside of the wind tunnel where they may be mounted in a traversing gear. The exterior surface of all round model stacks should be roughened in order to delay flow separation to points on the leeward side of the stack cross-section. This will reduce scale effects due to neglect of the Reynolds number as a significant similitude parameter.

2. Observations

The great attraction of wind-tunnel tests of plumes subjected to cross-wind and building wake interactions is the ease with which, by simple inspection, critical conditions may be discovered and corrected. Particularly at incipient downwash, relatively small changes in velocity ratio and/or stack height are often sufficient to change a bad situation into an acceptable one, and it becomes easily possible to determine optimum stack heights confidently, and with a minimum of experimental effort, to within a narrow margin of uncertainty (typically $\pm$ 5 feet for a model built at a scale of 1 : 180). This point is somewhat exaggeratedly, though certainly convincingly, demonstrated by the photographs of Figs. 3 and 4 for a large change in velocity ratio, and by the two pictures of Fig. 7 for a large change in stack height.

When considered desirable, visual observations may be augmented by measurements of the distribution of effluent concentrations over the model. However, the experimental apparatus required for this kind of work is complex, and the time involved may easily prove prohibitive where a large number of operating conditions need to be investigated.

CONCLUSIONS

Relatively simple wind-tunnel tests are required in order to determine with confidence the minimum heights of chimneys and stacks which will prevent the occurrence of aerodynamic downwash of gaseous effluents. Under the simplified model law applicable to such tests, buoyancy may be neglected or approximated by momentum effects, and velocity ratio appears as the only significant similitude parameter. Similarly, the otherwise strict requirement for geometric similarity between model and prototype may be relaxed by requiring only similitude of the gross configuration of buildings and structures. Adding to this the ease with which critical conditions may be detected and corrected, the technique of wind-tunnel modelling of stack gas discharge emerges as a very powerful tool in the control of air pollution from chimneys and stacks.

ACKNOWLEDGEMENTS

The writers and their colleagues are indebted to many agencies and industrial enterprises which, over the years, have encouraged and supported their work in building aerodynamics of which the present paper describes an important facet. However, special thanks are due to the Hydro-Electric Power Commission of Ontario which prompted, in 1958, the construction of their first micrometeorological wind-tunnel facility; and to the National Research Council of Canada which, through various grants, made much of the background research here reported possible.

REFERENCES

1. SHERLOCK, R. H and STALKER, E. A., The control of gases in the wake of smoke stacks, *Mechanical Engineering*, Vol. 63, No. 2, February 1941, p. 147.
2. STROM, G. H. and HALITSKY, J., Important considerations in the use of the wind tunnel for pollution studies of power plants, New York University Research Division, 1954.
3. MOSES, H., CARSON, J. E. and STROM, G. H., Effects of meteorological and engineering factors on stack plume rise, Feature Article, *Nuclear Safety*, Vol. 6 (1), 1964.
4. LEUTHEUSSER, H. J. and BAINES, W. D., Similitude problems in building aerodynamics, *Proc. Amer. Soc. of Civil Engineers*, Vol. 93, No. HY3, 1967, p. 35.
5. BRIGGS, A. G., A plume rise model compared with observations, Paper 65-44, Annual Meeting, Air Pollution Control Association, 1965.
6. PRATTE, B. D. and BAINES, W. D., Profiles of the round turbulent jet in a cross flow, *Proc. Amer. Soc. of Civil Engineers*, Vol. 93, No. HY6, 1967, p. 54, with corrections published in *Proc. Amer. Soc. of Civil Engineers*, Vol. 94, No. HY3, pp. 815–817, May 1968.

DISCUSSION

R. E. ALSTON (*Northwest Nitro-Chemicals Ltd., Medicine Hat*):

A stack is usually erected to disperse the stack emission high enough into the atmosphere such that the resulting ground level concentration is less than a pre-determined amount. At the present time, there are various methods in which the ground level concentrations can be predicted or rather what the stack height should be. It was my understanding that the Colley, Aziz, Lord and Leutheusser papers were investigating methods for improved predictions of what happens to the emission after it leaves the stack. When it is necessary to erect a stack for dispersion of a pollutant, the person for whom the stack is being erected and the Department of Health are concerned that the stack height will be sufficient to do the job properly.

Stacks are relatively expensive items and once installed are difficult to alter or modify. Usually a board division is required for the allotment of the necessary monies. Board members generally are not familiar with the technical details but make decisions on recommendations of their engineering personnel who, in turn, would have to rely upon the recommendations of the personnel conducting the wind tunnel or computer experiments.

I assume the computer and wind tunnel experiments are being conducted since present methods of determining stack heights leave something to be desired.

Being involved in pollution work, part of my assignment involves stacks and stack emissions. It is of importance to know, if possible, the probability that a stack that has been erected based on wind tunnel experiments will behave the same as the model tested previously in a wind tunnel.

AUTHOR'S REPLY:

The major shortcoming of all available analytical methods for determining stack heights is that they cannot account for the adverse effects on plumes due to aerodynamic downwash of the stack effluents. This phenomenon is caused by the large-scale eddy motion which exists in the wakes of buildings and structures. If stacks are too short or the velocity ratio is too small, these large eddies may entrain an emerging plume and bring it down to the ground while its pollution concentration is still unacceptably high. To prevent this occurrence and, hence, to make analytical methods more nearly applicable, the stack height must at least be such that the plume can escape the disturbing influence of the wake eddies.

The only method available to date by which this critical minimum stack height can be determined with confidence in each individual case is an experimental one. It involves scale-model tests of the stack and its surroundings in either wind or water tunnels, performed at Reynolds numbers which must be sufficiently large to produce turbulent flow. This technique is described in detail in the paper. Provided the tests are undertaken in accordance with the applicable model law, the agreement between model and proto-type performance can be expected to be perfect. However, stacks are usually tested only over a certain range of anticipated operating and meteorological conditions and not for all of the possible proto-type conditions. Hence, a given stack can certainly fail to perform properly if the prevailing proto-type conditions fall outside the range of variables for which the stack was originally designed with the aid of model tests.

NUMERICAL SIMULATION OF ATMOSPHERIC POLLUTION FROM INDUSTRIAL SOURCES

D. G. COLLEY and K. AZIZ   *University of Calgary*

ABSTRACT

The partial differential equations describing the conservation of momentum, energy and mass are solved for a portion of the atmosphere around an exhaust stack. The flow is assumed to be laminar and two-dimensional. The equations are solved by finite difference methods for several different initial and boundary conditions. The results indicate that certain aspects of the problem are well represented by this model.

INTRODUCTION

Simulation of atmospheric motions by hydrodynamic models is the basis of numerical weather prediction and many other problems associated with atmospheric motions. These problems are the subject of many current investigations and workable computer models of the atmosphere are being generated in some cases [1, 2]. The problem to be discussed in this paper is that of modeling a small portion of the atmosphere around one or more stacks discharging a polluting gas into the atmosphere. The objective of the investigation is to supplement information now available from wind tunnel testing and from completely empirical models of the plume. The project is still in its initial stages and many problems are still to be investigated before a reliable model is available for general use. We have, however, obtained some interesting results which are briefly reported in this paper. A more complete account of this work is contained in another report [3].

The flow is assumed to be laminar in this study and the equations of change are solved in two space dimensions (one vertical and one horizontal). The authors realize that the turbulent phenomena taking place in the atmosphere may not be described by the Navier-Stokes equations. Nevertheless, many interesting aspects of the problem can be realistically represented by the solution of laminar flow equations.

MATHEMATICAL DESCRIPTION OF SYSTEM

The conservation of mass, momentum and energy in a two-dimensional mesoscale section of the atmosphere shown in Fig. 1 is described by

$$a^2 \frac{\partial^2 \psi}{\partial x^2} + \frac{\partial^2 \psi}{\partial z^2} = -\xi \tag{1}$$

$$\frac{\partial \xi}{\partial t} + au \frac{\partial \xi}{\partial x} + w \frac{\partial \xi}{\partial z} = \frac{1}{Re}\left(a^2 \frac{\partial^2 \xi}{\partial x^2} + \frac{\partial^2 \xi}{\partial z^2}\right) + \frac{a}{Fr}\frac{\partial \theta}{\partial x} + \frac{a}{Fr_{ab}}\frac{\partial C}{\partial x} - \frac{L_z a}{\Delta V \, \rho_o \, V^{*2}}\frac{\partial V_s}{\partial x} M_s \rho_s \tag{2}$$

127

$$\frac{\partial \theta}{\partial t} + au\frac{\partial \theta}{\partial x} + w\frac{\partial \theta}{\partial z} = \frac{1}{P_r R_e}\left(a^2\frac{\partial^2 \theta}{\partial x^2} + \frac{\partial^2 \theta}{\partial z^2}\right) + \frac{L_z}{V^* \theta^* \rho_o C_p \Delta V} H_s M_s \qquad (3)$$

$$\frac{\partial C}{\partial t} + au\frac{\partial C}{\partial x} + w\frac{\partial C}{\partial z} = \frac{1}{S_c R_e}\left(a^2\frac{\partial^2 C}{\partial x^2} + \frac{\partial^2 C}{\partial z^2}\right) + \frac{L_z}{V^* C^* \Delta V} C_s M_s \qquad (4)$$

where the stream function, ψ, is defined such that

$$u = -\frac{\partial \psi}{\partial z}$$

and

$$w = a\frac{\partial \psi}{\partial x}$$

This choice automatically satisfies the continuity equation for an incompressible fluid, i.e.

$$a\frac{\partial u}{\partial x} + \frac{\partial w}{\partial z} = 0$$

The vorticity, ξ, is related to the two components of velocity by

$$\xi = \frac{\partial u}{\partial z} - a\frac{\partial w}{\partial x}$$

The pressure gradient terms in the Navier-Stokes equations are eliminated by the introduction of stream function and vorticity. The number of partial differential equations required to describe the system is also reduced from four to three by the use of this transformation. In the general case the source terms in equations (2), (3), and (4) are functions of position and time. In the case studied here these terms are zero everywhere except at the point where pollutants are introduced into the atmosphere by a stack.

The derivation of these equations is discussed in some detail in a report by Colley and Aziz [3]. The well-known Boussinesq approximations are employed to simplify the general equations. One of the basic assumptions made is that the density is constant everywhere except in the buoyancy term. The terms that account for changes in density are

$$\frac{a}{Fr}\frac{\partial \theta}{\partial x} \quad \text{and} \quad \frac{a}{Fr_{ab}}\frac{\partial C}{\partial x}$$

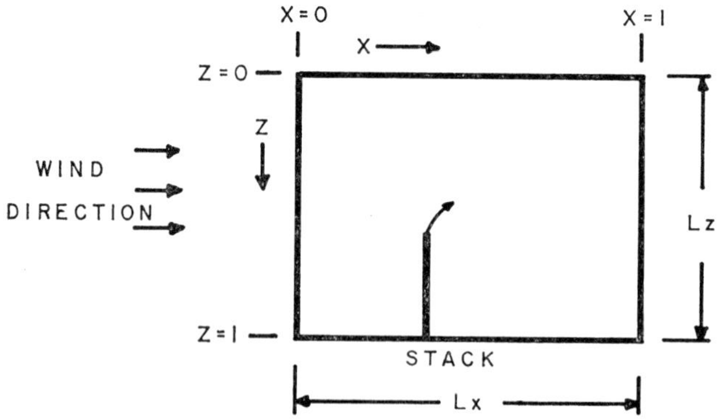

FIG. 1. The stack and surrounding area being modelled.

in the vorticity transport equation (eq. 2). The density changes in the bouyancy terms are accounted for by the first order equation of state.

$$\frac{\rho}{\rho_o} = 1 + \beta_1 \left(\theta - \theta_o\right) + \beta_2 \left(C - C_o\right)$$

where

$$\beta_1 = -\frac{1}{\rho_o} \frac{\partial \rho}{\partial \theta}\bigg|_{\theta_o, C_o}$$

and

$$\beta_2 = -\frac{1}{\rho_o} \frac{\partial C}{\partial \rho}\bigg|_{\theta_o, C_o}$$

The coefficients β_1 and β_2 are included in the two Froude numbers. In addition to the assumptions already stated we have also assumed that the viscosity, μ, thermal conductivity, k, and heat capacity, C_P, of the fluids are constant.

INITIAL AND BOUNDARY CONDITIONS

In order to solve the system of partial differential equations (1, 2, 3 and 4) we must specify the values of stream function, vorticity, temperature and concentration for all values of x and z in the domain of interest at time $t = 0$ (initial condition) and for all times at the boundary of the domain (boundary conditions). In addition, the rate at which material and/or heat is injected into the system through source terms must also be specified for all times. The boundary and initial conditions are usually specified in terms of velocity, temperature and concentration; from this we must derive the necessary conditions for stream function and vorticity. The initial conditions selected for this investigation are given below.
1. Temperature at time $t = 0$ is given by

$$\theta = A \left(1 - z\right)$$

where A can take on the values $+ 1 \cdot 0$, $- 1 \cdot 0$ or zero. This allows the study of all possible lapse conditions. The results described in this paper are for $A = 1 \cdot 0$.
2. The concentration of pollutant at time $t = 0$ is given by

$$C(x, z, 0) = 0 \cdot 0$$

This means that the system is initially free of pollutants.
3. Two different initial horizontal velocity profiles considered are:

$$\text{Case 1: } u(x, z, 0) = (1 - z)^2$$

$$\text{Case 2: } u(x, z, 0) = 1 - z^2$$

In both cases $u = 0$ at ground level and $u = 1 \cdot 0$ at the top of the system.
4. The vertical velocity is zero initially

$$w(x, z, 0) = 0 \cdot 0$$

The initial conditions on vorticity and stream function may be derived from 3 and 4 above.

The vorticity at time $t = 0$ for the two cases is given by

$$\text{Case 1: } \xi(x, z, 0) = -2(1 - z)$$

$$\text{Case 2: } \xi(x, z, 0) = -2z$$

The stream function at time $t = 0$ for the two cases is given by

$$\text{Case 1: } \psi(x, z, 0) = \frac{1}{3}(1 - z)^3$$

$$\text{Case 2: } \psi(x, z, 0) = -z + \frac{1}{3}z^3$$

The value of dependent variables at the boundaries are presented below.

1. The temperature at the boundaries is given by

$$\theta(0, z, t) = \theta(1, z, t) = A(1 - z)$$
$$\theta(x, 0, t) = A$$
$$\theta(x, 1, t) = 0 \cdot 0$$

2. The concentration at the boundaries is given by

$$C(0, z, t) = C(x, 0, t) = C(x, 1, t) = 0 \cdot 0$$

$$\frac{\partial C}{\partial x}(1, z, t) = 0 \cdot 0$$

3. The horizontal component of velocity at the boundaries is given for the two cases by

$$\text{Case 1: } u(0, z, t) = u(1, z, t) = (1 - z)^2$$
$$u(x, 0, t) = 1 \cdot 0$$
$$u(x, 1, t) = 0 \cdot 0$$
$$\text{Case 2: } u(0, z, t) = u(1, z, t) = (1 - z)^2$$
$$u(x, 0, t) = 1 \cdot 0$$
$$u(x, 1, t) = 0 \cdot 0$$

4. The vertical component of velocity is zero at all boundaries,

$$w(x, 0, t) = w(x, 1, t) = w(0, z, t) = w(1, z, t) = 0 \cdot 0$$

Again the conditions imposed on u and w are used to establish those on ξ and ψ. The vorticity at the boundary for the two cases is given by

$$\text{Case 1: } \xi(0, z, t) = \xi(1, z, t) = -2 \cdot 0(1 - z)$$
$$\xi(x, 0, t) = -2 \cdot 0z$$
$$\xi(x, 1, t) = 0 \cdot 0$$

Case 2: $\xi(0, z, t) = \xi(1, z, t) = -2 \cdot 0z$

$$\xi(x, 0, t) = 0 \cdot 0$$

$$\xi(x, 1, t) = -2 \cdot 0$$

The stream function at the boundary for the two cases is given by

Case 1: $\psi(0, z, t) = \psi(1, z, t) = \dfrac{1}{3 \cdot 0}(1 - z)^3$

$$\psi(x, 0, t) = \dfrac{1}{3 \cdot 0}$$

$$\psi(x, 1, t) = 0 \cdot 0$$

Case 2: $\psi(0, z, t) = \psi(1, z, t) = -z + \dfrac{1}{3 \cdot 0}z^3$

$$\psi(x, 0, t) = 0 \cdot 0$$

$$\psi(x, 1, t) = -1 + \dfrac{1}{3 \cdot 0} \text{ or } -2/3$$

In a real problem the boundary and initial conditions must be obtained from existing meteorological conditions. We have selected reasonable values here for testing the computer models. Other possibilities exist and these may be easily incorporated in the model.

METHOD OF SOLUTION

The partial differential equations describing the system are non-linear and coupled. No methods are known for obtaining exact solutions to such a system. A very versatile technique that has been used for the solution of many complex problems is the finite-difference method. In this technique the domain of interest is divided into a grid network and a finite difference approximation for each of the partial differential equations is written at each grid point. (The grid network used for this problem is shown in Fig. 2.) This operation yields a system of algebraic equations for unknown values of the dependent variables at each grid point. There are many different finite-difference methods and choosing a suitable method is no simple task. This problem is discussed in more detail in the report by Colley and Aziz [3]. The finite-difference method used here is known as the alternating direction implicit method (ADI). There are many variations of this procedure. We have used the procedure proposed by Brian [4] and Douglas [5] as modified by Aziz [6]. The solution of the stream function equations by an ADI procedure requires the selection of a series of iteration parameters. We have selected these parameters by the method of Wachspress [7].

RESULTS AND DISCUSSION

Transient and steady state concentration profiles are presented for several different atmospheric conditions and for three types of stack gas. These results were obtained by imposing either Case 1 or Case 2 initial and boundary conditions on the model and by varying the values of three of the five dimensionless parameters that control the behaviour of

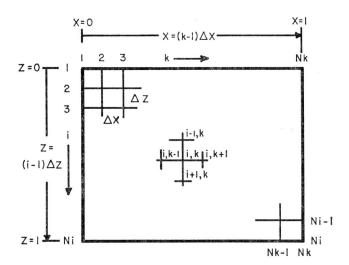

Fig. 2. The grid network used in modelling.

the system. In all the systems discussed in this paper the aspect ratio, $a = 0 \cdot 5$, corresponding to a system with a length twice the height; the Prandtl number $Pr = 0 \cdot 714$, corresponding to a system containing air; and the first Froude number $Fr = 1000$, corresponding to
a system in which temperature does not effect density. The effects of the remaining three
dimensionless parameters Re, Sc and Fr_{ab} on the plume were investigated by varying their
values in the computer model.

Transient results are shown in Fig. 3 (a to f)* for Case 1 initial and boundary conditions
with $Re = 50$, $Sc = 0 \cdot 75$ and $Fr_{ab} = 1000$. These values of the dimensionless parameters
describe a system in which:

    (a) The prevailing wind is relatively light due to the low value of Re.
    (b) Diffusion of the stack gases into the surrounding air is slightly greater than it should
        be ($Sc = 1 \cdot 0$ is closer to the true value for laminar dispersion).
    (c) The effect of concentration on the density is essentially zero due to the large value of
        Fr_{ab}.

Under these conditions the plume rises slightly as shown in Fig. 3f.

The effects of altering the Schmidt number and the second Froude number on the plume
behaviour are shown in Fig. 4. Figure 4a shows the effect of increasing Sc number from $0 \cdot 75$
to $1 \cdot 0$. The result is that the plume becomes narrower and the maximum value of concentration increase as Sc number is increased from $0 \cdot 75$ to $1 \cdot 0$. The plume rise was not affected
by increasing Sc number.

The effect of introducing light and heavy stack gases was investigated for $Sc = 1 \cdot 0$.
Figure 4b with $Fr_{ab} = 0 \cdot 75$ shows the result of a lighter than air stack gas. The plume rise
is slightly higher than in Fig. 4a. The opposite result is shown in Fig. 4c where $Fr_{ab} =
-0 \cdot 75$. The plume rise is now less than in Fig. 4a.

The effects of a different velocity profile on the concentration profile were also studied
by changing the initial and boundary conditions to those corresponding to Case 2. These

---

    * See Table 1 for maximum concentrations in profiles, Table 2 for coding scheme.

TABLE 1. LIST OF MAXIMUM CONCENTRATIONS

Fig. number	Maximum concentration (dimensionless)
3a	0·151
3b	0·208
3c	0·233
3d	0·236
3e	0·236
3f	0·236
4a	0·294
4b	0·290
4c	0·299
5a	0·253
5b	0·251
5c	0·254
6a	0·250
6b	0·255

conditions represent a velocity profile that increases much more rapidly with height and is closer to a neutral wind profile than the one considered in Case 1. Comparison of Figs. 4 and 5 clearly show the effect of this change in velocity profile on the plume. The gases now leave the stack parallel to the ground and flow directly downwind. The gases leave the stack and start to rise immediately for the Case 1 conditions. The concentration gradient in front of the stack was also much sharper with these new conditions. The Reynolds number was decreased in this case from 50 to 20 to maintain stability.

The effects of lighter and heavier than air stack gases were again studied with the Case 2 conditions. The results are shown in Figs. 5b, 5c, 6a and 6b. In Figs. 5b and 5c with Fr_{ab} = 0·1 and −0·1 respectively, the plume behaviour is quite similar to that shown in Figs. 4b and 4c. However, further decreases in the magnitude of Fr_{ab} caused rather strong convective motions resulting in partial looping of the plume. The density of the stack gases cause the plume to rise or fall in the immediate vicinity of the stack but the resultant plume rise at the right boundary is essentially the same as in Fig. 5a where the stack gas density is the same as that of air. Further studies dealing with convection effects are presently being carried out in a system with an aspect ratio of 0·25.

TABLE 2. CODING SCHEME FOR CONCEN-
TRATION PROFILES

Symbol	Concentration range
L	0 — 9% of C_{max}
2	10 — 27% of C_{max}
4	37 — 45% of C_{max}
6	55 — 63% of C_{max}
8	73 — 81% of C_{max}
H	90 — 100% of C_{max}
blank = all intermediate ranges.	

133

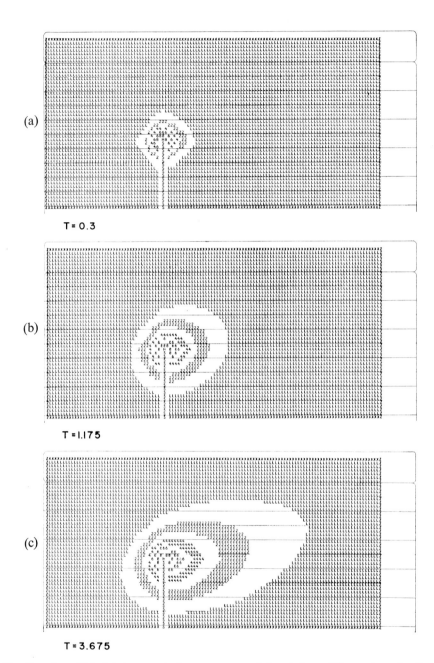

(a)

T = 0.3

(b)

T = 1.175

(c)

T = 3.675

FIG. 3. a, b, c. Calculated concentration maps around the stack at different times for $Re = 50$, $Pr = 0.714$, $Sc = 0.75$, $Fr = 1000$, $Fr_{ab} = 1000$

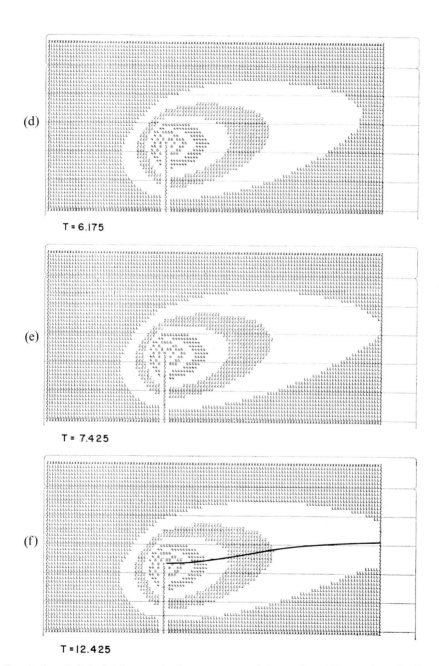

FIG. 3. d, e, f. Calculated concentration maps around the stack at different times for $Re = 50$, $Pr = 0.714$, $Sc = 0.75$, $Fr = 1000$, $Fr_{ab} = 1000$.

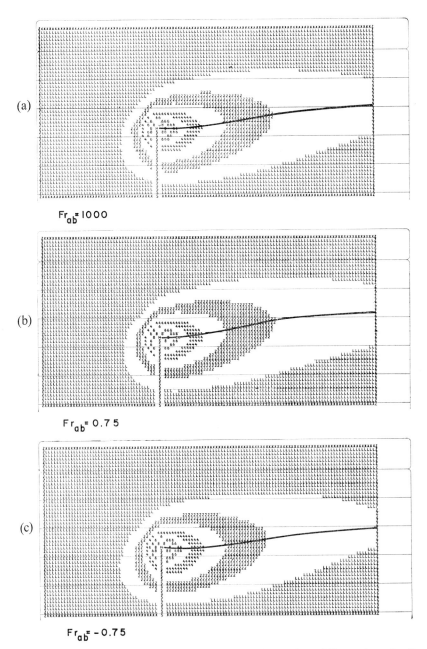

(a) $Fr_{ab} = 1000$

(b) $Fr_{ab} = 0.75$

(c) $Fr_{ab} = -0.75$

FIG. 4. a, b, c. Calculated concentration maps around the stack at different times for $Re = 50$, $Pr = 0.714$, $Sc = 1.0$, $Fr = 1000$.

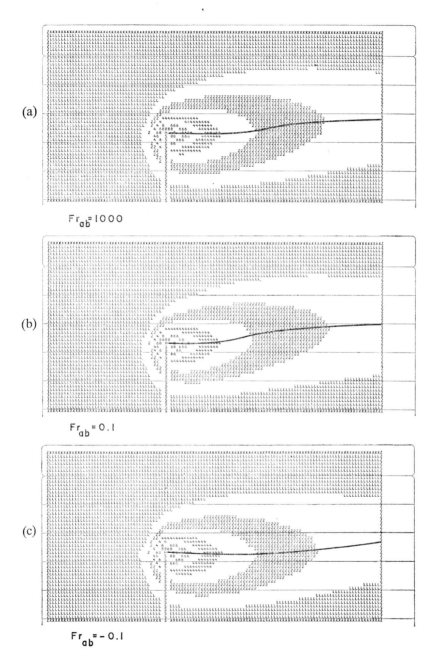

(a)

$Fr_{ab} = 1000$

(b)

$Fr_{ab} = 0.1$

(c)

$Fr_{ab} = -0.1$

FIG. 5. a, b, c. Calculated concentration maps around the stack at different times for $Re = 20$, $Pr = 0\cdot714$, $Sc = 1\cdot0$, $Fr = 1000$.

137

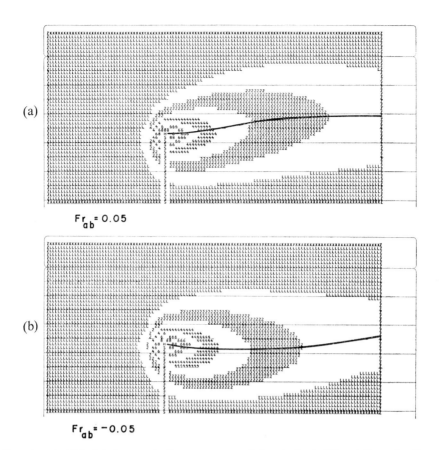

FIG. 6. a, b. Calculated concentration maps around the stack at different times for $Re = 20$, $Pr = 0.714$, $Sc = 1.0$, $Fr = 1000$.

The interpretation of these results as they apply to real systems has been complicated by the fact that only systems with small Reynolds numbers can be simulated. Initially it was hoped that a 150 meter by 300 meter or larger system could be simulated directly. For the Re number investigated in this study this yields a rather low wind velocity of 10^{-6} meters/sec. We are now looking into alternate approaches, such as the one proposed by Strom and Halitsky [8] for wind tunnel modeling. This, however, introduces other assumptions in the model. Other approaches being considered include the study of turbulent transport processes in the model.

NOTATION

a aspect ratio Lz/Lx, dimensionless
β_1 coefficient of density change due to temperature ($°C^{-1}$)
β_2 coefficient of density change due to concentration (M^3/gm)
C concentration, dimensionless
C^* characteristic concentration (gm/M^3)
C_p heat capacity ($cal/gm°C$)

```
TIME INCREMENTED TO 0.100E 02 SECONDS
THE REYNOLDS NUMBER IS      20.0000
THE PRANDTL NUMBER IS       0.7140
THE SCHMIDT NUMBER IS       1.0000
THE FROUDE NUMBERS ARE FR  1000.000  AND FRAB     -0.050
TEMPERATURE PROFILE
0.0        0.0        0.0        0.0        0.0        0.0        0.0        0.0        0.0        0.0        0.0
1.0000E-01 1.0866E-01 1.1817E-01 1.2531E-01 1.2246E-01 1.1020E-01 9.6095E-02 8.5133E-02 7.9220E-02 7.9244E-02 1.0000E-01
2.0000E-01 2.1726E-01 2.3616E-01 2.4967E-01 2.4218E-01 2.1718E-01 1.8990E-01 1.6930E-01 1.5883E-01 1.6023E-01 2.0000E-01
3.0000E-01 3.2556E-01 3.5323E-01 3.7137E-01 3.5622E-01 3.1838E-01 2.7998E-01 2.5226E-01 2.3979E-01 2.4494E-01 3.0000E-01
4.0000E-01 4.3298E-01 4.6776E-01 4.8754E-01 4.6201E-01 4.1274E-01 3.6642E-01 3.3512E-01 3.2404E-01 3.3556E-01 4.0000E-01
5.0000E-01 5.3851E-01 5.7712E-01 5.9480E-01 5.5853E-01 5.0131E-01 4.5122E-01 4.2054E-01 4.1438E-01 4.3388E-01 5.0000E-01
6.0000E-01 6.4074E-01 6.7840E-01 6.9083E-01 6.4754E-01 5.8731E-01 5.3824E-01 5.1251E-01 5.1378E-01 5.4034E-01 6.0000E-01
7.0000E-01 7.3833E-01 7.6991E-01 7.7606E-01 7.3308E-01 6.7556E-01 6.3285E-01 6.1545E-01 6.2397E-01 6.5335E-01 7.0000E-01
8.0000E-01 8.3045E-01 8.5244E-01 8.5359E-01 8.1840E-01 7.7202E-01 7.4083E-01 7.3237E-01 7.4420E-01 7.6961E-01 8.0000E-01
9.0000E-01 9.1717E-01 9.2814E-01 9.2722E-01 9.0695E-01 8.8080E-01 8.6472E-01 8.6239E-01 8.7097E-01 8.8568E-01 9.0000E-01
1.0000E 00 1.0000E 00 1.0000E 00 1.0000E 00 1.0000E 00 1.0000E 00 1.0000E 00 1.0000E 00 1.0000E 00 1.0000E 00 1.0000E 00
THE NUSSELT NUMBER IS      1.0242
CONCENTRATION PROFILE
0.0        0.0        0.0        0.0        0.0        0.0        0.0        0.0        0.0        0.0        0.0
0.0        9.1893E-07 1.9142E-05 3.4414E-04 2.4263E-03 4.8711E-03 6.3142E-03 6.9266E-03 7.1504E-03 7.2656E-03 7.3865E-03
0.0        3.2435E-06 6.4545E-05 1.1640E-03 7.3599E-03 1.2489E-02 1.4614E-02 1.5096E-02 1.5004E-02 1.4837E-02 1.4736E-02
0.0        9.7653E-06 1.8452E-04 3.3909E-03 1.8967E-02 2.5880E-02 2.6526E-02 2.5279E-02 2.3816E-02 2.2609E-02 2.1688E-02
0.0        2.6078E-05 4.6496E-04 8.9451E-03 4.4755E-02 4.7615E-02 4.2426E-02 3.7117E-02 3.2920E-02 2.9724E-02 2.7377E-02
0.0        6.0398E-05 9.9749E-04 2.0783E-02 9.5262E-02 7.6376E-02 5.9733E-02 4.8391E-02 4.0442E-02 3.4564E-02 3.0590E-02
0.0        1.1756E-04 1.7189E-03 3.8649E-02 1.6633E-01 9.9364E-02 7.1561E-02 5.5045E-02 4.3680E-02 3.5340E-02 3.0284E-02
0.0        1.8491E-04 2.1870E-03 2.8371E-02 1.0894E-01 9.1617E-02 7.0076E-02 5.3130E-02 4.0464E-02 3.1156E-02 2.6190E-02
0.0        2.2237E-04 2.1567E-03 1.8397E-02 6.2092E-02 6.6852E-02 5.5017E-02 4.1570E-02 3.0631E-02 2.2688E-02 1.8986E-02
0.0        1.7015E-04 1.4336E-03 9.5263E-03 2.8882E-02 3.4962E-02 2.9971E-02 2.2512E-02 1.6199E-02 1.1724E-02 9.8787E-03
0.0        0.0        0.0        0.0        0.0        0.0        0.0        0.0        0.0        0.0        0.0
U VELOCITY PROFILE
1.0000E 00 1.0000E 00 1.0000E 00 1.0000E 00 1.0000E 00 1.0000E 00 1.0000E 00 1.0000E 00 1.0000E 00 1.0000E 00 1.0000E 00
9.9000E-01 9.9000E-01 9.9000E-01 9.9000E-01 9.9000E-01 9.9000E-01 9.9000E-01 9.9000E-01 9.9000E-01 9.9000E-01 9.9000E-01
9.6000E-01 9.6000E-01 9.6000E-01 9.6000E-01 9.6000E-01 9.6000E-01 9.6000E-01 9.6000E-01 9.6000E-01 9.6000E-01 9.6000E-01
9.1000E-01 9.1000E-01 9.1000E-01 9.1000E-01 9.1000E-01 9.1000E-01 9.1000E-01 9.1000E-01 9.1000E-01 9.1000E-01 9.1000E-01
8.4000E-01 8.4000E-01 8.4000E-01 8.4000E-01 8.4000E-01 8.4000E-01 8.4000E-01 8.4000E-01 8.4000E-01 8.4000E-01 8.4000E-01
7.5000E-01 7.5000E-01 7.5000E-01 7.5000E-01 7.5000E-01 7.5000E-01 7.5000E-01 7.5000E-01 7.5000E-01 7.5000E-01 7.5000E-01
6.4000E-01 6.4000E-01 6.4000E-01 6.4000E-01 6.4000E-01 6.4000E-01 6.4000E-01 6.4000E-01 6.4000E-01 6.4000E-01 6.4000E-01
5.1000E-01 5.1000E-01 5.1000E-01 5.1000E-01 5.1000E-01 5.1000E-01 5.1000E-01 5.1000E-01 5.1000E-01 5.1000E-01 5.1000E-01
3.6000E-01 3.6000E-01 3.6000E-01 3.6000E-01 3.6000E-01 3.6000E-01 3.6000E-01 3.6000E-01 3.6000E-01 3.6000E-01 3.6000E-01
1.9000E-01 1.9000E-01 1.9000E-01 1.9000E-01 1.9000E-01 1.9000E-01 1.9000E-01 1.9000E-01 1.9000E-01 1.9000E-01 1.9000E-01
-0.0       -0.0       -0.0       -0.0       -0.0       -0.0       -0.0       -0.0       -0.0       -0.0       -0.0
W VELOCITY PROFILE
0.0        0.0        0.0        0.0        0.0        0.0        0.0        0.0        0.0        0.0        0.0
0.0        -4.2417E-02-4.7038E-02-4.0321E-02-7.9736E-03 2.6163E-02 4.1333E-02 3.9825E-02 2.9354E-02 1.6369E-02 0.0
0.0        -8.3211E-02-9.4563E-02-8.1393E-02-1.0414E-02 5.7141E-02 8.3230E-02 7.7614E-02 5.5630E-02 2.8583E-02 0.0
0.0        -1.2011E-01-1.4213E-01-1.2249E-01-1.1292E-03 9.5140E-02 1.2405E-01 1.1040E-01 7.5722E-02 3.3254E-02 0.0
0.0        -1.5005E-01-1.8695E-01-1.5975E-01 2.4915E-02 1.3669E-01 1.5885E-01 1.3426E-01 8.6891E-02 2.9074E-02 0.0
0.0        -1.6874E-01-2.2167E-01-1.8518E-01 6.4891E-02 1.7112E-01 1.8093E-01 1.4553E-01 8.7627E-02 1.7503E-02 0.0
0.0        -1.7095E-01-2.3310E-01-1.8827E-01 9.7517E-02 1.8618E-01 1.8599E-01 1.4256E-01 7.8485E-02 2.6086E-03 0.0
0.0        -1.5307E-01-2.0752E-01-1.6307E-01 8.7173E-02 1.8137E-01 1.7327E-01 1.2539E-01 6.1990E-02-9.6384E-03 0.0
0.0        -1.1558E-01-1.5364E-01-1.1818E-01 5.9572E-02 1.4509E-01 1.3665E-01 9.3857E-02 4.1545E-02-1.4251E-02 0.0
0.0        -6.2267E-02-8.1484E-02-6.1671E-02 2.9728E-02 8.0560E-02 7.5759E-02 5.0206E-02 2.0376E-02-1.0077E-02 0.0
0.0        0.0        0.0        0.0        0.0        0.0        0.0        0.0        0.0        0.0        0.0
```


FIG. 7. Typical print out of computed results.

- Cs concentration of sourcc (gm/M^3)
- g normal gravity (M/sec^2)
- H_s heat content of source (cal/M^3)
- k thermal conductivity (cal/M sec °C)
- L_x length of system (M)
- L_z height of system and characteristic length (M)
- M_s strength of source (M^3/sec)
- μ viscosity (gm/M sec)
- ρo mean density (gm/M^3)
- ρs stack gas density at atmospheric temperature and pressure (gm/M^3)
- t time (1)
- t^* characteristic time and $= Lz/V^*$ (sec)
- θ temperature (1)
- θ^* characteristic temperature (°C)
- u horizontal component of velocity (1)
- V^* characteristic velocity (M/sec.)
- V_s exit velocity of stack gases (M/sec)
- w vertical component of velocity (1)
- x horizontal distance (1)
- z vertical distance (1)
- ΔV element of volume $(DX \cdot DZ \cdot 1)$ (M^3)

Dimensionless Groups

$$Fr = \frac{V^{*2}}{gL_z\beta_1\theta^*} \qquad \text{First Froude Number}$$

$$Fr_{\text{ab}} = \frac{V^{*2}}{gL_z\beta_2 C^*} \qquad \text{Second Froude Number}$$

$$Pr = \frac{\mu Cp}{k} \qquad \text{Prandtl Number}$$

$$Re = \frac{L_z V^* \rho_o}{\mu} \qquad \text{Reynolds Number}$$

$$Sc = \frac{\mu}{\rho_o D_{AB}} \qquad \text{Schmidt Number}$$

REFERENCES

1. QUARLES, D. A., Jr., SPIELBERG, K., A computer model for global study of the general circulation of the atmosphere, *IBM J. of Research and Development*, **11**, 3, 1967.
2. MURRY, F. W., Numerical simulation of cumulus convection, Rand Corporation, Memorandum RM-5316-NRL, 1967.
3. COLLEY, D. G. and AZIZ, K., Numerical simulation of atmospheric pollution from industrial sources, Report No. 1, Dept. of Chemical Engineering, University of Calgary, Calgary, Alberta, 1968.
4. BRIAN, P. L. T., A finite difference method of high order accuracy for the solution of three-dimensional transient head conduction problems, *A.I.Ch.E.J.*, **7**, p. 367.
5. DOUGLAS, J., Jr., Alternating direction method for three space variables, *Num. Math.* **4**, p. 41, 1962.
6. AZIZ, K., A numerical study of cellular convection, Ph.D. Thesis, Rice University, 1965.
7. WACHSPRESS, E. L., *Iterative solutions of Elliptic systems*, Prentice Hall Inc., New York, 1966.
8. STROM, G. H. and HALITSKY, J., Important considerations in the use of the wind tunnel for pollution studies of power plants, *Trans. ASME*, **77**, 781–795, 1955.

AIR POLLUTION FROM BIVALENT SULFUR COMPOUNDS IN THE PULP INDUSTRY

F. E. MURRAY   *University of British Columbia*

ABSTRACT

In the production of wood pulp by the kraft process, odorous sulfur compounds are formed and may be released to atmosphere. These noxious compounds include hydrogen sulfide, methyl mercaptan, dimethyl disulfide and dimethyl sulfide. They can be detected in the atmosphere at concentrations of a few parts per billion. The formation of these compounds in the various process steps and the points at which they may be released to atmosphere are discussed. The chemical characteristics of the offending compounds are outlined as they relate to the development of control methods. Control methods now in use and the results obtained and those under development are discussed in some detail.

INTRODUCTION

The production of pulp and paper is one of the most important industries in Canada and is of particular importance in British Columbia. There are basically two processes by which wood chips are processed to produce chemical cellulose. In the various sulfite processes, the delignifying agent is a solution of sulfur dioxide combined with various metal ions. Air pollution from this process is usually minimal particularly in the newer soluble-base sulphite processes. In the kraft process which is increasing in use throughout the world, the wood chips are cooked in a solution containing sodium hydroxide and sodium sulfide in about a four-to-one proportion. A flow sheet showing the essential steps in the kraft pulping process is given in Fig. 1.

Because kraft cooking solution contains sulfide and bisulfide ion, the process produces a number of highly malodorous compounds which are similar to those produced in the oil and gas industry. These include hydrogen sulfide, methyl mercaptan, dimethyl sulfide and dimethyl disulfide. All of these compounds produce obnoxious smells at very low concentrations. Methyl mercaptan and hydrogen sulfide have odor thresholds in the vicinity of 5 parts per billion in air.

POLLUTANT SOURCES

There are three primary points of odor production in a kraft pulp mill although the points of odor release may be far more numerous. These primary sources are the digestion process, the direct-contact evaporator and the recovery furnace.

In the digester, methyl mercaptan is produced by bisulfide ion combining with methoxy groups on the lignin molecule according to the reaction:

$$Lig - O - CH_3 + NaSH \longrightarrow CH_3SH + Lig - O - Na.$$

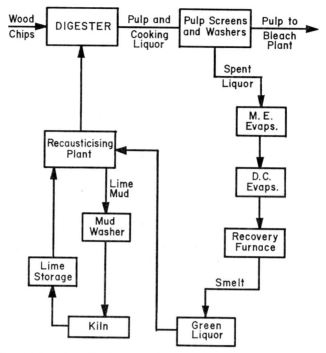

FIG. 1. Flow sheet showing essential steps in kraft pulping process.

Since there is a large excess of sodium hydroxide present in the cooking liquor, the mercaptan formed exists primarily as sodium mercaptide. In the form of mercaptide, the mercaptan reacts with further methoxyls on the lignin to produce dimethyl sulfide according to the reaction:

$$Lig — O — CH_3 + NaSCH_3 \longrightarrow CH_3 — S — CH_3 + Lig — O — Na.$$

As a result of these two reactions, a mixture of methyl mercaptan and dimethyl sulfide is produced in the digestion process. The amounts produced during cooking will generally increase with time, temperature and the concentration of sulfide in the liquor [1, 2].

These odorous compounds, dissolved in the black liquor, flow with the discharging pulp to the blow tank. There and in the subsequent operations, part of the dissolved mercaptan is oxidized to dimethyl disulfide. Hence, the spent cooking solution (black liquor) in the blow tank contains dissolved methylmercaptan, dimethyl sulfide and dimethyl disulfide and the gas phase above the liquor, though mainly steam, also contains these compounds.

Figure 2 shows how these odorous compounds will be distributed throughout the pulp mill and released to atmosphere under normal operation. The most serious release of these gases will usually occur at the digester blow system and at the multiple effect evaporators.

In the second source of primary odor formation (the direct contact evaporator) black liquor containing sodium sulfide and bisulfide is evaporated by contacting it with the flue gas stream from the recovery boiler. The commercial devices for this include cascade, cyclonic and venturi evaporators.

The recovery furnace gases contain large amounts of carbon dioxide. This acidic gas is absorbed in the alkaline sulfide liquor during direct-contact evaporation and the pH of the

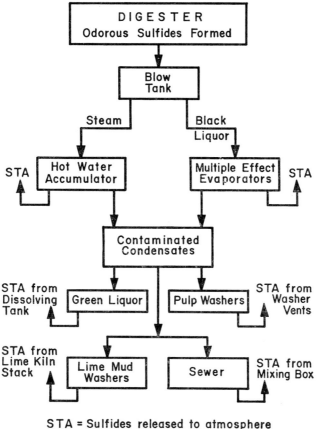

FIG. 2. The distribution of odorous gases formed in the digester.

liquor decreases [3]. As this occurs, the equilibrium partial pressure of hydrogen sulfide over the liquor increases in accordance with the relationship,

$$P_e(\text{H}_2\text{S}) = K\frac{C_{\text{Na}_2\text{S}}}{C_{\text{OH}^-}}$$

where $C_{\text{Na}_2\text{S}}$ is the total sulfide concentration and C_{OH^-} the hydroxide ion concentration in the solution. With the increasing value of $P_e(H_2S)$, large amounts of hydrogen sulfide are stripped from the black liquor by the stream of flue gas and carried to atmosphere.

From the direct contact evaporator, the concentrated black liquor is sprayed into the recovery furnace where the organic constituents burn to produce steam and the inorganic pulping chemicals are recovered as smelt. Recovery furnaces must operate so that there is no excess oxygen in the region of the smelt bed. This means that some of the burning of mixed organic and sulfur compounds must occur under reducing conditions. Pyrolysis under these conditions causes formation of large amounts of bivalent sulfur compounds [4] such as hydrogen sulfide and the organic sulfides mentioned before. These compounds will escape to the atmosphere in the flue gas stream unless they are oxidized in the gas-burning zone of the furnace. Hence, unless the furnace is very well controlled it can emit large amounts of malodorous bivalent sulfur compounds [5].

CONTROL MEASURES

It is apparent that control must be effected at several points in the kraft mill cycle at which it is unavoidable that malodorous sulfides are present. For the organic sulfur compounds formed in the digestion process, control must be effected on the noncondensible gases from the digester and blow tank and from the multiple effect evaporators and on the foul condensates that are formed in contact with these gases. The non-condensible gases may be collected and burned either in a lime kiln or furnace or they may be oxidized catalytically [6]. Catalytic oxidation has several advantages including smoother combustion control and opportunity for sulfur dioxide recovery. Typical behaviour of these compounds in an experimental catalytic reactor is shown in Fig. 3. Aqueous chlorine has also been used with success [7] in treating these noncondensible gases but is generally less effective than combustion.

The aqueous condensates may be steam stripped [8, 9] to remove the odorous compounds and the gas stream from the stripper passed through a furnace. Recently, studies have been underway to attempt to destroy the malodor in these condensates by oxidation using molecular oxygen [10]. Work to date has been somewhat limited but results, as shown in Fig. 4, appear to show promise. Oxidized condensates would be reused in the plant so that the dissolved sulfur would be returned to the mill chemical inventory.

The emission of hydrogen sulfide from black liquor during direct contact evaporation can be very substantially reduced by oxidation of the sulfide in the black liquor [3]. If the value of $C_{\mathrm{Na_2S}}$ is reduced to a very low value by oxidation, then since

$$P_e(\mathrm{H_2S}) = K\frac{C_{\mathrm{Na_2S}}}{C_{\mathrm{OH^-}}},$$

$P_e(\mathrm{H_2S})$ also becomes very small and stripping of hydrogen sulfide from the liquor is proportionally reduced.

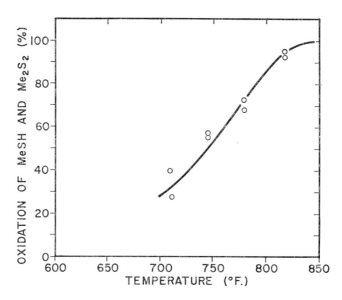

FIG. 3. Catalytic oxidation of gaseous organic sulfur compounds from kraft pulp mills.

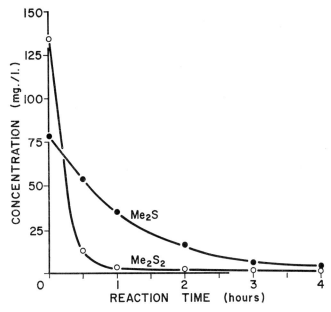

FIG. 4. Oxidation of organic sulfur compounds with molecular oxygen in aqueous solution.

Although oxidation is quite effective in reducing the emission of hydrogen sulfide from direct contact evaporators, as is illustrated in Fig. 5, there is a strong trend to-day to eliminate this type of evaporator and conduct all evaporation by indirect or multiple effect methods. This is a highly desirable trend in view of the very low odor threshold of the emitted sulfides.

The problem of the recovery furnace is a problem of good operation and combustion control within the furnace design capacity [5]. Figure 6 shows the effect of furnace loading on hydrogen sulfide emission and Fig. 7 shows the relationship between the oxygen and hydrogen sulfide content of the furnace flue gas stream. A good deal more study is needed to improve operating control of recovery furnaces.

As is indicated in the above discussions, much has been accomplished to reduce odorous emissions from kraft pulping operations. New developments now in the laboratory promise to effect better control in years to come. We cannot now build a completely odorless kraft pulp mill but we are coming rapidly to the point where this may be possible.

REFERENCES

1. McKean, W. T., Jr., Hruitford, B. F., Sarkanen, K. V., Price, L. and Douglas, I. B., Effects of kraft pulping conditions on the formation of methyl mercaptan and dimethyl sulfide, *Tappi* 50, 8, p. 400, 1967.
2. Douglas, I. B., Private communication, 1965.
3. Murray, F. E. and Rayner, H. B., Emission of hydrogen sulfide from kraft black liquor during direct contact-evaporation, *Tappi*, 48, 10, 1965, p. 588.
4. Feverstein, D. L., Thomas, J. F. and Brink, D. L., Malodorous products from the combustion of kraft black liquor, *Tappi*, 50, 6, 1967, p. 258.

145

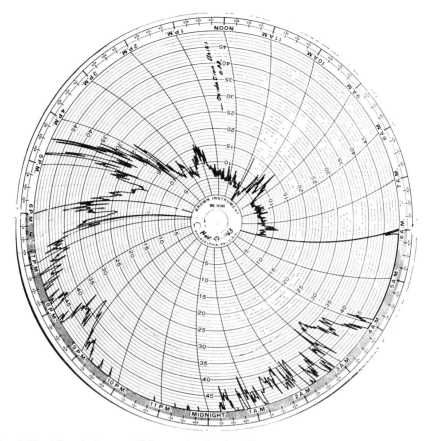

FIG. 5. Chart from hydrogen sulfide recorder showing effect of black liquor oxidation on hydrogen sulfide content of the recovery stack gases. Full scale = 600 $\mu g/l$. Oxidation towers operated from 6.00 a.m. until 12.30 p.m.

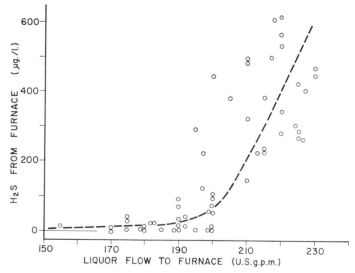

FIG. 6. The emission of hydrogen sulfide from a kraft recovery furnace as the flow of liquor to the furnace is varied.

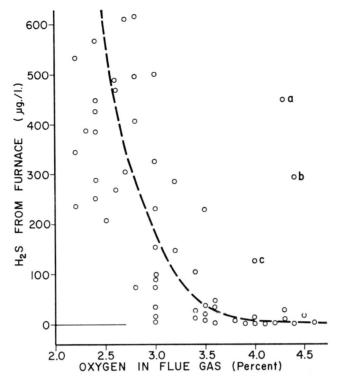

FIG. 7. Relationship between the oxygen and hydrogen sulfide content of the recovery furnace flue gases.

5. MURRAY, F. E. and RAYNER, H. B., The emission of hydrogen sulfide from kraft recovery furnaces, *Pulp and Paper Mag. of Can.*, **69**, 5, 1968, p. 71.
6. HARKNESS, A. C., MURRAY, F. E. and GIRARD, L., Catalytic oxidation of sulfurous air pollutants, *Atmospheric Environment*, **2**, 1968, p. 303.
7. MURRAY, F. E., Method of deodorizing sulfide-containing gases, Canadian Patent 643,389, June 19, 1962.
8. MAAHS, H. G., JOHANSON, L. N. and McCARTHY, J. L., Sekor III: Preliminary engineering design and cost estimates for steam stripping kraft pulp mill effluents, *Tappi*, **50**, 6, 1967, p. 270.
9. LINDBERG, S., How Uddelholm destroys air and water pollutants at the Skoghall works, *Pulp and Paper Mag. of Can.*, **68**, 7, 1968, p. 125.
10. MURRAY, F. E. and RAYNER, H. B., The oxidation of dimethyl disulfide with molecular oxygen, *Pulp and Paper Mag. of Can.*, **69**, 9, 1968, p. 64.

MANAGEMENT VIEWS ON POLLUTION CONTROL

J. E. BAUGH   *Canadian Fina Oil Limited, Calgary*

ABSTRACT

Pollution is defined as the release of foreign substances, the nature or quality of which would be damaging to health, property or environment. Control of pollution is the joint responsibility of the public, government and industry and co-ordinated efforts of all three are essential. Government must (1) decide on jurisdictional responsibility at various government levels (2) accelerate efforts to reach a Canadian National Code for Pollution Control and (3) develop reasonable regulations to enforce the code, and administer such regulations promptly, fairly and consistently. Industry must increase its recognition of the need for control and co-operate with government in the establishment of pollution codes. Pollution control will cost a lot more money in the future. Most industry leaders are cognizant of the problems and cost and are already taking action within their own sphere to do their part. It is suggested that industry stands ready to actively support responsible government leadership in keeping pollution under control in Canada.

INTRODUCTION

I would like to qualify somewhat the title of this paper which was assigned to me by the committee in charge of this session on Industrial Air Pollution. Firstly, the views which I will be expressing are largely my own and do not necessarily represent those of industrial management in general. However, from what I have read and from what I have learned from limited discussions with management people in my industry, at least some of my views are shared by others.

Secondly, although pollution can and does originate from many sources, my comments are largely oriented toward industrial pollution control; that is, control of the release of waste materials from industrial and manufacturing activity.

Thirdly, I am speaking largely on the subject of air pollution, although some general comments may well apply to any type of pollution.

Pollution is not a new word. Over 2700 years ago a Jewish prophet in Israel in 776 B.C. more or less correctly prophesied the destruction of the kingdom of an idolatrous king known as Jeroboam II. In the Old Testament, Book of Amos, the prophet Amos told King Jeroboam II:

[Ch. 7, V. 17:] Therefore saith the Lord;
Thy wife shall be an harlot in the city, and
thy sons and thy daughters shall die by the
sword and thy land shall be divided by line;
and thou shalt die in a polluted land.

There has been a horror of dying in a polluted land for many years. From the concern demonstrated by the participation in this Banff Conference on Pollution, of such a large group of persons from the ranks of government, science, education and industry, I hope we in Canada will be able to look toward a future safe from the prospect of dying in a polluted land.

Nevertheless, there is a great concern throughout Canada and the rest of the industrialized world about the growing incidence of air, water and soil pollution. Any air traveller today has seen the evidence in the form of the brownish smog lying over almost every airport where his plane touches down. Government leaders who are tuned to public opinion are concerned.

To quote President Lyndon B. Johnson of the U.S.A.:

> "Of all the dangers our advanced civilization has created, none is more serious than the pollution of our air. We can purify our water before we drink it. We can restore the scarred and lacerated landscape. But we must breathe the air as it comes to us, polluted or not . . ."

In addressing Congress in support of the "Air Quality Act" of 1967, President Johnson said:

> "The pollution problem is getting worse. We are not even controlling today's level of pollution. Ten years from now, when industrial production and waste disposal have increased and the number of automobiles on our streets and highways exceeds 110 million, we shall have lost the battle for clean air unless we strengthen our regulating and research effort . . . . Air pollution is the inevitable consequence of neglect. It can be controlled when the neglect is no longer tolerated."

I agree that pollution, and particularly air pollution is increasing, that it has already reached serious proportions in some areas, that it may affect health and increase the incidence of certain diseases and that society as a whole is concerned and wants the leaders of government and business to take whatever action is necessary to maintain a clean, healthy environment. I am convinced that this is the view of industrial management in Canada. The problem is how this may be achieved. It is so easy to make sweeping statements such as, "This must be stopped". But in a mobile, industrial society, it is another matter to devise a reasonable plan of control.

WHEAT IS POLLUTION?

From an absolute or purist viewpoint, any release of material foreign to the local environment, into that environment, could be defined as pollution. From this standpoint even the North American Indians were polluting the atmosphere with their camp fires before the arrival of white man and his industrial activity. But practically speaking, I would not believe any reasonable person would consider this a fair basis for a definition of pollution.

A modern industrial society inevitably must release by-products and waste materials into its surrounding environment in quantities ranging from minute, to significant, to even substantial.

Thus pollution, as it is being considered at this meeting, must be defined as being release "in excess of allowable limits" of these foreign substances into the environment. That is, we must accept the fact that there will be some pollution from an absolute point of view associated with modern industrial activity and even modern everyday living—as witness the massive release of products of combustion from automobile engines, which has become an integral part of all of our lives.

I would define pollution as—the release of foreign substances into the environment in such quantities as to be damaging to property, life and/or health of man or his surroundings. DeMicheal [1] defined air pollution as:

"... the unfavorable and harmful alteration of environment caused by man's emitting into the air foreign materials in liquid, gaseous or solid states, in amounts exceeding the air's capacity for dispersion."

I believe the key word in any definition of pollution has to be the word "harmful".

ACCEPTABLE LEVELS

If pollution then, by definition, is the release of damaging or harmful amounts of waste products, then it follows that non-damaging levels of foreign materials must be established and controls designed to limit emission to these levels. Clearly, any hazard to public health is not acceptable. Likewise, damage to public or private property by release of wastes must not be permitted.

In the less severe situation, which might be called the level of "public nuisance" arising from release of waste materials, a more relaxed level of control should be adopted. Release of a simple harmless material such as wood smoke from a fireplace might, as an example, be an area where no control should be necessary, even though the combined effect of many fireplaces could cause a haze or smoke pall, and thereby be a public nuisance to some people. I would rather liken this to the situation where a neighbour paints his house a shocking pink. Now this may to someone be a source of great annoyance and therefore "a public nuisance"; it clearly is not harmful or damaging and therefore should be outside control.

This point is mentioned because people sometimes tend to become very alarmed about pollution and frequently campaigns may be launched by purists who, without any basis in fact, refuse to be satisfied with any amount of release of waste products from an industrial operation.

These are, no doubt, the same people who, twice in the past few years, have rejected deliberate "pollution" of the Calgary city water supply by addition of minute quantities of sodium fluoride, and their forbears who similarly rejected chlorination of the municipal water supplies of that day.

In considering acceptable levels, it must be remembered also that the state of pollution of man's environment at any time is the result of the sum of all the pollutants being emitted at that time together with the residue of earlier emissions that has not been dispersed or destroyed by decay or other mechanisms. One must bear in mind this additive effect and, in some cases, a cumulative effect—so that in fact we must look into the future and predict what the outcome of this accumulation process will be.

However, the main point that I wish to make here is that there are, and there must be, acceptable levels of pollution established to allow the inevitable growth and expansion of our industrial society and that these lines must be reasonably drawn to prevent damage to health or property, but at the same time, to not unreasonably burden industry with red tape, restrictions and extra cost. This becomes one of the major difficulties because it is often difficult even to say what substances are the pollutants, let alone in what concentration they are acceptable or harmful.

POLLUTANTS AND SOURCES

In discussing the subject of air pollution control from a management point of view, I believe it is appropriate to consider what the main pollutants are and what is their source. This will, perhaps, serve to identify the areas of responsibility and place management's position in the proper perspective. According to publications by the Government of the U.S.A., the data in Table 1 is considered to be representative for the U.S.A. and I expect Canada will have a very similar pattern:

TABLE 1. POLLUTANTS AND SOURCES

Pollutant	%	Source	%
Carbon monoxide	52	Transportation	59·9
Oxides of sulphur	18	Manufacturing	18·7
Hydrocarbons	12	Generation of electricity	12·5
Particulates	10	Space heating	6·3
Oxides of nitrogen	6	Refuse burning	2·6
Other gases	2		
Total	100		100·0

From this table it can be seen that automobiles are the source of the vast majority of carbon monoxide. More than one-half the sulphur dioxide comes from the fuel oil used in electric power generation. The rest of the sulphur dioxide comes from industrial processes largely, and to a lesser extent, space heating and refuse incineration. There are two basic approaches to control of sulphur dioxide emission; either control of the sulphur content of the fuel and control of the chemical processes producing sulphur dioxide or cleaning the waste gas to remove the sulphur dioxide. Manufacturers are actively investigating various means to remove sulphur compounds from fuels and from stack gases at reasonable costs.

It is, I believe, pertinent to note, however, that manufacturing and electric power generation combined are estimated to contribute to only some 30% of the total emission in the U.S.A. Whereas this is a sizeable contribution to the pollution problem, it is still only one-half the contribution of transportation.

WHO IS RESPONSIBLE FOR CONTROL?

Responsibility for the sensible control of pollution falls into the hands of three general groups, each of which must play a part to lead to a successful result.

1. Public Responsibility

The first group is the general public, both as a group and as individual members in that group. The public must be concerned and informed. The alarmists previously mentioned must be put in their proper place and their emotional outcries countered by considered actions by responsible citizens and officials. There are many areas where ordinary citizens can personally fight pollution, whether it be an urban dweller avoiding burning the family trash in the lane, or the careful farmer operating in such a way as to minimize soil drifting and surface erosion of his land with the subsequent silting and pollution of our rivers, or avoiding the indiscriminate use of chemical weed killers and pesticides in his farming operation.

The ordinary citizen must take every opportunity to become informed about pollution, and the press as a segment of what I call the general public, must undertake to provide responsible reporting and factual information. I am concerned that the press is too often guilty of reporting the emotional statements of the alarmists, whether the subject be a sanitary land fill project or a new industrial plant, with the results that irreparable damage is done to many a worthy project.

2. Government Responsibility

The second area of responsibility for pollution control is that of government. Pollution is properly a matter of concern to governments at all levels since this is where the public interest is taken care of and it is only through government that a co-ordinated sensible control system can be achieved. The main functions of government at least with respect to industrial operations, are quite obvious; namely, to set acceptable levels, to prescribe regulations, to monitor and record the actual levels, to investigate and evaluate programs of pollution control and to inform and educate the citizens and industrialists alike on such matters.

I believe that the presence of several distinguished government people at this conference is evidence that there is a real appreciation and concern for the grave responsibility that government has in this matter.

The Federal Department of Energy, Mines and Resources, has already taken significant steps in co-ordinating government activities in the pollution field. At the meeting of the Canadian Council of Resource Ministers about a year ago [2], the Minister introduced several proposals to the provinces concerning joint studies and research on water pollution. I am not at all familiar with details of the Provincial and Federal programs which are underway but I certainly endorse the principles.

However, in carrying out their roles with respect to industrial pollution control, I would like to respectfully suggest that government should pay particular attention to the following areas where, in my view, there is need for leadership and improvement:

(a) *Jurisdiction.* Government must decide at what level regulations are to be made and enforced, and standards set and to co-ordinate these on a national scale.

For example, in the U.S.A. one feature of the Air Quality Act of 1967 [3], foresaw the national government establishing broad air quality regions or atmospheric areas on the basis of meteorological and topographical factors. These regions were to be independent of any political boundaries and were to have co-ordinated emission controls within the region with state and municipal authorities operating within the region on a co-ordinated basis.

I believe such an approach is essential in Canada, with indeed, international co-ordination between Canada and our neighbor to the south in some parts of the country.

(b) *Standards.* A set of national standards for control of air, water and soil pollution must be adopted, also with international co-operation negotiated where necessary (e.g. control of pollution of the Great Lakes).

Pollution in Canada is a national and international, as well as a regional problem and it must be uniformly dealt with.

(c) *Consistency.* Regulations must be established and administered consistently as between communities, industries and provinces. For example, it is inconsistent to require a new plant or industry to comply with certain anti-pollution measures when other older established installations are exempt or ignored by virtue of predating the current regulation.

(d) *Inspection.* Monitoring and inspection of industrial installations must be scientifically conducted, impartial, and must take into account all possible sources of pollutants in the area. Inspection and monitoring must be done by competent people with a sound knowledge of the measurements and analyses they are taking.

(e) *Basis for rules.* Control of pollution should be based on rules developed from factual observations as well as theoretical predictions.

(f) *Prompt handling of industry applications:* It is redundant, perhaps, to say that in business, time is money. But sometimes government agencies seem to ignore this. An application for approval of a pollution control plan, when such is required by statute or regulation, must be dealt with quickly and a decision handed down to the applicant forthwith. It may be a rejection, an approval or a request for further supporting information, but it should not be anything else. Industry may be criticized (quite properly sometimes) for leaving such matters too late and then pushing for a quick decision. But whatever the reason, the requirement is the same; a decision is needed quickly.

(g) *Economics.* Government officials must give some consideration to economics of control measures they prescribe. Especially, when established industries are affected, and short of a real threat to public health, they must be given some reasonable time to adjust or modify their operations. It is reasonable to expect that as an area becomes increasingly industrialized, there are more sources of potential pollutants and the restrictions may have to be made progressively more severe.

3. Industry Responsibility

The third and most directly concerned group in the problem of industrial pollution control is, of course, the business and industrial segment of the community. With this group lies the real obligation to society to take action to prevent pollution of industrial origin and to preserve a safe environment for the future generations. The management of industry today must assume their obligation forthwith. Given an atmosphere of reasonable and co-operatively derived government regulations, I believe industry will do a responsible job. This responsibility takes many forms, some facets of which are as follows:

(a) *Appreciation of the problem.* Every industry must accept as a fact of modern manufacturing life, the premise that pollution is not acceptable, and therefore steps must be taken to see that it does not occur.

(b) *Co-operation with regulatory agencies.* Industry must learn to co-operate with the government by full compliance with all sensible standards and in monitoring their own operations to prevent pollution. Industry cannot view the regulatory agencies as "the enemy" but rather as an interested party with the same objective, namely, to prevent pollution.

(c) *Setting standards.* In the area of setting standards to keep emission of waste materials to an acceptable level, the industrial concerns surely must have a great deal to contribute. Keeping of records and preparing statistical analyses of monitoring data to relate plant performance to observations of the presence or absence of pollutants, is a function which could be undertaken by individual industrial concerns to assist regulatory bodies. Industry generally will have available more technology surrounding its own operation than does government and this should be brought into play. I believe that each industrial concern should be charged with the responsibility of monitoring its own operation and filing reports with regulatory agencies.

(d) *Industrial planning.* For new industrial operations, the most important time to consider pollution control is at the time of designing the new plant. The process can be selected to minimize quantity of harmful waste effluent. The plant location can be selected having regard to waste disposal requirements and the additive effect of all the sources of pollutants in the same vicinity. The raw materials and plant fuel to be used can be selected with pollution in mind.

In brief, when a new project is planned, one of the design and location considerations should be pollution control.

(e) *Technological development.* It is apparent that industry in some areas has reached or exceeded the point of saturation in respect to further disposal of waste materials into the atmosphere, into the neighboring waters of lakes, rivers or oceans, or onto the land. Therefore it becomes a requisite that technological improvement must be made in both the manufacturing processes and in the products sold. In the latter instance, perhaps products will have to be chemically redesigned to avoid pollution by their ultimate consumer. As an example, the use of tetra-ethyl-lead, the familiar additive to motor gasoline used to achieve satisfactory anti-knocking characteristics, and octane may have to be curtailed. The petroleum refining industry is considering replacement, at least in part, of the T.E.L. treated hydrocarbons with aromatic hydrocarbons which are a lesser source of carbon monoxide and hydrocarbon pollutants. This is an example of an area where industry surely can and will contribute technologically in trying to identify the pollutants and developing alternate processes or products for their control.

WHAT IS THE COST OF POLLUTION CONTROL?

I do not know of any statistical publication setting forth the amount of money being spent on pollution control today. But certainly it must be a substantial part of the cost of all our manufactured goods, and it will undoubtedly be an increasing amount. Perhaps it is more pertinent however to ask, "How much is pollution costing us?" If I can again draw on published information of the U.S. Department of Health, Education and Welfare, the current cost of air pollution is $65.00 per person per year. Applied to Canada, this would suggest a cost of 1.3 billion dollars per year as the price Canadians pay for damage to crops, property, health, extra cleaning, extra electric power for lights because of an overcast sun, etc. If this is the case, it becomes abundantly clear that it would be better to pay the cost of abatement of air pollution, than to pay for pollution itself.

It is also clear that, whatever industry pays for abatement, the cost will be handed on to the consumer. It is difficult to generalize on the actual direct cost of pollution control, which will vary drastically from one industry to another and from one area to another.

In my own industry in Western Canada, the crude oil and natural gas processing plants have installed facilities for dispersal of waste residue gases costing in the order of 3% to 5% of the capital cost of the plant. In some cases, fuel gas to incinerate these waste gases might represent 3% to 4% of the total operating costs of the plant if it were valued at the current selling price for natural gas at the plant.

In the January 1968 issue of the *Petro/Chem. Engineer* [4], several industry leaders in the United States were interviewed on the subject of cost of pollution control (among other things). Mr. T. B. Nantz, President of the B. F. Goodrich Chemical Company stated that although his company has

> "always been cognizant of need for built-in controls in our operations to curb or eliminate pollutants, we've added engineers and specialists in our several plants to see where we can improve. We've restated our goals. And we're investing a sizeable amount of money, over the next several years, to keep our operations in alignment with new, stricter controls that are sure to come."

In the same magazine, Mr. T. J. Innes, Jr., Executive Vice-President of the Enjay Chemical Co. stated that

> "the high cost of restrictive but necessary air and water standards would doubtless force up the costs of many goods and services in the future."

It is inevitable that increased costs of production will be reflected in the price of the product to the consumer. Therefore, as industry is forced to meet new and increased capital and operating costs to control pollution, then the buying public will, in fact, be paying that cost and properly so in my opinion. But it is also a well established fact that in our competitive society, industry will look for other ways to avoid the added costs, especially when investment in pollution abatement facilities will yield little or no return.

In view of Mr. R. G. Widman, Manager, Petroleum and Chemicals Division, Arthur G. McKee & Co., this will " . . have an incentive to create new technology which combines adequate return on capital with air and water pollution abatement."

Mr. E. T. Layng, Executive Vice-President of Hydrocarbon Research, Inc. stated that, ". . . industry will be forced to spend large sums of money to cope with pollution problems. I predict that many valuable by products will be found."

I believe that these few quotations [4] are representative of the position of responsible industry management. They are alive to the problem, are prepared to meet the challenge and to concentrate on technology improvements and byproduct development as one means of pollution control, and as a means to partially pay the cost.

It is apparent that not only will industry be required to increase the amount of money spent on the direct cost of pollution control, but so will government spending have to increase. Municipal works for sewage treatment and disposal and power generation will have to be expanded and improved. Immediately, additional government spending on technology for developing standards will be required. This is the obvious starting point for a sensible control system. This will, no doubt, lead to additional spending for surveillance and monitoring which I have previously suggested should be largely done by the industrial establishments as part of their operating routine.

CONCLUSIONS

In conclusion, I would like to summarize my views and recommendations as follows:

(1) Canada sorely needs a strong co-operative program between the various levels of government and industry to establish national pollution control standards. I believe the appropriate Federal Government Department should aggressively promote further action

with the Provinces to undertake this project. Industry should become involved at all levels but could best participate at the Provincial level, through the means of small joint industry-government working committees to develop acceptable standards to meet the specific regional and provincial needs all within the national framework.

(2) I would like to see the public better informed on pollution and believe the Provincial governments could serve a very useful purpose by publishing their current findings and observations as well as expanding their public information service. We occasionally see a great hue and cry in the daily press about some citizen or citizens having suffered grievously due to industrial pollution. I believe that the appropriate Provincial authorities should investigate such matters and issue public reports and statements on their findings. Pollution control measures should not be established on emotional grounds but on the basis of scientific and technological facts.

(3) The industrial community must accept pollution control as a mandatory part of doing business and co-operate and assist government in setting acceptable standards and operating in such a way as to be within these standards. Many fine national engineering codes and standards have been established by joint action of industry and government, e.g. the recently adopted Canadian pipeline code (officially C.S.A. Std. Z183, Oil Pipe Line Transportation Systems), covering specifications for designing and constructing high pressure pipelines. This was developed over the course of several years by joint effort of many individuals from industry, including producing, pipeline, manufacturing, transportation, contracting companies, together with the Federal and Provincial governments within the framework of the Canadian Standards Association. Perhaps a "Canadian Code for Pollution Control" could be developed on similar basis. Technological study and development should be pursued vigorously by industry to find ways to dispose of industrial wastes than literally putting them in the nearest part of the sky, water or land.

(4) Pollution control is going to cost money, perhaps directly as much as 3% of the value of manufactured products. These costs will be passed on to the consumers of manufactured products. Public funds will have to be made available in increased amounts to administer the program as well as to take direct action to control pollution by public works.

(5) Responsible industry leaders are all aware of the above conclusions and are prepared to take their part in solving this growing problem in a planned and organized way. They are looking to government for leadership. Their co-operation and support will be forthcoming in many ways as long as the public requirements are reasonable and consistently applied.

REFERENCES

1. DeMicheal, Don, Environment gone wrong, *Actual Specifying Engineer*, November 1967.
2. "National Conference on Pollution and our Environment", Canadian Council of Resource Ministers, Montreal, October 1966 (in three volumes), Queen's Printer, Ottawa, 1967.
3. Middleton, John T., The government and the pollutors, *Actual Specifying Engineer*, November 1967.
4. Chambers, Peter S., HPI executives look at '68, *Petro/Chem. Engineer*, January 1968.

EFFECTS OF AIR POLLUTION ON HEALTH

A. J. de VILLIERS *Dept. of National Health and Welfare, Ottawa*

ABSTRACT

Sufficient evidence is available to indicate that the varying degrees of atmospheric pollution do affect health adversely. It contributes to excesses of deaths, increased morbidity and the earlier onset of chronic respiratory diseases. There is evidence of a relationship between the intensity of the pollution and the severity of attributable health effects and a consistency of the relationship between these environmental stresses and the diseases of the target organs. While experimental results are not reviewed in detail, there is, nevertheless, a considerable body of knowledge available to support and explain the effects observed in man.

INTRODUCTION

A discussion of health effects should be based on an understanding, however incomplete, of the fundamental meaning of "health". It may be pertinent, therefore, to reflect that the very process of living is characterized by the interplay between the individual and the stresses to be found in his external environment. To "counterbalance" these stresses, highly complex physiological or internal adaptive mechanisms are evoked in order to maintain an optimal equilibrium (or homeostasis). Fitness or "health" of the individual depends, therefore, on the effectiveness of these counterbalancing forces. Maladjustment, on the other hand, may lead, as Hatch [1] pointed out in his concept of the multiple factors in the etiology of disease (Fig. 1), to failure of the normal defences, disturbed function, disease and/or death.

Our total environment does not remain constant but is in a continual state of change; a state influenced increasingly by man's rapidly-growing technology, the harnessing of all forms of energy and the development and use of our natural resources.

Associated with these changes, and those in medical science and technology which accompanied them, is a changing pattern and distribution of health effects or diseases. By reducing the toll of the acute diseases, for example, we have increased the life-expectancy of man, but in doing so, we have increased the incidence of the chronic degenerative diseases among the elderly. The early emphasis on the single or relatively simple predominant causes of illness and death, such as the pneumococci and the tubercle bacilli—the two leading causes of death at the turn of the century—has shifted to diseases of multiple causation exemplified by the chronic cardiovascular-respiratory diseases and malignant neoplasms. These are the leading causes of death on the North American continent today and also those affecting the target organs involved in the conflict between man and the noxious elements in his atmospheric environment. They are, therefore, of central interest to our discussion of the health effects of air pollution.

Fundamental to these developments are the questions: to what extent the chronic respiratory diseases are becoming manifest as a normal uncontrollable accompaniment of the aging process; to what extent the quality of the air in our larger cities may significantly influence

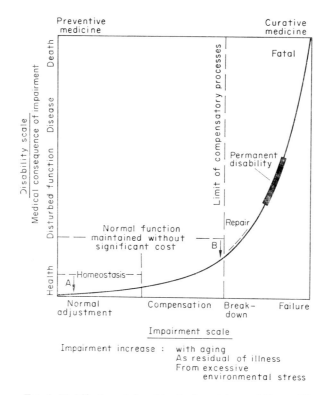

FIG. 1. Multifactor relationships in the etiology of disease [1].

the occurrence of deaths, the development of sickness and shorten the life expectancy of urban dwellers. In more practical terms—to what extent may polluted air be responsible for the toll taken in terms of human misery by chronic ill health which places an enormous burden on the economy of the country, in cost of medical care and lost national productivity caused by absenteeism and disablement.

To establish the significance of a pollution-effect relationship, it would be necessary to demonstrate excess risk, a dose-response relationship, consistency of the association and, where possible, the production of similar effects in susceptible experimental animals. This has been difficult in the case of human populations exposed to community air pollution, largely because of an imprecise, cumbersome and costly methodology and the presence of a multiplicity of factors operating at very low doses and dose rates. Specific pollutants in low concentrations do not often exceed the threshold limits established as guide lines for use in industry. At such low dose rates, discernible biological or health effects may not become apparent for long periods of time. Furthermore, most of the information available to date has been reported in terms of the general factor "urban pollution". This factor is comprised of the effects of individual pollutants or their combinations, the effects of greater population density with the consequent greater incidence and likelihood of respiratory infections, and other less specific urban factors. These are, in addition, complicated by various occupational, climatic and personal pollution (or smoking) factors and the problems of additivity, enhancement (synergism) or the development of tolerance.

NORMAL DEFENCE MECHANISMS AND RESULTS OF FAILURE

Before discussing the known health effects of air pollution, it would be of interest to review briefly some of the basic processes involved in the interplay between the atmospheric environment and the internal environment of man.

Air normally contains approximately 20% oxygen, 80% nitrogen, with trace amounts of other gases, of which carbon dioxide ($0\cdot3\%$) is the most important. Suspended in air are particulates and droplets dispersed from natural sources or by man's industries and activities. Relatively clean air may contain up to 70,000 particles per cubic foot, but counts vary depending on the environment and nature of industry or activity. The atmosphere of our cities may contain a large number of added liquids, gases and solids as by-products of combustion processes and chemical reactions in the air. The quality and quantity of "pollutants" added in this manner is directly proportional to the amount and type of fuel burnt, the efficiency of the combustion process, the size of the community, the density of housing, industry and motor vehicle traffic and is notably influenced also by topographic and meteorologic factors (inversion, etc.).

The average man moves approximately 8000 litres of air in and out of his lungs per day in order to provide for the exchange of gases (O_2 and CO_2) necessary to sustain life. Much of the particulate and droplet material, together with minute quantities of gases absorbed onto it or dissolved in it, may be deposited in the respiratory tract. The amounts so deposited will depend upon the particle size of the aerosols, the concentration to be found in the air and the duration of exposure. Particles below one micron usually penetrate the deep lung regions. In this way, toxic materials dissolved in or adsorbed onto aerosols may reach the deep portions of the lung where they may exert deleterious effects over a potentially vast lung surface area.

Under ordinary circumstances, the cleansing mechanisms of the lungs are highly efficient. The larger solid particles and droplets are screened out by nasal hair or the mucous secretions of the upper respiratory tract. Particles reaching and deposited in the deeper portions of the lungs are normally conveyed towards the throat—where they are swallowed or expectorated. A continuously moving blanket of mucuous acts as a conveyor-belt for deposited material and is, in turn, propelled by the hair-like processes ("cilia") characteristic of the cells lining the air passages. This movement is facilitated by respiratory excursions, coughing and sneezing. Particles may also be engulfed and removed by scavenger or phagocytic cells or remain embedded in the interstitial tissues of the lungs. It is only when these defenses are damaged or overwhelmed by high concentrations and/or repeated exposure to deleterious substances that changes or deviations from the physiological or normal occur.

Depending upon the severity of the insult or of subsequent and repeated insults and a number of individual susceptibility or host factors, the biological effects may manifest themselves as local irritation and inflammation of the air passages; injury to the lining cells of the alveoli and the underlying vasculature causing pulmonary edema and predisposing to invasion by pathogenic micro organisms; reversible bronchial constriction; or as biochemical lesions which may result in the morphological or pathological manifestations of fibrosis, destruction of tissue (as in emphysema) or cell mutation or neoplasia. These effects can be elicited by a bewildering range of substances to be found in the atmospheric environment.

MEASURABLE AIR POLLUTION HEALTH EFFECTS

To understand the measurable effects of pollution on health, we need to distinguish between effects on the natural development of chronic respiratory disease in the previously healthy individual, and the effects of polluted atmospheres on the health status of the individuals with an altered threshold of reaction; notably, the individual with an already existing chronic respiratory or cardiac disease. These aspects are embodied in the suggestion made by Anderson [4] on the basis of accumulated epidemiological evidence that the measurable effects of air pollution should be considered to operate in seven stages as listed in Table 1. These stages are consistent with the multiple factor etiology, referred to earlier, and provides a convenient structure for the consideration of health effects in relation to the different types and intensities of polluted atmospheres.

TABLE 1. STAGES IN THE MEASURABLE EFFECTS OF AIR POLLUTION
ON HEALTH [4]

Stage 0	No measurable effect
Stage 1	Awareness of pollution at a level sufficient to lead individuals to change residence or place of employment
Stage 2	Reversible alteration in physiological functions
Stage 3	Untoward symptoms of bodily dysfunction
Stage 4	Irreversible alteration in vital physiological functions
Stage 5	Chronic disease
Stage 6	Acute sickness or death in debilitated persons
Stage 7	Acute sickness or death in healthy persons

Two major general types of community air pollution occur—a *"reducing" form* consisting largely of soot, fly ash, other material and sulphur dioxide—an atmosphere characteristic of London-type "smog"; and an *oxidizing form* containing carbon monoxide, hydrocarbons and photochemical decomposition products such as oxides of nitrogen, ozone, peroxyacetyl nitrate and olefins characteristic of the Los Angeles-type "smog". The combustion of sulphur containing fossil fuels for industrial and domestic purposes largely contributes to the former, and automotive exhausts in association with an abundance of sunlight to the latter. Various mixtures of these predominant types may occur but it is essential to note, from the health point of view, that the quality and quantity of pollutants in the atmosphere may vary from city to city or region to region, each of these delimitations constituting its own kind of local ecosystem.

Effects of Reducing-type Atmospheres

The most dramatic effects of pollution have been reported in association with the reducing types of atmospheric pollution. These effects are examples of Anderson's stages six and seven, shown in Table 2, and include the well-known episodes or *disasters*. Characteristically, these episodes occurred during the fall or winter months, in the Northern temperate zones; and unusually high concentrations of pollutants were associated with certain meteorological or inversion conditions. These conditions usually lasted three to five days with effects attributable to the smog following after an initial delay of one to two days.

The first documented fatal fog occurred during the week of February 7, 1880. During the week of the fog, deaths due to diseases of the respiratory organs rose to exceed the corrected weekly averages of the previous two weeks by 1118 [2, 3].

162

TABLE 2. AIR POLLUTION EPISODES*

Date	Place	Attributed mortality
February 1880	London, England	1000
December 1930	Meuse Valley, Belgium	63
October 1948	Donora, Pennsylvania	20
November 1950	Poza Rica, Mexico	22
December 1952	London, England	4000
November 1953	New York	220 [5]
January 1956	London, England	1000
December 1957	London, England	700–800
December 1962	London, England	700
January 1963	New York	300 [6]
November 1966	New York	168

* Adapted from Anderson [2].

By far the best-known episode, however, was the disaster that hit London in December 1952 [7, 8]. The cause of this disaster was a temperature inversion which occurred over the southeastern part of England. It lasted four days and was particularly severe in the London area. During these four days, a number of people became acutely ill and died. So many were affected that it resulted in an excess over expected mortality of approximately 4000 deaths. The majority of these deaths, and the greatest number of illnesses, occurred among the elderly and in those with pre-existing cardiorespiratory diseases or disabilities (Stage 6 effect). Deaths due to pneumonia and bronchitis increased almost four- and ten-fold, respectively, over those of the previous week. Smog analyses revealed increases of the sulphur dioxide and particulate levels several orders of magnitude over those previously reported. Despite these increased concentrations, however, the general levels of these pollutants, observed during the episode, were not such that conventional toxicologic data would have predicted the resulting illnesses and deaths.

As an hypothesis, Amdur [9] suggested that the air pollution effects were due probably to a potentiation of the toxic propensities of sulphur dioxide (converted to sulphuric acid in the presence of fog droplets and catalysts) which had penetrated the deep lung regions, dissolved in or attached to submicronic particles in the fog aerosol. This suggestion has been supported in part by the observation during more recent episodes, that the lesser severity of the later episodes appeared to correlate well with the much more marked reduction in the particulate content (over that of the sulphur dioxide concentrations), achieved since the implementation of the Clean Air Act in Great Britain. However, a consideration of sulphur dioxide and particulates alone in relation to the health effects of the above episodes, undoubtedly oversimplifies the problem and it will remain to be seen what other pollutants (including various catalytic substances) may be implicated in the future. It is interesting to note, nevertheless, that advance warning, based on these measurements of increased levels of pollution, may also have helped to reduce the mortality in the later episodes. During the 1962 episode, for example, cardiorespiratory patients were specifically advised to remain indoors at home.

The Meuse Valley incident occurred during the first six days of December 1930. A heavy mist lay over this industrialized valley in Belgium and became particularly severe on the second day when illnesses started to occur. It was estimated that several thousand illnesses occurred; there were sixty deaths. Again, as in other disasters associated with this kind of pollution, the illnesses and deaths attributed to the fog occurred chiefly among the elderly and those with pre-existing heart or lung disease.

A combination of industrial effluent, topographic and meteorologic factors was also responsible for the 1948 episode in Donora [10], a small town on the Monongahela River south of Pittsburgh, Pennsylvania. The fog lasted about six days and, as in the other disasters, excess fatalities were among the elderly and debilitated. A large number of presumably normal individuals were also affected as it was estimated that 6000 of the 13,000 residents were affected by the fog, with a case fatality rate of $3 \cdot 33$ per 1000 cases [11]. Post-mortem examination suggested that the deaths were due to asphyxia caused by changes in the stiffness of the lungs, brought about by an inflammatory response to the irritant aerosol. In discussing this, Anderson has suggested that a "smog disease" may indeed exist as an entity among respiratory cripples in heavily polluted urban areas.

The Poza Rica, Mexico, incident occurred in 1950 and was due to a coincident but accidental release of hydrogen sulphide at the time of severe atmospheric inversion conditions. It is listed and discussed as an air pollution episode but should, perhaps, more appropriately be considered as accidental pollution by a more specific chemical agent. The comparatively brief period of the episode, nevertheless, claimed 22 lives; 320 persons were hospitalized (Stage 7 effect).

Apart from these excesses of deaths during pollution episodes, positive correlations between an urban factor including, of course, air quality, with *mortality* and a number of causes of death, have now been well established. Earlier studies described the excess urban over rural deaths in the United Kingdom, as well as the association among city dwellers of an increased risk of lung cancer presumed to be related to the carcinogenic polycyclic hydrocarbons present in urban atmospheres [12]. A long-term study of the relationships between residents, occupation and smoking habits and the mortality from chronic diseases among Canadian veterans [13] has also indicated a higher death rate among those persons who had lived five or more years in a city with a ratio of 1 : 12. This association between urban residents and mortality rates in excess of those of rural residents was independent of smoking habits. The urban-rural ratio in the above study for lung cancer mortality was $1 \cdot 5$. In the United States, Manos [14], reviewing mortality for 163 areas in the United States for the years 1949–51 inclusive, by degrees of urbanization, was also able to demonstrate the association of an urban factor and an urban-rural gradient in association with an increased incidence of lung cancer and a number of other disease categories. In a later work, Manos and Fisher [15] reported a high frequency of positive correlations between a number of different indices of air pollution, taking into account also city characteristics, and socioeconomic factors, and the following causes of death: malignant neoplasms of the esophagus and stomach; trachea, bronchus and lung; arterio sclerotic heart disease, including coronary disease; and chronic endocarditis, not specified as rheumatic. They pointed out, however, that more critical tests would be required before assuming a definite causal relationship.

Much of the demonstrated excess of mortality may be due to a *higher frequency or prevalence* of respiratory diseases occurring under higher intensity pollution conditions in certain urban communities. Many investigators, using a standard respiratory questionnaire in conjunction with simple lung function tests, have been able to demonstrate significant relationships between the prevalence of chronic respiratory diseases and urban pollution (Stage 5 effect). There is also some evidence that the prevalence is directly related to the intensity of pollution and the size of the community. At lower levels of pollution, as found in the smaller communities in North America, however, the differences between relative pollution levels may not always be large enough to demonstrate an effect on the frequency distributions of these diseases or overcome the overwhelming influence of such added variables as personal pollution or smoking.

The findings of the Windsor-Detroit health study [16] carried out under the aegis of the International Joint Commission during the years 1951–1954, were inconclusive for the above and other reasons. In this study, the sickness incidence was compared between each sample of 200 randomly-selected families in each high and low pollution area defined for the purpose of the study on either side of the border. These families were interviewed on a bi-weekly basis during the period of the study in order to obtain the necessary sickness information. While some health effect was demonstrated on the Detroit side, where sickness rates were generally at a higher level in the more polluted area, the study, on the whole, was inconclusive. Some of the reasons for this became clear during the course of the study. In the Windsor area, for example, the high pollution area did not have consistently high pollution readings and when pollution levels increased, a concomitant increase in pollution level occurred in the low pollution area.

Bates et al. [17] discussed differences in the severity of bronchial disease among a group of Canadian veterans resident in the four Canadian cities, Toronto, Winnipeg, Montreal and Halifax, and indicated that the cases from Winnipeg, by far the cleanest of the cities in respect of industrial dustfall and SO_2 levels, appeared to be less severe than the groups from the other three cities. Caution was, however, expressed about the possible influence of medical treatment and climatic factors, as well as the adequacy of the air quality information available at the time of the study.

Ferris and Anderson [18] studied the prevalence of respiratory disease in Berlin, New Hampshire, a moderately polluted city and later made comparisons [19] with that observed in Chilliwack, B.C., a city of comparable size. Chilliwack had a much lower dustfall and sulphur dioxide pollution exposure during the period of the study (ratios of 6·6 and 10·0, respectively [20]), and comparisons made indicated a tendency towards a slightly lower respiratory disease prevalence than in Berlin, N. H., but the differences were small.

In his recent review of the subject, Ferris [21] compared the New Hampshire findings with those of the United Kingdom and found that the U.S. prevalence was very similar to that of rural England. However, while an age gradient could be demonstrated to occur for various symptoms in the United Kingdom, this could only be demonstrated for the symptom, breathlessness, in New Hampshire, suggesting that the type of response or health effect may differ in quality. When comparing the symptom groupings, simple bronchitis and complex bronchitis, it was clearly demonstrated that with increasing levels of pollution, more severe effects were to be found (Fig. 2). Simple bronchitis refers to chronic phlegm production whereas complex bronchitis includes, in addition, some evidence of breathlessness and a period of increased cough or phlegm, lasting at least three weeks for two or more winters.

From the clinical point of view, real differences appear to exist. The findings of Fletcher [22] and others suggest that there is a higher incidence of recurrent disabling chest infections or so-called complex bronchitis in England than in the United States. Further, when the mortality rate due to chronic bronchitis in Great Britain was compared with that in Denmark [23], it was found that the rate for Denmark was only one sixth of that for the rural areas of Great Britain and that in Denmark, rural-urban differences could not be demonstrated.

165

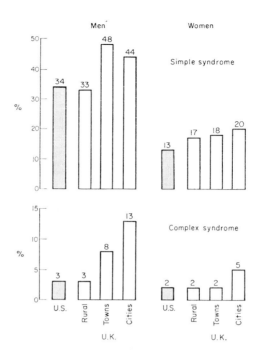

FIG. 2. Prevalence rates standardized for age and lifetime cigarette consumption [22].

Of considerable interest in these studies, then, is the fact that the biological effects may differ qualitatively and quantitatively from region to region and country to country. Chronic respiratory disease is much more evident in England than the United States. Men between the ages of 45 and 54, for example, living in Britain have five times the death rate for certain chronic respiratory diseases and twice the lung cancer death rate, as compared with those in North America.

Some of the above differences, as seen earlier, are attributable to higher pollution levels in the United Kingdom, and some are undoubtedly due to differences in diagnosis—chronic bronchitis having been more commonly quoted as a cause of death in England. In the United States, the chronic respiratory disease component of the individual's cause of death often appears with emphasis on emphysema as a contributory cause of death only. Dean [24] pointed to another possible factor when he suggested that the British-born migrant carries with him a greater liability to lung cancer or to be deleteriously affected by factors in his ambient air environment. He also carries with him his smoking habits.

Other approaches to the establishment of positive correlations between pollution and health have included the use of such indices as the *utilization of medical services*, the *day-by-day reporting of untoward symptoms*, and the study of special indicator or sensitive population groups (such as panels of chronic bronchitics, asthmatics, school children and identical twins) and *pulmonary function studies*. Positive correlations have, for example, been established between peaks in SO_2 concentrations and the particulate content of the atmosphere and hospital admissions and/or the occurrence of certain symptoms [26] (Stage 3 effect) among exposed populations. Minor ventilatory function changes have also been described among normal (Stage 2 effect) and chronic respiratory disease subjects exposed to a variety of environmental factors [27]. Previous studies have correlated the incidence of asthmatic attacks among adults with intensities of pollution [28]. Another recent study of asthma in children in Philadelphia revealed a nine-fold greater incidence of bronchial asthma during days of stagnant air and high air pollution than on control days of cleaner and less stagnant air [29]. The irritant and inflammatory effect of SO_2 in conjunction with the existence of a chronic respiratory disease component as, e.g. in the elderly, is said to be operative in these cases.

Sulphur dioxide is formed during the combustion of sulphur in fossil fuels and is a common constituent of polluted air. Small amounts of SO_3 are also formed, but together with the quantities produced by oxidation of SO_2 in the atmosphere (photochemical, catalytic), are rapidly converted to sulphuric acid. The associated presence of sulphuric acid and sulphate salts is the reason for the purported health effects, some of which are reviewed in Table 3. The threshold value set for SO_2 in industry is at $5\cdot0$ ppm, at which level exposure can occur without serious health effects during an 8-hour day, 40-hour week. The highest value obtained for SO_2 during the 1952 London disaster was only $1\cdot3$ ppm, but it was accompanied by a high smoke or particulate loading, optimal conditions for the conversion of SO_2 into sulphuric acid and/or a particular combination of a number of different factors operative on a 24-hour dose-time relationship or dose rate.

TABLE 3. SUMMARY OF SULPHUR DIOXIDE CONCENTRATION AND SUGGESTED HEALTH EFFECTS
(Other associated pollutants not specified)

Conc. in ppm	Time-dose relationship	Effect
$0\cdot015$–$0\cdot15$	Annual average	Increased morbidity [25, 30, 16]
$0\cdot20$–$0\cdot86$	3 consec. days	Air Pollution Episode; N.Y. 1953 [5]
$0\cdot25$	24-hour average	Increased total death rates, London 1963 [31]
$0\cdot3$–$1\cdot0$		Can be detected by average individual (taste) [32]
$0\cdot46$	Average for 15 days	406 excess deaths; pop 45 years + [33]
$0\cdot5$		Damage to sensitive parts [34]
$0\cdot5$–$0\cdot7$		Odour threshold; highly sensitive persons [35]
$0\cdot57$	5-day average	Air Pollution Episode; London 1952 [7, 8]
$0\cdot5$–$2\cdot0$	Calculated for 3–4 days	Air Pollution Episode; Donora, Pa. 1948 [10]
$1\cdot6$	10 minutes	Threshold for bronchoconstriction; healthy man [36
$3\cdot0$		Odour threshold; average individual [32]
$5\cdot0$	8 hour day; 40 hour week	T.L.V. for industrial exposure [37]
6–12	immediate	Irritation to nose and throat [32]
$20\cdot0$		Least amount irritating to eyes [32]
50–100	30–60 minutes	Maximum permissible; short exposure value [32
400–500		Immediately dangerous to life [32]

In addition to a combined action of different environmental factors, it appears that concentration (and, therefore, also dose-rate) and duration of exposure at higher dose rates, may also be of special importance. This is suggested by the data available for one pollutant —sulphur dioxide. Short-term levels of $0\cdot2$ ppm SO_2 and higher have been associated with apparently increasingly severe pollution episodes. Values of $0\cdot20$–$0\cdot86$ during three consecutive days were reported for the 1953 New York episode during which 220 excess deaths occurred; a 24-hour average of $0\cdot25$ ppm was associated with increases in total death rates in London; a 15-day average of $0\cdot40$ ppm was associated with 406 excess deaths among men 45 years of age and older and the 1952 London episode was associated with average values of 0·5 or slightly more during the 5 days of the disaster period. These values quoted for SO₂ alone do not, of course, reflect the degree of hazard accurately, and must be considered in conjunction with the degrees of particulate loading and other factors. The clarification of the role played by these other factors is essential to our understanding of the effects on health or reducing types of polluted atmospheres.

Exposure to Oxidizing Atmospheres

Unlike the pollution found in Britain and parts of the eastern United States, the oxidizing type of pollution, found characteristically in Los Angeles, has not been correlated with marked excesses of deaths, nor with excesses of lung cancer. Instead, much of the earlier emphasis was placed on the occurrence of a time-associated relationship between daily oxidant levels and the mean daily frequency of eye discomfort [38] (Stage 3 effect), the demonstration of certain disturbances in pulmonary function among chronic respiratory [39] disease patients and a low positive correlation between chemical measures of air pollution and the number of attacks of asthma among asthmatics [40].

Of, perhaps, considerably greater significance and potential portent are the reports of Brant and Hill [41], who found increased respiratory dysfunction and, in a later study [42], increased hospital admissions for cardiovascular diseases, under sustained high oxidant; low relative humidity; low temperature conditions, related on a post-exposure; bases of four weeks. He suggested that these conditions constituted a formidable and potentially catastrophic danger to public health in Los Angeles. In their recent study, Sterling *et al.* [43] and others, in essence, confirmed these findings when they found a definite correlation between pollution and fluctuations in rates of admission to hospitals for respiratory diseases and heart and other conditions thought to be relevant or possibly affected by air pollution. With, again, the exception of eye irritations and allergies, these ailments were primarily those that affected individuals with a low threshold or pre-existing disease or debility.

It is possible, therefore, that the oxidizing form of pollution is a lower intensity stress causing ill effects in debilitated individuals only after a delay of days to weeks. It appears, at any rate, to have a different mechanism of action than the reducing smogs, one which has not yet been shown to be clearly associated with the development of irreversible changes (Stage 4 effect) in the previously healthy individual.

Of considerable current interest is the role of carbon monoxide present as an important constituent in automobile exhaust gases. It has been suggested [44] that carbon monoxide may well be the most under-estimated pollutant of this era and evidence is gradually accruing in support of this contention.

The quantity present in automobile exhaust gases varies, as we know, with the air/fuel ratio and may, under certain conditions, amount to between 5000 and 70,000 ppm [32]. As a product of incomplete combustion, it is very widely encountered and is, as such, also an important component of inhaled cigarette smoke which may contain between 200–800 ppm. The current threshold limit value for industrial exposure is set at 50 ppm for an 8-hour day. Values up to 50 ppm or more are found on Los Angeles freeways and downtown areas for short periods of time and have also been reported in Montreal during last year's bus strike and, hence, the increase in automobile traffic. Levels in underground garages may reach 80–100 ppm (1-hour average) or up to 200 ppm (20-minute average) for short periods.

Carbon monoxide has a much greater affinity for hemoglobin than oxygen and exerts its effect by interrupting the normal oxygen supply to the tissues (anoxia). The gas is released, but slowly, and continued exposure leads to increasing degrees of saturation of the blood. Overt symptoms do not normally appear until a saturation of 10–20% has been reached. Individuals with existing lung or heart disease, associated with low grades of oxygen deficiency, are particularly prone to be deleteriously affected by increases in carbon monoxide. The heart muscle itself is an avid user of oxygen and heart pain (angina) may be induced or be made more severe with small concentrations of carbon monoxide. Repeated long-term exposure has been found to have an effect on the blood-forming tissues as well, resulting in an increased packed-cell volume. This has the tendency to thicken the blood and to increase the likelihood of clot formation and growth—yet another mechanism associated with morbidity and mortality from cardiovascular disease. It is, however, the extra work-load imposed on the heart muscle of cardio-respiratory patients, by levels of 5–10% carboxyhemoglobin that is of immediate concern to the health of these subjects.

Carboxyhemoglobin concentrations of below 5% may, in addition, affect task performance [45] and levels of 5–10% saturation may dangerously affect the alertness of automobile drivers [46]. These are levels that can be attained by cigarette-smoking or work in traffic tunnels. Blood taken from drivers responsible for traffic accidents revealed substantially higher levels of CO hemoglobin than individuals who thought they had been exposed to carbon monoxide or workmen who had some exposure to the gas at work. It has been pointed out that laboratory tests used in assessing the effects of CO on psychomotor activity may not reliably predict the influence of increased blood levels of CO-hemoglobin on mental alertness, since attention of the subject during testing may affect the test result, but be absent at the time of accidents when, indeed, attention is distracted.

It is clear that much more emphasis should be placed on the measurement and evaluation of the effects of this widely dispersed gaseous pollutant.

Other important constituents of the Los Angeles-type smog include the oxides of nitrogen and ozone. Automobiles are responsible for approximately 30–60% of the nitrogen oxides present in urban atmospheres. Nitrogen dioxide in high concentrations is a most toxic gas causing severe degrees of pulmonary edema but whilst the threshold level for 8-hour daily exposure in industry is set at 5 ppm, these values are never found in urban atmospheres.

Ozone, used as one of the indicators of the level of oxidizing pollution, is another important and potentially toxic component. It is an irritant to the eyes and mucous membranes and, at high concentrations, is a dangerous lung irritant. The recommended threshold limit value in industry is 0·1 ppm [41]; a level at which plant damage is said to occur. Pulmonary function has been shown to be affected at levels of 0·6–0·8 ppm for 2 hours and tolerance may develop at these and slightly higher levels. Animal experiments have indicated that, at levels of 0·7 to 0·9 ppm, ozone may predispose or aggravate a response to bacterial infection [47].

EFFECTS OF PERSONAL POLLUTION

No discussion of the health effects of polluted atmospheres can ignore the considerable effect of personal pollution or smoking. Smoking is of particular importance to the natural history of the chronic respiratory diseases. It has been well documented that considerable differences between smokers and non-smokers occur with regard to crude mortality and mortality from lung cancer [48, 49] and cardiovascular disease, the prevalence of certain symptoms indicative of chronic non-specific respiratory disease and with regard to measurable ventilatory function, has been well documented. An increasing risk of developing lung cancer with an increasing daily consumption of cigarettes has been demonstrated; so, too, has the fact that elimination of the hazard considerably reduces this risk.

So overwhelming and powerful is the influence of smoking as a factor in respiratory disease that it bears repeating that Anderson found the effects of smoking eliminated differences in the prevalence of respiratory disease between two cities, despite significant differences in air quality. It may be argued—with some justification, that the levels of pollution in these two communities were not sufficiently high to affect the prevalence of respiratory disease. However, a recent study [50] of another North American community in New Jersey showed quite clearly that when smokers were compared with non-smokers in a heavily polluted area, the cigarette smokers had a prevalence of chronic productive cough 8·3 times greater than the non-smokers.

It is also notable that pulmonary emphysema, as reported from the autopsy room, occurs primarily in those with a long history of smoking. Ishikawa [51] and his colleagues in Winnipeg have recently reviewed the incidence of emphysema in a series of 300 routine autopsies from St. Louis, Mo. and Winnipeg, respectively. This study revealed not only a higher prevalence, an earlier age distribution and a more severe form of the disease in the more highly polluted area of St. Louis, but also a much greater prevalence of emphysema among smokers when compared with non-smokers. While demonstrating additivity of effect, smoking in this case—if these comparisons can be made—did not overshadow the effect of pollution and other urban factors presumably operative at a higher level of intensity than those that were operative in the case of the Berlin-Chilliwak comparisons. These studies confirm not only a dose-response relationship for air quality but also the important additive effects of smoking.

It has recently been reported that individuals who do not smoke enjoy an advantage in prolonged life [53]. This was demonstrated in studies of the non-smoking Seventh Day Adventists in California, who live longer than smokers and who have a lower probability of developing lung cancer, pulmonary emphysema, other diseases of the respiratory tract as well as coronary artery disease. At age 40, their life expectancy is 6·1 years greater than that for other California men.

A similar effect is shown in Table 4 based on the study of the effect of smoking on the health of Canadian veterans. It may be seen (Fig. 3) that for each 1000 non-smokers of age 32·5, we would expect 155 to reach the age of ± 90 years, whereas the equivalent number reaching that age among the smokers of 20 or more cigarettes per day could be expected to be only 35.

THE INFLUENCE OF CLIMATIC, SOCIOECONOMIC AND OTHER FACTORS

The role of *climatic factors* (other than inversion conditions) on the prevalence of respiratory disease, is less well-defined. Climatic factors have been implicated in the effects of pollution on asthmatic attacks and appear to be integrally related to health effects of oxidizing pollution in Los Angeles. Tromp [53] and others in Holland demonstrated the influences of changing meteorological conditions, e.g. changes in temperature on the frequency and severity of episodes among a group of asthmatics. The above data indicate that climatic factors should be considered and controlled in future epidemiologic studies. Such studies should also consider the effects of *socio-economic factors*, selective migration and the

TABLE 4. ESTIMATED SURVIVORS* OF FOUR POPULATIONS OF A THOUSAND MALES EACH AT AGE 32·5; NON-SMOKERS, AND CURRENT CIGARETTE SMOKERS OF THREE INTENSITIES THROUGH ELEVEN SUCCEEDING AGES [13]

Age (years)	Estimated population surviving for males of four smoking categories			
	Never smoked	Currently smoke cigarettes only		
		Less than 10 per day	10–20 per day	More than 20 per day
32·5	1000·0	1000·0	1000·0	1000·0
37·5	986·5	991·6	988·0	986·2
42·5	956·1	975·2	971·3	971·7
47·5	953·8	954·0	944·1	934·8
52·5	905·1	911·8	893·6	882·5
57·5	847·6	834·4	816·1	808·4
62·5	787·1	743·6	703·3	686·6
67·5	715·2	631·9	578·4	563·2
72·5	602·3	487·6	437·2	422·2
77·5	467·8	326·3	308·0	280·6
84·3	291·6	148·1	139·1	132·9
90·3	155·4	74·1	59·6	35·4

* Based upon the age-specific death rates of non-smokers and persons of three cigarette smoking categories.

competing effects of occupational exposures. With regard to *occupational* influences, Anderson has indicated that one should not "assume that persons employed in occupations where they will be exposed to respiratory irritants" will necessarily have more respiratory disease as selection factors are operative within industry and that these may preclude such populations from epidemiological studies. Nevertheless, certain industrial environments unquestionably contribute to the development of acute, chronic and often disabling occupational lung disease.

Health Effects and Trace Elements

Of growing importance to health are the concentrations of trace elements to be found in urban environments. Of particular interest in this regard is lead, to be found in almost all gasolines used in North America. Almost 300,000 tons of the compounds are used each year and the element is, therefore, continually being returned to the atmosphere, constituting a source of lead absorption by inhalation. Lead is also deposited on city streets, washed down in sewers and, in certain cases, it gains access into drinking water supplies and, hence, into the food cycle (average daily consumption is 320 micrograms). Drinking water may contain 10 micrograms per litre on the average [54].

Large city atmospheric levels naturally vary with the amount of traffic and report of average values range from a few tenths of micrograms per cubic metre to as much as 15 micrograms per cubic metre of lead in a few cities. The average for urban atmosphere in the United States is estimated at 1·4 micrograms per cubic metre. Lead is, in addition, present in cigarette smoke (an average of 0·3 micrograms per puff).

"Normal" blood lead values are approximately 0·02 milligrams per cent (0·2 ppm). At 0·08 mg per cent and over, clinical symptoms may occur. Although there is no real

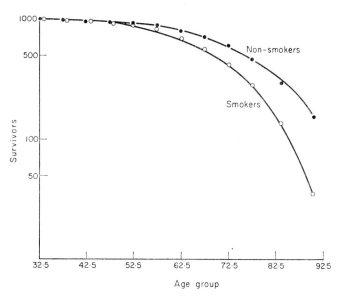

FIG. 3. Estimated survivors among non-smokers and smokers (more than 20/D) [13].

evidence that so-called "normal" blood values are increasing, the margin between safe and symptom-inducing levels appears slight and may require further reviews in years to come.

Other trace elements of importance to health include elemental nickel which, at low concentrations, may interfere with normal metabolism of inhaled polycyclic hydrocarbons [55]; cadmium, which, on the basis of the average concentrations found in 28 cities have been correlated with death rates from hypertension and arterio sclerotic heart disease [56]; vanadium, which acts as a respiratory irritant and asbestos.

Asbestos has given rise to considerable concern since the demonstration by Thomson [57] and others that "asbestoid" bodies can be found in the lungs of approximately 50% of city dwellers and since the demonstration by Wagner et al. [58], Selikoff et al. [59] and Newhouse et al. [60] and others of the association between exposure to asbestos and the incidence of mesothelial tumours of the pleura and peritoneum. Asbestos is used in many building materials and is an important component in the brake linings of automobiles. As such, this mineral has become ubiquitous, certainly as far as our urban atmospheres are concerned. Since the full significance of exposure to asbestos fibres, at the minimal concentrations to be found in urban atmospheres, are as yet undetermined, consideration should be given to including the monitoring of asbestos in air pollution control programmes. Other factors of considerable but, as yet, not clearly defined importance, are the polycyclic hydrocarbons and various bacterial agents. Much has been written about the presence of the polycyclic hydrocarbons in urban atmospheres, many of them with known carcinogenic activity. Despite this, however, "there is, as yet, no clear indication that their presence is significant, though their interaction with biological and physical substances might indeed be the mechanism of carcinogenesis". It is in regard to this that the role of also the micro-biological agents may indeed be of particular importance. It has been shown, for example, that exposure to Los Angeles smog can induce squamous cell carcinomata in experimental animals treated with PR-8 influenza virus [61]. The role of bacterial infections in the natural history of the non-specific chronic respiratory diseases requires further clarification as well.

TRENDS AND COSTS

It has been the purpose of this paper to discuss some of the measurable health effects of air pollution, to focus attention on some of the difficulties encountered in defining health effects and to show the essentially long-term or insidious nature of their onset. It has not been possible to review all aspects of health in the broad sense of the term, including welfare and the growing awareness of individuals of the disagreeable aspects of air pollution (at the perception or Stage 1 effect level). This type of effect is, nevertheless, of growing and of fundamental importance to the development of acceptable air quality criteria.

It has not been the purpose to discuss the problems of health in the future as it may be affected by the atmospheric environment against a background of increasing industrialization and population growth. However, it would be of interest to examine the present status with regard to discernible trends in diseases of interest to air pollution. The simplest, although crude indicator of present trends, is the mortality index.

On the basis of the premise that the quality of the atmosphere in larger urban communities is deleterious to health, particularly in terms of the diseases that affect the target organs—the cardiorespiratory diseases—it would not be unreasonable to use as a yardstick trends in mortality from diseases such as lung cancer, chronic bronchitis and emphysema and degenerative heart disease. In Canada, the trend in mortality for these diseases has been in a steadily upward direction (Fig. 4). While it must be emphasized that not all the increases are due to the influence of atmospheric pollution since diagnostic factors and changes in cigarette smoking habits and many other competing risks may play a part, the trend is, undoubtedly, important.

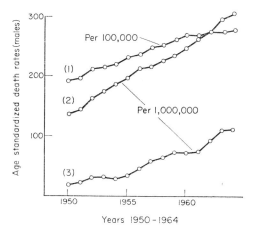

Fig. 4. Age standardized death-rates (males) for: (1) degenerative heart diseases; (2) lung cancer; and (3) bronchitis and emphysema.

With an increasing incidence of disease, there has also been a spiralling of the cost of ill health in monetary terms. With so many direct and intangible factors involved, it is obviously not possible to prepare an accurate cost-accounting for the ill health attributable to the various forms of atmospheric pollution. Nevertheless, air pollution is an important contributor to the natural history of the chronic respiratory diseases which, in turn, are responsible for about one quarter of all in-hospital patient days for all respiratory diseases per year. In 1965, for example, 3·2 million in-hospital days were recorded in Canada for all diseases of the respiratory system at an estimated cost of approximately 123 million dollars. Lost wages and losses in productivity due to these diseases were estimated at approximately one billion five hundred million dollars in 1967. To these must be added the costs for day-to-day out-of-hospital care and that of a variety of other indirect factors. Whatever proportion of the total economic burden may be attributable to the effects of air pollution, the costs are likely to be considerable.

CONCLUSION

Sufficient evidence is available to indicate that the varying degrees of atmospheric pollution do affect health adversely. It contributes to excesses of deaths, increased morbidity and the earlier onset of chronic respiratory diseases. There is evidence of a relationship between the intensity of the pollution and the severity of attributable health effects and a consistency of the relationship between these environmental stresses and the diseases of the target organs. While experimental results were not reviewed in detail, there is, nevertheless, a considerable body of knowledge available to support and explain the effects observed in man.

The trend, at present, is towards more chronic ill health and, as a result, considerably increased burden being placed on the economy of the country.

It would not be unreasonable to say, therefore, that we are already behind in our efforts to control and alleviate the effects of air pollution on health. It is evident that we shall need renewed impetus and efforts of the highest order directed at the development of new and improved control measures, better indicators and pollution based on more ongoing and prospective studies to determine health effects, more research for the elucidation of mechanisms of toxic action of pollutants and the development of experimental models to serve as the basis for preventive and corrective health measures.

As Sargent [62] pointed out, "The choices in the strategy are between costs—costs of regulation of output of pollutants, of selection of alternative sources of energy and raw materials, and of new technological design—and risks—risks of economic loss through environmental and material deterioration, of increased discomfort, dysfunction, morbidity and mortality in the biosphere, and of reducing renewable natural resources in the ecosystem that can meet man's subsistence requirements". "Whereas much is known about the costs of regulation, relatively little is known about the risks. For this reason, it is imperative that greater attention be given to environmental biology and particularly human adaptability."

REFERENCES

1. HATCH, T. F., Changing objectives in occupational health, *Amer. Industr. Hyg. Assoc. J.* **23**:1, 1962.
2. ANDERSON, DONALD O., The effects of air contamination on health: Part I. *Can. Med. Assoc. J.* **97**, Sept. 2, 1967, 528.
3. ANDERSON, DONALD O., The effects of air contamination on health: A review. Part II. *Can. Med. Assoc. J.* **97**, Sept. 9, 1967, 585.
4. ANDERSON, DONALD O., The effects of air contamination on health: Part III. *Can. Med. Assoc. J.* **97**, Sept. 23, 1967, 802.
5. GREENBERG, LEONARD and others. Report of an air pollution incident in New York City, November 1953, *Public Health Reports*, **77**, 1, January 1962, 7.
6. GREENBERG, L., FIELD, F., ERHARDT, C. L. and REED, J. I., Air pollution, influenza and mortality in New York City during January-February 1963. Presented at the 58th Annual Meeting, APCA, Toronto, June 22, 1965.

7. ABERCROMBIE, G. F., December fog in London and the Emergency Bed Service, *Lancet*, **1**, January 31, 1953, 234.
8. WILKINS, E. T., Air pollution and the London Fog of December 1952. *J. Roy. San. Inst.* **74**, 1, January 1954, 1.
9. AMDUR, MARY O., The influence of aerosols upon the respiratory response of guinea pigs to sulphur dioxide. *Am. Ind. Hyg. Assoc. Quarterly*, **18**, 1957, 149.
10. HEMEON, W. C. L., The estimation of health hazards from air pollution. *Arch. Industr. Health*, **11**, 1955, 397.
11. SCHRENK, H. H., Air pollution in Donora, Pa., Epidemiology of the unusual smog episode of October 1948: Preliminary Report by H. H. Schrenk and others. Federal Security Agency. Public Health Service, Bureau of State Services, Division of Industrial Hygiene, Public Health Service Bulletin No. 306, United States Government Printing Office, Washington, D.C., 1949.
12. STOCKS, P., Recent epidemiological studies of lung cancer mortality, cigarette smoking and air pollution with discussion of a new hypothesis of causation. *Brit. J Cancer*, **XX**, 4, December 1966, 27.
13. A Canadian Study of Smoking and Health, Department of National Health and Welfare, Ottawa, 1966.
14. MANOS, NICHOLAS E., Comparative mortality among metropolitan areas of the United States, 1949–51. 102 causes of death. U.S. Department of Health, Education and Welfare, Public Health Service, Bureau of States Services, Division of Special Health Services, Air Pollution Medical Programme, October 1957, Public Health Service Publication No. 562.
15. MANOS, N. E. and FISHER, G. F. An index of air pollution and its relation to health. *Air Pollution Control Assoc. J.* **9**, May 1959, 5.
16. REPORT OF THE INTERNATIONAL JOINT COMMISSION, UNITED STATES AND CANADA. On the Pollution of the Atmosphere in the Detroit River Area. Washington, Ottawa, 1960.
17. BATES, D. V., GORDON, C. A., PAUL, G. I., PLACE, R. E. G., SNIDAL, D. P. and WOOLF, C. R., Chronic Bronchitis. Report on the Third and Fourth Stages of the Co-ordinated Study of Chronic Bronchitis in the Department of Veterans Affairs, Canada. *Med. Serv. J. Can.* **XXII**, 1, January 1966, 5.
18. FERRIS, BENJAMIN G. and ANDERSON, DONALD O., The prevalence of chronic respiratory disease in a New Hampshire town. *Am. Rev. Resp. Dis.* **86**, 2, August 1962, 165.
19. ANDERSON, DONALD O., FERRIS, BENJAMIN G. and ZICKMANTEL, ROSALIE. The Chilliwak Respiratory Survey, 1963: Part III. The prevalence of respiratory disease in a rural Canadian town. *Can. Med. Assoc. J.* **92**, May 8, 1965, 1007.
20. ANDERSON, D. O. and FERRIS, B., Community studies of the health effects of air pollution—A critique. *Can. J. of Public Health*, 1966, 209.
21. FERRIS, B. G., Epidemiological studies on air pollution and health. *Arch. Env. Health*, **16**, 4, April 1968, 541.
22. REID, D., Diagnostic standardization in geographic comparisons of morbidity. *Amer. Rev. Resp. Dis.* **86**, 1962, 850.
23. CHRISTENSEN, O. W. and WOOD, C. H., Bronchitis mortality rates in England and Wales and in Denmark. *Brit. Med. J.* **1**, 1958, 620.
24. DEAN, G., Lung cancer in Northern Ireland. *Brit. Med. J.* **1**, 1966, 1506.
25. STERLING, T. D. *et al.*, Air pollution and urban morbidity: A First Report. *Arch. Env. Health*, **13**, 158, August 1966.
26. MCCARROLL, JAMES, CASSEL, ERIC J., WOLTER, DORIS W., MOUNTAIN, JOSEPH D., DIAMOND, JUDITH R. and MOUNTAIN, ISABEL M., Health and the urban environment. v. Air pollution and illness in a normal urban population. *Arch. Env. Health*, **14**, 1, January 1967, 178.
27. SPICER, WILLIAM S., Air pollution and meteorologic factors. *Arch. Env. Health*, **14**, 1, January 1967, 185.
28. DOERNER, ALEXANDER A., Air pollution and chronic lung disease. *Annals of Allergy*, **23**, October 1965, 475.
29. GIRSH, LEONARD S., SHUBIN, ELLIOT, DICK, CHARLES and SCHULANER, FREDERIC A., A study on the epidemiology of asthma in children in Philadelphia. *Journal of Allergy*, **39**, 1967, 347.
30. ZEIDBERG, L. D., PRINDLE, RICHARD A. and LANDAU, EMANUEL, The Nashville air pollution study, III: Morbidity in relation to air pollution. *Am. J. Pub. Health*, **54**, January 1964, 85.
31. LAWTHER, P. J., Compliance with the Clean Air Act. Medical aspects. *J. Inst. Fuel*, **36**, 341, August 1963.
32. PATTY, FRANK A., *Industrial Hygiene and Toxicology, II: Toxicology*. Second Revised Edition, Interscience Publishers, 1967.
33. GREENBURG, L., FIELD, F., ERHARDT, C. L. and REED, J. I., Air pollution, influenza and mortality in New York city during January-February, 1963. Presented at the 58th Annual Meeting, APCA, Toronto, June 22, 1965.
34. GOLDSMITH, JOHN R., GREENBURG, LEONARD, ALTSHULLER, A. P., SPICER, WILLIAM S., CASSELL, ERIC J. and LANDSBERG, H. E., Air pollution and health. American Thoracic Society. Medical Section of the National Tuberculosis Association, 1966, 302.

35. Dubrovskaya, F. I., Hygienic evaluation of pollution of atmospheric air of a large city with sulphur dioxide gas. In: *Limits of Allowable Concentrations of Atmospheric Pollutants*. Book 3. Ryazanov, V. A., ed. Levine, B. S., Trans. U.S. Dept. of Commerce. OTS. Washington, D.C. 1957, pp. 37–51.
36. Tomono, Y., Effects of SO_2 on human pulmonary functions. *Japan J. Ind. Health*, **3**, 77, February 1961.
37. THRESHOLD LIMIT VALUES FOR 1967. Recommended and intended values. Adopted at the 29th Annual Meeting of the American Conference of Governmental Industrial Hygienists, Chicago, Illinois, May 1–2, 1967.
38. Hammer, D. I., Portnoy, B., Massey, F. M., Wayne, W. S., Oelsner, T. and Wehrle, P. F., Los Angeles air pollution and respiratory symptoms. *Arch. Env. Health*, **10**, March 1965, 475.
39. Motley, H. L., Smart, R. H. and Leftwich, C. L., *J.A.M.A.* **171**, 1469, 1959.
40. Schoettlin, Charles E. and Landau, Emanuel, Air pollution and asthmatic attacks in the Los Angeles area. *Public Health Reports*, **76**, June 1961, 545.
41. Brant, John W. A. and Hill, Stanley R. G., Human respiratory diseases and atmospheric air pollution in Los Angeles, California. *Inst. J. Air. Wat. Poll.*, **8**, Pergamon Press, 1964, 259.
42. Brant, John W. A., Human cardiovascular diseases and atmospheric air pollution in Los Angeles, California. *Int. J. Air Wat. Poll.*, **9**, Pergamon Press, 1965, 219.
43. Sterling, T. D., Pollack, S. V. and Phair, J. J., Urban hospital morbidity and air pollution. A Second Report. *Arch. Environ. Health*, **15**, September 1967, 362.
44. Goldsmith, J. R., Report of Meeting on Carbon Monoxide. *Science*, **157**, August 18, 1967, 842.
45. Schulte, J. H., Effects of mild carbon monoxide intoxication. *Arch. Environ. Health*, **7**, 524, 1963.
46. Lawther, P. J., Abstracted in Notes and Comments. Motor exhausts and health. *The Medical Officer*, Feb. 25, 1966, 101.
47. Coffin, D. L. and Blommer, E. J., *J. Air Pollut. Contr. Assoc.* **15**, 523, 1965.
48. Doll, R. and Hill, A. B., Mortality in relation to smoking. Ten years' observations of British doctors. *Brit. Med. J.* Nos. 5395 and 5396, 1399–1410 and 1460–1467, May and June 1964.
49. SMOKING AND HEALTH, Report of the Advisory Committee to the Surgeon-General of the Public Health Service. P.H.S.P. No. 1103.
50. Gocke, T. M., Factors which aggravate chronic bronchitis. Emphysema in industry. Indus. Hyg. Foundation of Am., Inc. *Medical Series Bulletin* No. 10, 1966, 57.
51. Ishikawa, S., Personal communication. University of Manitoba.
52. APHA CONFERENCE REPORT 1967. Lifespan of adventists prolonged by not smoking. *Public Health Reports*, **83**, 3, March 1968, 225.
53. Tromp, Solco W., Biometeorological aspects of respiratory diseases, Reports Biometeorological Research Centre, No. 3, March 8, 1966.
54. PUBLIC HEALTH SERVICE DRINKING WATER STANDARDS. U.S.P.H.S. Publication No. 956, 1962.
55. Stokinger, H. E., Mountain, J. T. and Dixon, J. R., Newer toxicologic methodology. *Arch. Environ. Health*, **13**, Sept. 1966, 296.
56. Carroll, Robert E., The relationship of cadmium in the air to cardiovascular disease death rates. *J.A.M.A.* **198**, 3, October 17, 1966, 177.
57. Thomson, J. G., Asbestos as a modern urban hazard. *S. Afr. Med. J.* **31**, Jan. 19, 1963, 77.
58. Wagner, J. C., Sleggs, C. A. and Marchand, P., *Brit. J. Industr. Med.* **17**, 1960, 260.
59. Selikoff, I. J., Churg, J. and Hammond, E. C., *J. Amer. Med. Assoc.* **188**, 1964, 22.
60. Mewhouse, M. L. and Thompson, H., Mesothelioma of pleura and peritoneum following exposure to asbestos in the London area. *B.J.I.M.* **22**, 1965, 266.
61. Kotin, P. and Falk, H. L., *Dis. Chest*, **45**, 236, 1964.
62. Sargent, Frederick, Air pollution: A problem for human ecology. *Arch. Environ. Health*, **14**, 1, January 1967, 35.

176

A SYSTEMS ENGINEERING APPROACH
TO URBAN SOLID WASTE COLLECTION AND DISPOSAL

J. W. MACLAREN and D. P. SEXSMITH *James F. MacLaren Ltd., Toronto*

ABSTRACT

The paper establishes in initial outline a system of activities that must be integrated on a planned basis to contribute to the production of a single set of optimum outputs based on known or assumed inputs, to permit the establishment of the most practicable system of solid waste management. It then proceeds to define the scope of these activities so as to make clear the inherent complexity of such a study and the need for establishing it on a wide scope basis. These activities will demonstrate the necessity for considering the detail and constraints of regional planning and socio-economic conditions of the area, the establishment through inputs derived from these sources of optimum collection and disposal schemes, the intereffect of disposal methods on other resources, benefit/cost relationship of the various possible schemes and the manner of financing the schemes. The process of refining and referring the alternative solutions to arrive at an optimum conclusion will then be demonstrated, together with the obvious restrictions that still dilute the effect of such an approach.

INTRODUCTION

The science of modern refuse collection and disposal for urban areas has, during the past ten years, undergone major improvement through a sudden awakening to the immensity and complexity of the problem. The burgeoning quantities of solid waste requiring collection by public and private agencies have increased in the past ten years from $2 \cdot 5$ to over 5 pounds *per capita* in average urban areas, representing a clear demonstration of the affluence of our society. Rapid changes in packaging, indifference in domestic procedures, decline in markets for salvaged materials, rejection of certain liquids from sewer disposal are major factors contributing to this increase.

This effect has created the necessity for substantially improving collecting procedures, including frequency and handling aspects, thereby triggering a significant boom in the development of available hardware and the complex problem of its proper selection. In disposal, the increasing volumes of refuse have resulted in a rapid depletion of sanitary land fill space and reserve design capacity of processing and/or disposal devices previously considered adequate for years to come. Such increase has made evident the necessity for operating fills on a sound engineering basis to improve compaction and space efficiency, to protect the public health and to guard against nuisance and resulting public objection. The current and proper total environment considerations of pollution control have also had a significant effect on the approach to refuse disposal practises.

In addition to being overloaded, incineration and composting devices are being forced to accept refuse the character of which has changed materially from the refuse that design was predicated upon. This has necessitated the development of improved equipment with by-product recovery and again many types of hardware have become available requiring complex selection studies to determine "best choice".

Finally, the grave problem of soil and ground water pollution from sanitary landfills, the air pollution and ash disposal problem resulting from incineration, the problem of liquid toxic waste disposal to avoid environmental contamination have made evident the growing necessity in refuse disposal for rigid and complex interacting controls on the pollution of air, soil and water.

This latter awareness has disclosed the political, social and economic problems of refuse collection and disposal. Pollution aspects and public awareness in the face of growing quantities create impracticable conditions for disposing of refuse within fixed political boundaries. Refuse disposal and therefore collection have in fact, whether politically acknowledged or not, become a regional problem.

The foregoing refers to privately collected as well as publicly collected wastes and the necessity of ensuring capacity for processing and disposal of privately collected wastes in public facilities.

By developing a regional plan for refuse collection and disposal, the use of land, labour and equipment can be optimized for the overall benefit of the area in economic, social and health aspects. The significance of the complex problem can be properly analyzed through a reduction in the number of assumptions or constraints. Advantage can be taken of a larger scale operation administered under one major authority with whom private collectors can establish their position. Finally, it is possible thereby to develop a long-term master plan for ten to twenty years that will optimize costs, financing, and organization and permit conformity with overall regional planning.

This introduction indicates the wisdom of developing a master plan for urban and regional collection and disposal of solid wastes in full consideration of all the engineering alternatives that may be available. It also dictates, however, the necessity of considering the feasibility of these alternatives in the light of time and social, political, psychological, economic, and legal aspects. The diversity of these various inputs clearly demonstrates the complexity of the situation and the need for a systems approach based on the contributing skills of not only engineers of several disciplines but specialists from many other fields united into a project team with an effective means of internal communications. It is well to emphasize this latter point. A systems approach is required not only due to the complexity of the problem and its alternate solutions but to establish planned communication for a multidisciplinary team.

SYSTEMS OUTLINE

The jargon of the economist, the sociologist, the operations researcher and the systems analyst are confusing to the engineer in the application of his technology to the development of a modern systems approach to a public problem such as refuse collecting, processing and disposing. Yet, most systems analysts consider the project engineer the key to the formulation of the systems study plan and its operation.

Although the systems technique has been employed for more than thirty years, the intense application of the California experience of the aerospace industries to public problems commencing in 1964 has brought definite prominence to the value of the systems approach in complex public socio-economic and engineering studies. If a system can be developed whereby the level of a specific public service can be balanced with other services in relation to its relative value to the public as a whole and the financial resources available, efficiency in engineering planning and public service can be established at a high level.

Systems engineering has been defined by one expert as "the activity of planning and designing the arrangements of things and people which operate collectively as a system, to the end that the collective outputs of the system in operation will yield significantly greater values than the system in operation at present".

The systems approach then is a reasonable scheme of establishing requirements and goals, determining and evaluating alternatives and selecting the optimum course to follow. Its essence is the subdivision of a broadly defined system into definite tasks so that individual and functional work units will effectively provide input to an overall integrated system.

The full exploration of all reasonable alternatives and the search for an optimum solution entails repeated computations of the predictions of the system for the different possible values of the variables considered controllable. Indeed, because of this action, it has become commonplace to associate systems analysis with computer-based information systems.

As an example to demonstrate the foregoing remarks in the light of a possible refuse collection and disposal study and plan for regional urban application, Fig. 1 entitled Proposed Systems Activity Plan is enclosed herewith. This figure outlines the complex nature of the inputs and disciplines which must be considered in the development of an optimum solid waste management system and shows the advantage of defining the specific tasks and determining their relative interdependence.

Rather than representing a collection of discreet and isolated tasks, the programme follows a logical format in which the interrelation of all tasks is clearly appreciated which permits attainment of the project's goal in the most efficient manner. In this connection, it is important particularly to recognize that certain project tasks require the development of mathematical models, the outputs of which must become available at the most opportune time to serve the next activity or task.

SUB-ACTIVITY SCOPE

It is evident in the project activity plan that a number of major activities divided into several or more tasks must be carried out in parallel during the period of the study, but that all these activities relate to the mainline activity "THE PLAN". This mainline activity involves the sequential appraisal and evaluation of alternative engineering systems for refuse collection and disposal and all other activity lines are corollary to it.

A discussion of each of the major activities to disclose their contribution to the development of the plan might appear warranted at this point.

1. Planning and Economics

Under this activity, the boundaries of the political subdivisions to be included in the study are established. Because of the nature of this study and the problems associated with a regional plan for refuse collection and disposal, the demographic sub-areas employed may not necessarily agree with political sub-divisions. The relationship between population, land use and refuse generation is very direct. An inventory of present land use practices and the predictions of future use are mandatory to the forecasting of future economic and demographic growth patterns.

From these considerations sources or points of generation of refuse can be defined and qualitative relationships established for anticipated future developments. Prior to actually evaluating future refuse quantities, the development must be estimated in respect of population, land use, economic activity and industry type and keyed to existing planning that may apply in the area. Information established to that point can provide input for forecasting future refuse quantities.

Associated with improvements in refuse collection and disposal are a number of direct benefits such as improved property values, public health protection and decreased capital and operating costs through central management and a number of intangible benefits relating to improved environmental conditions, improved traffic planning, recreational benefits through reclaimed fills, etc. These benefits when listed and evaluated (a scoring system can be applied to intangible benefits) can then serve as the basis for determining incremental benefits for each of the sub-areas and the subsequent benefit-cost analysis of each of the alternative engineering systems to be evaluated.

2. Refuse Quantities

Prior to projecting future waste loads, the present level of production of refuse must be developed. This task can be accomplished by a complete and detailed accumulation of data by sub-area from all sources within the study region. This will require origin surveys of private collections as well as an assessment of public collections according to route and area served. These quantities must be related to type and quality such as garbage, trash, etc. These data are then reduced for the computer in order to facilitate utilization in subsequent predictions of refuse type and quantity for various sub-areas. With the quantitative input of typical unit loads anticipated on the basis of future land use and economic planning for the subdivisions of the region, a computerized programme can be established to forecast anticipated loads. These loads will be projected by area subdivision, land use and refuse type to permit evaluation of ultimate collection methods and processing and disposal capacities and practices.

3. Collection

This activity requires initially the identification, assembly and collation of all available background data, reports and other useful information relating to the collection of refuse whether by public or private agencies. Execution of this task entails the development of a master inventory listing with essential cross-referencing of all agencies which currently collect refuse, all physical facilities and methods employed by them for this purpose and all routing, frequency and methods employed now and planned for by these same agencies.

From these data, improved methods can be outlined for study consideration including items applying to local collection such as route, equipment type and size, crewing, refuse location for collection based on population density and land use, frequency of collection relating to refuse type, collection versus transfer indices based on ton/mile costs and haul methods that might be employed on an incremental basis for future increase in loads. Eventual development of complete engineering alternatives will require referral and revision of the collection methods to achieve optimization.

4. Processing and Disposal

In this parallel division of the study again all available background data relating to the processing and disposal of refuse by public and private agencies alike will be assembled. This undertaking will require a detailed examination of the operation of all processing and disposal facilities and the examination of any plans for their further development or augmentation. Additionally, the quantity and quality records of material received by these facilities will be studied and listed. Efficiency checks will be carried out in relation to compaction, gas travel, ground water pollution for disposal in fills and burning rates, air pollution control efficiencies and ash volumes for processing in incinerators.

From these data, the applicability of new and improved methods can be determined and alternative processing and disposal methods can be developed. Consideration can be given to the necessity of meeting increasing environmental standards in relation to local control agencies.

5. Quality Objectives

The selection of trial environmental quality objectives with relation to refuse disposal effects as well as other pollutants can unquestionably have a considerable influence on the design of the alternative engineering systems, especially in relation to processing and disposal and the manner in which these systems can be operated. Consideration must be given to the various federal, provincial and local agencies and to their responsibilities in the area. A set of trial quality objectives can be established for the region and where practicable for the sub-region.

From these objectives and in view of existing conditions, pollution emission levels from various processing and disposal alternatives can be established on a further trial basis. However, the selection of the trial quality objectives would, of necessity, have to be founded on the basis of current thinking and without a full appreciation of the impact of any proposed plans, of plans conceived of during the study or of the future actions of the control agencies based on their consideration of ultimate quality goals. Therefore, as these indeterminates are reduced, it would be appropriate to review and revise these objectives. This review process will develop from a "feed back" of information resulting from the succession of appraisals which will be made of alternative engineering systems to which they may be related. Proposed engineering systems which cannot meet the requirements of the revised objectives would have to be rejected.

6. Financing Procedures

The preliminary phase of the financial studies required to develop a master plan for refuse collection and disposal would consist of the collection, review and analysis of available financial information relating to the cost of operating existing collecting, processing and disposing facilities within the study area. From a listing and inventory of these figures, unit guideline estimates can be prepared for consideration in the initial selection and development of alternative physical plans for refuse control. This material will be subjected to review in the light of local criteria and constraints established after analysing public debt structures, assessed valuations and tax rates obtaining with public agencies in the study area. In addition, government structure will be reviewed with respect to financing powers and the potential for outside assistance including subsidy will be tested. The ultimate evaluation of the financial feasibility of alternate engineering systems is a vital element preceding the formulation of the master plan. Alternative financing plans for each proposed engineering system must be considered and related to the availability of capital, applicable interest rates, annual revenues, timing of capital expenditures, statutory requirements and public opinion. The final phase of the financial studies would be directed to the selection and refinement of the financing plan including the allocation of cost applicable to each of the proposed engineering systems. Decision on the financing plan appropriate for each alternative engineering system would include recommendations regarding type and source of capital funds, type and source of annual operating funds, legislative changes relating to financing, relative timing of financing with the proposed construction schedule and illustrations to show the financial effect on various beneficiaries of the project.

7. Governmental Structures

The jurisdictions of a number of governmental agencies may overlap in relation to the creation of a regional refuse control plan. To evaluate the effects of this government pattern on the development of alternative master plans, and to provide the basis for revising or developing new or revised government structures, these structures must be inventoried and their several jurisdictions, powers, resources and legal characteristics outlined. These structures would then be reviewed and amendments considered, or if necessary new structures suggested so as to permit optimum administration of the various alternative engineering plans. Eventually, one or more alternative government administrative structures would be selected for each alternative physical system proposed based primarily on extent of legal change required, degree of departure from present government structure and an evaluation of continuing level of conflict in government structures. Finally, a selection of the government structure considered most appropriate for each alternative physical plan will be made and justified in terms of other government structures that were analyzed and found to be less suitable.

8. Basic Data Operations

The magnitude and interdisciplinary range of the proposed study make it essential that an operational plan for data control and management be established at the beginning of the study. Such a plan can provide a central depository for applicable existing data and that developed from within the study group. The plan can also be designed to provide in addition to storage and retrieval, the necessary statistical and numerical routines required to put data into a form suitable for convenient use by all members of the study group. This system provides efficient data management and utilization for the conduct of a study of the scope proposed. Maintaining a central file or catalogue of available data can minimize duplication of data collection efforts, provide for effective interchange of data between the numerous task groups, assist in testing for data inadequacies or inconsistencies and thus provide direction to data review and collection programs, provide ready access to all data used or generated within the study, ensure adequate documentation of all study tasks and results to and including evaluations of alternative management systems and provide more efficient and accurate compilation of data for reports and publications. Also at the completion of the study the basic data "bank" can be invaluable resource to the implementation of the selected refuse management plan and its later administration.

MAINLINE ACTIVITY—"THE PLAN"

The foregoing activities as described serve to provide the necessary inputs to permit the logical but sequential development and evaluation of alternative engineering systems for refuse collection, processing and disposal. Initially, it is necessary to develop a set of alternative systems and/or elements which may comprise potentially attractive engineering systems for refuse management. The variations which may be possible within this set can encompass a wide spectrum of schemes ranging from a "no plan" alternative to those which may be so advanced as to be unrealistic for attainment even with the most optimistic perspective. The number of alternatives which can result from the possible combinations can be enormous, especially when consideration is given to collection methods and routes, processing alternatives and disposal choices. For this reason, it is wise to confine the initial selection to reasonable alternatives by limiting the alternatives through the early input of practicable collection systems. The initial skeleton alternatives can then be reduced through the initial design process which provides the first critical screening of alternatives. Inputs relating to processing and disposing and permissible concentrations of residual pollutants can provide stabilizing constraints so that a manageable series of technologically feasible systems for refuse management develop. These systems are then subjected to the process of appraisal in which the response of the environment and the objectives to be achieved are weighed. It is unlikely that a computerized approach can be achieved at this stage but the rather ancient tool of experienced judgement may be a prime factor in establishing this reduced series.

A further comparison of quality response to the trial objectives under various plan conditions will, based on an appropriate scoring system, result in the elimination of a number of alternatives. For instance, a system which collects, transports, processes and/or disposes of all the solid wastes generated, without polluting the surrounding environment in excess of prescribed standards can be scored at par. It must then be scored independently for cost effect and social effect and the three parameters evaluated separately to determine its ultimate standing. With the imposition of the score, many schemes will be found wanting and can be eliminated.

At this point in the study, there will be identified a number of distinctive alternative systems, each feasible of construction, each carrying a certain construction cost and a financing operation and maintenance cost and each capable of meeting the basic requirements of the environment. These will be moved forward to undergo economic scrutiny out of which should emerge a clearer understanding of the values and costs related to each. Evidence of the variation in systems can be established in determining the staged costs of the various systems still under consideration and the relative financial advantages in such staging. The remaining alternative systems can then be subject to economic evaluation in the context of related benefits and costs. An appraisal can be made of benefits derived through each alternative where appropriate; incremental benefits achieved by changes in quality will be related to corresponding incremental costs. Because of the complexity of the situation, rigorous benefit-cost analysis are not applicable. Instead it is necessary to identify in discreet and separate fashion with each alternative system those benefits which may be classified as direct or indirect and tangible or intangible. Those benefits which may be quantified in dollar terms, or other tangible measures of utility can be carried into formal analysis. The remaining benefits, intangible but exceedingly important in a social sense, will have to be carried forward as qualifiers on each of the alternatives. Subsequent evaluation in the face of financial planning and government structures will make use of such information. The final selection of the recommended refuse management plan is multidisciplinary and involves both objective and subjective appraisal. The role of the political and financial analysts becomes dominant with economic and engineering experts being reduced to a subordinate position at this stage. Finally, with the selected plan a practical schedule of implementation must be developed to conform to the needs of the area and its financial constraints.

Although the example activity chart has not been prepared to show the complex referral system necessary to keep the study in balance, the interdependence of tasks indicates the sensitivity of the whole system to any major task unbalance and the necessity for constant referral. In actuality the system must "breath".

CONCLUSION

From the foregoing descriptions, it can be inferred that a systems approach to solid waste management will prove to be a panacea to the problems of an inadequate "garbage system". Unquestionably systems engineering has aided this type of study materially but unfortunately the major hazard with this tool is that there is a natural desire to re-engineer the entire world of things and people, thus making the study unnecessarily complex, costly and time-consuming. The challenge is actually to evaluate a smaller number of important changes that will provide significant improvement.

Finally, probably the greatest threat to the validity of any study relating to public engineering lies beyond the capability of the systems approach to solve. That is the bewildering and baffling problem of establishing the physical boundaries of the study area on some technically justifiable basis.

REFERENCES

1. DUDLEY, R. H., HEKIMIAN, K. K., A Systems Approach to Solid Waste Management, Engineering Foundation Research Conference, University School, Milwaukee, Wisconsin, July 1967.
2. JAMES F. MACLAREN LIMITED, Report on Refuse Disposal for Municipality of Metropolitan Toronto, May 1967.

POLLUTION CONTROL AND ABATEMENT
WITHIN THE PLANNING PROCESS

W. T. PERKS, *Urbanist, National Capital Commission, Ottawa.*

ABSTRACT

Although man adjusts to his environment, urbanization has countless adverse affects which result in physiological disfunction and psychic disorder. We are unsure or often unaware of the long-term effects on man of urbanization or pollution. While pollution is one of the major issues of urban planning, the profession has not moved very quickly in examining the quality of cities other than in its visual attributes. Pollution is viewed as a control problem and not as a component of a resources management system. Will technological determinism and cost-benefit alone continue to shape our planning approaches to pollution or will we establish resource management policies that are more than idealistic schemes? We are aware that ecological, ethnological and economic theories provide the cornerstones of resource management but they have not as yet integrated into a satisfactory, pragmatic public philosophy. An integral approach must account for the quantifiable payoffs of resource development and for processes of dialogue and concensus to make planning policies acceptable to all.

INTRODUCTION

It is only in the last fifty years or less that large-scale urbanization has become the characteristic settlement pattern. The pace and magnitude of changes in the environment during this period have been unprecedented and overwhelming. While an ever-increasing number of injurious factors have been introduced through rapid technological and economic expansion, there has been too little time for conscious adaptation to environmental change. The consequences have been phenomenal rises in pollution, physiological stress and psychic disorder. Many believe that changes in the human condition caused by these large urban agglomerations and by technology have already out-stripped our capacity to redress the imbalance between man and his environment. Still others believe that detrimental modifications in the genetic structures of plant, animal and human species are being caused by certain practices which intervene in the evolutionary process itself [1].

What then are the characteristics of environmental change caused by pollution? How is planning brought to bear on the problem? The city is the generator of pollution, while the urban region and areas beyond it are the victims. The catalogue of ills and stresses associated with urban living is an impressive one [2], and there is much statistical evidence to suggest causal relationships between certain pollutants and many of these disorders. Pollutants produce their effects through a number of carrier media. This fact alone gives rise to situations of varying significance from one community to the next, depending upon the degree to which health is threatened or depending upon the end uses being considered for the media themselves. Pollution has no universal definition, and uniform standards to combat it are difficult—if not impossible—to apply. Jurisdictional problems are created by the movement of pollutants through air and water, which in turn raises questions as to basic concepts of resources ownership or ultimate responsibility for the effects of resource practices. As pollution defines its own region it adds a new dimension to the planning of urban activities and regional resource development. Finally, it appears that some anti-pollution measures can themselves produce "new pollution monsters"*.

I. THE PLANNING PROCESS

Against the complex background of bio-technico and jurisdictional considerations, the planner plays out his role of the generalist, the visionary, the coordinator. In the past, that role has been more often than not a passive one, as evidenced by the limited contribution of planning to pollution abatement. Zoning and "control" by-laws were the weapons customarily deployed against a transcendent threat to environmental equilibrium. Today, however, urban planning is moving away from the predominantly control and beautification functions by which it is usually known. New urges in society and an expanding knowledge of urban and regional phenomena has given to planning new purposes and new techniques.

The New Planning

The urge for economic equalization has recently become a powerful force for stimulating the economy of depressed cities or regions and for developing equal opportunities of economic and cultural fulfilment within large cities. The rising densities of urban areas, together with their declining quality of environment have precipitated fiscal and management crises. Meanwhile, the leisure society of tomorrow is demanding a whole new set of resource management policies to meet the changing patterns of recreation and social life. To meet these challenges, there is now improved knowledge on the interrelatedness of urban and regional activities: economic disciplines and systems analysis have opened new avenues of technique leading to the introduction of dynamic characteristics into an urban or regional plan. These techniques are seen in the automated information systems, land use models and regional accounting models.

Despite these new levels of sophistication, planning has no general rules to offer for dealing with pollution. If there has been too little action taken on pollution, it is not because society is technologically ill-equipped—on the contrary. To some extent we have unconsciously cultivated a technological determinism at the expense of vital socio-cultural considerations which provide the necessary link between man and technology. This thesis and its relation to pollution are dealt with in section II. In section III, some approaches to dealing with regional pollution problems are discussed. Concluding remarks deal with the basic tenets of an approach to resource management which could improve our techniques for dealing with environmental improvement.

What is the planning process? Let us first be clear on one point: an urban or regional plan is not just the planner's baby. It is everyone's concern. That concern is ultimately for the taking of decisions that influence the shape and quality of our environment. The underlying premise of plans is that decision makers operate in a world where rationality prevails. In other words, they seek to clarify objectives among many alternative courses of action, and they seek ways to measure the effectiveness of these decisions while not losing sight of the intangibles.

* Reference to algae pollution generated by dissolved plant nutrients from sewage treatment facilities (e.g. Lake Ontario).

The Plan and the Process

The plan is first an expression of social, economic and political objectives judged appropriate and feasible by the regional community. These objectives relate to the spatial distribution of activities (land uses). By necessity, they also relate to the conditions for regulating the development or conservation of major resources. The second dimension of the plan is a series of statements (policies) spelling out the instrumentalities and priorities of implementation; what legislation is best suited or required to accomplish objectives; and what responsibilities for monitoring, controlling, coordinating and updating the plan must be accorded various agencies in the region. A third dimension of the plan is its substantive content—the way in which it tells us how the future environment will differ from the present, how the human condition is likely to be affected by the plan.

The fourth dimension is its dynamic quality. The plan must set the norms and provide for mechanisms which periodically evaluate the effectiveness of decisions. There is a need to test objectives against unanticipated change, to modify them as needs dictate. As projects are implemented, the success of the plan is measured according to how these have responded to objectives, as well as by the adaptability of the plan itself to changing needs and conditions.

The selection of objectives is fundamental to the process, for these touch upon the full spectrum of resources management. The planner's role is to synthesize and interpret the evolving social and economic forces which give rise to trends in the spatial distribution of activities. He assesses the constraints, potentialities and likely repercussions of development trends. He addresses himself to the general question: what would the environment be like after a specified period of time, under conditions of freely-evolving social and economic forces and no planning intervention? From this assessment he introduces a set of planning objectives. Some will conform to desirable trends, others will modify trends and still others may propose to suppress undesirable trends. It is in the latter sets of objectives that the substantive quality of a plan is highlighted. In most simple terms, this quality is a vision of the future—a future of improved opportunities for creating growth and a higher quality of environment.

The planner's set of objectives and objectives formulated independently by other agencies in the community should then pass into the political forum for evaluation and selection. To the degree that benefits and costs associated with each objective are explicit and comprehended, a final decision to select one set of objectives over another will be efficaceous. In this process the planner endeavours to provide the quantitative and qualitative bases for evaluating alternative courses of action. Ideally the planning process is completed only after the regional population has had an opportunity to evaluate proposals, provide a feedback to the plan-making team and finally, to arrive at a consensus on objectives that must be retained in the plan.

II. PRESENT FRAMEWORK FOR ACTION ON POLLUTION

Pollution is one set of retrogressive forces in the environment which must be dealt within the planning process. There appear to be two basic perspectives on the nature and significance of pollution, and each in its own way has an important influence on planned approaches to control and abatement. To deal effectively with pollution, understanding of these two viewpoints is an essential point of departure.

Pollution as it Relates to Perception

On the one hand, pollution is seen as an attribute of environment perceived through human value systems and judged according to our conception of what the human condition is, or ought to be. As one resources expert has explained it, "Judgement as to the severity of a perceived aspect of the environment varies greatly from person to person. Two people in the same metropolitan area may see air pollution as high or low, while agreeing that it constitutes an impairment of the habitat" [3]. In this sense, the pollution phenomenon has subjective meaning and little scientific relevance. Scientifically speaking, we are dealing with wastes, by-products or forms of energy which, as a rule, can be identified and quantified, but our perception of all these takes on special (but widely varied) meaning only when we begin to regard them as injurious. When are they regarded as being injurious? Generally, it is when statistical evidence linking environmental pollution to chronic or degenerative diseases is convincing. Unfortunately, pathological effects become convincing only when large populations have been observed over long time periods. While waiting for the statistics, losses of productive human resources continue to mount.

Thus, considerable importance can be attached to evaluating changes as they occur or are anticipated. Because of man's inconstant attitudes, it is difficult to get a reading on the public viewpoint while changes are actually occurring. Nevertheless, attitudes are real and they can be made more influential in the course of deciding how to improve the environment. Conversely, they can also be influential, if properly assessed and recorded, in the event of planned or anticipated events expected to diminish the quality of environment.

The point is that urban planners give virtually no attention to finding out how the environment is actually perceived by the people expected to improve it. Yet a great deal of expert assertions are made as to what the people want and need. It is too often disregarded that pollution abatement and control is but one element among a host of conflicting preferences for improving the quality of life and the environment. Only some preferences can be transformed into active projects at a given point in time. Pollution itself divides into numerous subsets of preferences, and the "pay-offs" which can be associated with each often cannot be compared in qualitative or quantitative terms. If we are to be effective in planning a better environment, a great deal more effort must be made to assess how pollution and the environment are actually perceived by people.

The task is not a simple one. In public administration, where major issues of resources management are decided, we have not yet developed adequate techniques for finding out what beliefs and attitudes are actually held. This engenders a falling back on expert opinion too often constrained by a framework which imputes "rational" and "irrational" attitudes to management of the environment. The more ambiguous the goal, the less apt this dichotomous approach becomes, and most goals associated with pollution abatement are ambiguous. Water management provides an interesting example. Many objectives are usually fused, while each can be variously or capriciously emphasized according to the shifts of administrative purpose: treatment of polluted rivers can be seen as reducing hazards to health, rendering streams useful for recreation, restoring their quality for fish, or restoring their quality for more economic, multiple uses by downstream users. To what extent all these are related to people's perception of the environmental qualities involved and the benefits to be derived for one community (as opposed to another) is seldom appreciated. In the planning process, therefore, relating explicit goals to explicit attitudes becomes a necessary functional step in achieving environmental change.

Pollution as it Relates to Science and Technology

The second stance—around which most environmental improvement programmes have thus far revolved—is the technological one. A pollution technologist more likely inclines to the view that pollution can be quantitatively determined through measurable effects on biological systems. He would argue that because man fails to perceive pollution or chooses to ignore it, this does not negate its existence. Moreover, he can probably estimate to what degree pollution of air, water and soil are outstripping our capacity to regenerate or restore these resources. His standard of evaluation is the "natural condition"—the environment as it was before the intervention of man or some arbitrary standard of health. This kind of standard has a built-in dilemma which, as we will see, obscures some relevant research issues.

Although the "natural condition" is a useful theoretical basis for measurement, it is useless as an ideal for environmental improvement. Yet it persists in the ideology of pollution reform. We are exhorted to "restore rivers to their natural condition" and to "prevent the atmosphere being used for any kind of waste disposal". Costs involved are frequently underplayed in relation to the ideal. For example, it has been estimated that complete treatment of all effluents in the United States could cost about $20 billion a year—the equivalent of the national annual expenditure on public and secondary education [4]. If restoring the elements of our environment to their pristine state is an extreme goal, accepting unmitigated pollution of air, water and soil is equally extreme. Are we suggesting that all losses in economic productivity, natural resources and human fulfillment arising from unrestrained pollution can be tolerated? Certainly not . . . but in deriving solutions somewhere in between the extremes, we are too prone to seek out decisions at the professional level where the appeals of scientific methodology and quantification are very appealing.

As Kneese reminds us, many environmental quality decisions are taken by persons who feel a "strong professional identification". What is beyond their professional competence (but perhaps quite relevant to the decision outcome) is too often ignored. Their perspective and preferences, although solidly based in the theoretical and technological framework of their field, become the exclusive determinants of plans laid before the public. This is not suggesting that the professional has been responsible for public action or non-action in the matter of pollution—only, that collectively we tend to readily accept his perceptual framework as all-embracing and sufficient for the shaping of decisions. As a corollary to this, professional-technological judgments often contain untested assumptions about public preferences. While the engineer's proposal for cleaning up a river invariably contains his view of the public valuation of the situation, when the moment arrives for citizens to decide, they are limited to approving or disapproving the plan but not its underlying rationale which might very well touch upon assumed preferences. However the citizen reacts, he can neither endorse or refute the conclusions of the technologist: he makes no contribution to, nor does he participate in the formulation of a rationale. This situation explains in part why many anti-pollution measures go down to defeat.

Limitations of technological concepts for planning. Not only have we placed inordinate reliance on the technological approach to environmental quality in the past, but in some important respects the scientific and educational inputs to the problem are tending to ignore other equally pertinent areas of investigation. Consider the suggestion that pollution is "Any modification which makes the environment unfit for reasonable uses" [5]. This might be considered as good a definition as any, but it is a limited notion of what constitutes pollution, and it can steer the course of scientific enquiry along utilitarian lines to the exclusion of equally important environmental considerations. The concept is inadequate because it views environment as a utility and not as something to be cultivated or enriched in a symbiotic relationship with man. It demonstrates our preoccupation with the conquest of technology over resources—man over nature—our lack of understanding of environmental systems. Within the framework of this recommendation one finds a list of eleven areas where development of additional technology is needed, but not one recommendation for scientific research into the perceptual norms and cultural attitudes which, in the final analysis, determine what pollution is and what we can do about it.

Moreover, many "reasonable uses" already constitute forms of pollution in the sense that they degrade our aesthetic sensibilities, contribute to psychic disorder or disrupt the intermittent communion with nature that urban dwellers require. Highway billboards, commercial strip boulevards, slag heaps and junkyards on the landscape, discordant sights and sounds of the urban scene, the pre-eminence of property and rights of exploitation which preclude access to, and disfigure the rural environment, the use of rivers for transportation of logs to the exclusion of other uses, etc. These are uses in the environment, the legitimacy of which is seldom questioned. They never figure in the science and technology of pollution studies. The scientist, the technologist and the planner should be wary of any approach to pollution study which first accepts a totally anthropocentric, utilitarian view of environment and secondly, which does not explicitly admit as proper to it, the interrelationships of man and other life forms in an ecological system.

In another definition, formulated in response to research and education needs, pollution is held to be "alteration of the natural environments, air, water or soil, so that they are rendered offensive or deleterious to man's aesthetic senses or uses or to animals, fishes or crops which man wishes to preserve" [6]. Although this approach tends to recognize a broader basis for evaluating pollution, it suggests that there are somehow "natural environments" proper to the study of alterations and, by implication, "artificial environments" that presumably are not. A search for convenient scientific catalogues seems to result in dissection of the problem into elemental compartments, and the significance and meaning of environment becomes shaded. For in an ecological sense, because man is a natural phenomenon, the environments he shapes or creates are also natural. This applies to the city and regional environments with their complex structure of ecological systems. Since the equilibrium state of these systems is germane to the resolution of pollution problems, it would be prudent to recognize the inseparability of the elements, man and environment, in the scientific and educational programmes for anti-pollution research.

We are also advised that anti-pollution research is concerned with establishing "criteria of the limits of tolerance" to alterations in the environment. This in itself is a badly needed area of study, but one finds it difficult to reconcile with statements to the effect that "Research is limited to providing the know-how", that "it is not concerned with mechanics, authority or exercise of authority . . . to prevent or control pollution" [7]. The direction taken here is perhaps supportable on purely technological grounds. Nevertheless, it fails the planner and the administrator who are looking not only for technological "know-how" but for the foundations of public attitudes which relate human perception of the environment to viable anti-pollution options. Without these foundations we will continue to plunge headlong into technologically attractive adaptations and to flounder about in an effort to mobilize public support for anti-pollution projects. Obviously, science and education must be concerned with more than just developing know-how. There is a very real need for scientific enquiry into human perception of the environment, preferably within regional contexts of varying urban composition and resources base. And, if there is to be planned, acceptable economic approaches to improving our environment, the scope of scientific research and education must be enlarged to include our institutional capabilities to use the technology we now have.

Responsibility and Cost

On the question of who should support the cost of pollution abatement, professional viewpoints appear to polarize around two general statements: "pollution must be controlled economically" or "polluters should bear the costs of their pollution damage" [8]. The first too often implies that virtually nothing should be done in cases where polluting agents would suffer competitive disadvantages as the result of imposed control measures. This position is neither equitable nor ultimately reconcilable with the proposal that "limits of tolerance" be respected. In the first instance, it is highly unlikely that all types of polluting agents or all communities are in the same competitive position. Thus, discrimination between agents or between communities, is likely to arise. In the second, the implication is that irrespective of what tolerance levels are established, health and welfare could very easily go by the board if competitive situations dictate. In general, the position opts for "seniority" rather than "priority".

The second position [9] was formulated by the President's Science Advisory Committee (1965) which recommended, "Disposal of polluting wastes and . . . the expense of disposal should be reckoned as part of the cost of doing business." Implementation of this policy would certainly require complex, costly technological innovation, in addition to extensive biological research into what actually constitutes a polluting waste under differing environmental conditions. But over and above these considerations, it is doubtful that a polluting agent can really be considered a free agent in every sense of the word. Our approach to defining the responsibilities of any resource user should recognize that both the benefits and the social costs attributable to him are publicly as well as privately created and in part due to the complex interplay of institutional, cultural, technological, entrepreneurial and economic forces external to the agent. In the contemporary society of closely interrelated government and private sector economies, it is no longer realistic to think in terms of exclusive areas of public and private responsibilities for the consequences of resource practices.

Limitations of cost-benefit analysis. One other aspect of pollution abatement which requires clearer understanding is the technique of cost-benefit analysis. Private costs associated with pollution have been estimated in many cases and have been widely publicized with a view to stimulating public action. The follow-through sometimes involves cost-benefit calculations designed to effect support for particular abatement projects. Quite apart from the fact that many pollution costs are indirect and never figure in an individual's private accounting, the technique has serious limitations. Although a few industries may have been persuaded to carry out corrective measures which produce benefits through a recovery process, general experience indicates that the benefit calculations of privately financed anti-pollution proposals are usually untenable.

As for abatement projects financed by the public sector, there are two reasons why cost-benefit analysis alone is inadequate. For any given project, evaluated in itself, the social costs and social benefits can rarely (if ever) be totally quantified. In fact, the intangible costs and benefits, which never enter into the analysis, may indeed be the most "significant" ones.

there are finite limits to the flow of funds and resources in the public sector which ...he dynamic of choosing among many alternative projects in the process of achieving community goals. It should be recognized that in this context, cost-benefit analysis is worthless because it is suited only for ranking courses of action designed to attain the same ends [10]. Given two different projects—a new roadway vs. a sewage treatment plant, for example—each costing the same amount but money for one only, cost-benefit analysis provides no basis for deciding which is "best". Unfortunately, public administrators constantly have to decide on "best" projects in order to fulfil their responsibilities, and unless better methods of ranking alternatives for different ends are adopted, the real benefits of decisions will be speculative and uncertain.

Summary

The present conceptual framework and direction of scientific research should be enlarged if we are to mobilize greater action on pollution. Pollution is a function of cultural precepts as well as scientific knowledge, and while the latter is developing rapidly, the significance of the former is not well enough appreciated. More meaningful steps for improvement of the environment within the planning process can be taken if we move to close the gap between technology and man. Degradation of the environment, while scientifically comprehended at many levels, is ultimately discerned with varying significance by populations at the regional level where particular social needs and economic conditions create the basic determinants of resource practices. In the final analysis, the economics of pollution abatement cannot be easily separated from these determinants; by implication, simplistic rules of assigning cost and responsibility may prove most difficult to uphold or to apply universally.

III. THE PLANNING OPPORTUNITY

In this section, an attempt is made to uncover some of the opportunities of a planning approach to environmental improvement. Pollution is considered as an attribute of resource practices which themselves become the subject of a planning rationale for policy decisions. A unique, sectorial approach to pollution control is considered to be an inadequate rationale. Concensus is proposed as the dominant characteristic of a viable plan structured according to alternative opportunities afforded by the physical, cultural and economic assets of a given region.

Criterion of Economic Regional Opportunities

The rationale for regional approaches to environmental improvement lies in efficient, more effective measures which cannot be achieved by setting standards or imposing taxes upon individual agents or local decision-makers who cause spillover effects. In economic terms, there are advantages of scale which agents or communities cannot realize while acting on their own. In social and jurisdictional terms, the satisfaction of human needs dependent upon access to resources located beyond one residential jurisdiction (city or Province) can be realized by viewing neighbouring communities as interdependent entities. Regional-scale solutions in the field of water management are the most prevalent, while the first step towards similar solutions in air pollution can be seen in the U.S. Air Quality Act (1967).

In the case of water resources, emphasis has been on assessing damage costs and control costs arising from pollution. Indications are that damage costs (costs to the user obliged to

192

improve the quality of water) involved in a polluted stream system seldom justify, on economic grounds alone, the installation of upstream sewage treatment plants. For example, one study [11] has shown that water withdrawal for municipal uses at downstream locations as a ratio of upstream sewage treatment volumes would have to be anywhere from 16 to 1 to as high as 250 to 1 if treatment costs were to be justified. In the case of industrial users, damage costs are likewise unlikely to justify pollution abatement [12]. Moreover, it often appears that sensitivity of industrial processes is greater where pollutants of natural origin are concerned, such as chlorides, magnesium, colouration due to organic constituents, etc. Looking at social values, such as recreation, there is still a great deal of research required to bring the economic benefits of anti-pollution into clearer focus. To cite one promising example, for the Delaware estuary it has been estimated that boating charges of $2.50 per day could possibly justify achieving 3 ppm of dissolved oxygen.

In some long-term policy studies concerning water control costs it is indicated that universally applied standards may not be the best approach. In the case of industrial pollutants, there are widely varied control costs from one industrial establishment to the next, due to factors such as plant design and age, recovery materials in the process, fuels and raw materials used and market conditions. These factors suggest that uniform effluent standards could well impose higher unit costs of control on some plants than others. A promising alternative approach is to apply "effluent charges" which allow agents to optimize adjustments to the situation in accord with standards developed from regional needs and particular stream conditions. This type of system is applied in the Ruhr basin. It is based on a multiplicity of criteria and standards, including one stream totally devoted to waste disposal. The criteria respond to the region's unique industrial and municipal characteristics, its biophysical resources and population needs. At the same time, it creates incentives for polluting agents to reduce the quantity of undesirable effluents they contribute to the basin.

A study of the Potomac basin, in which a great many alternatives were examined, produced several combinations of solutions less costly than the sum of conventional waste disposal projects proposed for each polluting agent in the whole system. Included in these combinations was a proposal for maintaining high levels of dissolved oxygen at less cost by introducing air into the river rather than treating wastes at the effluent discharge points.

Similar alternatives to uniform regulations might also prove feasible in air pollution situations. Again, based on regional determinants, such as climatology and the form, character and intensity of urban-industrial and agricultural activities, a policy of air user charges might be established. These charges could be varied according to peak loads of air congestion and micro climate variations and could conceivably be related to the relative property damage caused by specific pollutants. In other instances, it might prove more feasible and less costly to modify the inputs of the industrial process rather than treat the waste-products. This is analogous to the approach taken with hard detergents where persuasion was exercised on manufacturers to switch to bio-degradable products.

Where regional plans for anti-pollution measures hold out the possibility of more economic solutions, they in turn create their own sets of problems. These are of an institutional or social order and relate to "distributive equity". If, for instance, effluent charges in a regional system produce surplus, how should it be divided up? When a stream is selected to specialize in carrying and disposing of wastes, how are riparian owners dealt with? Where there are no direct revenues from the use of renewed water, land or air resources brought about by public investment, who should benefit?—only those who have the income and leisure time which afford the means and opportunity to enjoy those resources? Do the

193

benefits of a regional scheme justify setting up and running supplementary administrations where unique provincial or municipal jurisdictions cannot cover the region?

In the foregoing, some of the potentialities and repercussions of regionally-based approaches to pollution have been discussed from the point of view of better "economics". There are other considerations which play into the process of planning the environment, and these will be dealt with next. To sum up at this point: studies of many environmental management problems strongly suggest that optimal solutions can probably not be realized by the imposition of universal rules and standards on the individual industries and individual communities responsible for pollution. It seems that improvement measures can be better founded on regional opportunities which give rise to their own standards for balancing costs and gains, which inhere their own set of social and economic circumstances and which give rise to alternatives determined by the region's over-all resource potentials. Legislation aimed at environmental improvement should be framed in this perspective.

Ecological and Cultural Criteria

While the tendency may often be to focus on the economics of a planning proposal, there are two additional considerations. The first concerns the physical habitat or ecology of the environment. The second is the cultural framework. An ecological approach to planned resources utilisation seeks to maintain equilibrium among the inter-related biological sub-systems of the environment, such that survival of all species making up the "ecosystem" is assured. Accordingly, certain pollutants and resource practices can be seen as tending to upset the desired equilibrium. By disrupting the equilibrium, such practices impair the life-sustaining capacity of land, air and water and lead eventually to diminution or extinction of plant and animal life forms.

The cultural framework establishes those themes according to which we collectively value the different resources of our habitat and set the conditions for their use. For instance, we may think of "efficiency", "progress" and "conservation" as typical referential datum for evaluating pollution impacts on the environment. The role of culture is quite significant in shaping our perception and means of exploiting natural resources. It has many attributes, ranging from moral and aesthetic precepts through to technological and institutional foundations. When the planning of resources is viewed within a cultural framework, practices which may either conserve or destroy are valued by the people concerned in terms of their particular system of activities. In this approach, when we suggest what ought to be done about pollution we are endeavouring to establish practices consistent with the major themes found in the wide range of activities making up our culture.

According to a scheme suggested by Walter Finey, the pollution phenomenon can therefore be viewed as a component of resource practices which are "possible or not" (ecology), "adoptable or not" (culture), and "gainful or not" (economy) [13].

Planning could proceed by choosing one criterion while ignoring the other two. Alternatively, the planner could resort to "ad hoc" principles or intuition and dismiss the need for any rational justification of his endeavours. This would likely lead him to recommend contradictory policies in an unsystematic framework of "common sense" statements (extreme example: "all our rivers should be restored to their natural condition"; "the costs of treating wastes should be reckoned as part of the cost of doing business"). As a third possibility, planning can attempt to retain all three criteria and balance them off against each other in the process of goal-formation. The difficulty is that by the nature of these separate criteria, their optimum conditions do not necessarily coincide—that is, their benefits to the community with respect to any regional resource management policy cannot be compared in like qualitative or quantitative terms. There is no common denominator which relates the aesthetic properties of cleaner air or an untarnished landscape to the costs of eliminating smoke pollutants.

Opportunity of Concensus Planning

Through the planning process we hope to provide a rationale for decision-making, for choice of alternative objectives. Controlling pollution and restoring polluted environment constitutes one set of alternatives among many in a regional plan. To weigh separate objectives within the total range of alternatives, recourse can be made to rather sophisticated techniques which make explicit both the tangible and intangible benefits of each objective [14]. Where the intangibles and a "vision of the future" are concerned, we are, in the final analysis, attempting to relate objectives to values held in the community. Although the planner's intuitive knowledge of the community frequently provides the basis for these objectives, they should be formulated in response to attitudinal expression at various levels in the community. This can be approached by direct and indirect research into behavior and aspirations. In effect, it is the testing of planning hypotheses by reference to cultural themes such as referred to earlier.

The test of possible objectives in a plan reposes upon the attitudinal triad of "good", "sure" and "right" [15]. The plan must be convincing in these respects. Out of this develops a sense of obligation to the ideal presented by planned environmental improvement. Only by this kind of development can resource practices insinuate themselves into people's thinking and thereby reinforce the social order which makes fulfillment of the plan possible. Insofar as pollution is concerned, the planning process is concerned with setting a framework for judging what practices—by communities, by individuals, by industrial agents—are privately gainful and opportunistic as opposed to being moral and altruistic. It is this "philosophical" input to the planning process that distinguishes it from limitative cost-benefit solutions and purely technological adventures.

If a plan is to be ultimately realized—if it is to "make a difference"—its ideal, its objectives and conditions (fiscal, legislative, social and institutional commitment, etc.), must be clearly understood. In short, concensus within the regional or urban community is a requisite. Without this attribute there can be little or no willing conformity to resource practices which yield greater environmental stability but without "security of expectations" which is a prerequisite to every viable social order. Coercive plans may be successful but they seldom achieve legitimacy. It might also be added that they are invariably expensive relative to their yields.

Summary

It is imperative that decisions in environmental improvement be taken on the basis of rational planning. Regional opportunities would seem to provide the basis for devising plans with optimal solutions to pollution problems. A respectable rationale for planning the environment is offered by approaches through ecological, cultural and economic theories. Neither of the three provides an all-embracing guide for policy development but nevertheless, must serve as ideal standards in the process of selecting objectives. To reconcile what ought to be with what can be, a plan must win the consent of those for whom it is prepared. Concensus provides the adhesion between expectations and practical possibility and ensures the social commitment necessary to effect meaningful change in the quality of the environment.

REFERENCES

1. DOBZHANSKY, T., *The Biology of Ultimate Concern*, The New American Library, 1967.
2. BAKÁCS, T., *Health and Welfare*, Paper No. 11, Centennial Study and Training Programme on Metropolitan Problems, Bureau of Municipal Research, Toronto, 1967.
3. WHITE, G. F., Formation and role of public attitudes, essay in *Environmental Quality in a Growing Economy*. Resources for the Future, Inc., The Johns Hopkins Press, 1966, p. 119.
4. KNEESE, A. K., Research goals and progress towards them, essay in *Environmental Quality in a Growing Economy*. Resources for the Future Inc., The Johns Hopkins Press, 1966, p. 71.
5. Canadian Council of Resource Ministers, Recommendations, p. 167, of the Working Paper on the National Conference on Pollution, 1966. Report of Guideline Group 1–6 on Science and Technology.
6. Ibid., Report of Guideline Group 5–2, pp. 205, 206.
7. Ibid., p. 205.
8. Ibid., Reports of Guideline Groups 3–2 and 5–2, pp. 181, 205.
9. Ibid., Report of Guideline Group 3–1, p. 179.
10. HILL, M., A goals-achieving matrix for evaluating alternative plans, *Journal of the American Institute of Planners*, January 1968, pp. 19–29.
11. FRANKEL, R. J., Water quality management: Engineering-economic factors in municipal waste disposal, *Water Resources Research*, Vol. 1, No. 2, 1965.
12. Resources for the Future Staff Studies in the U.S., described by Allen K. Kneese, op. cit., p. 73.
13. FINEY, W., *Man, Mind and Land*, the Free Press of Glencoe, Illinois, 1960; see also DUNCAN, O. D., Human ecology and population studies, in *The Study of Population*, edited by Philip M. Hauser, University of Chicago Press, 1959.
14. HILL, M., op. cit., pp. 21–29.
15. FINEY, W., op. cit.